Defining Integrated-into-Writing Constructs

Evidence at the B2–C1 Interface

Also in this series:

Criterial Features in L2 English
John A Hawkins and Luna Filipović

Language Functions Revisited
Anthony Green

Immigrant Pupils Learn English
Bronagh Ćatibušić and David Little

The CEFR in Practice
Brian North

English Profile in Practice
Edited by Julia Harrison and Fiona Barker

Critical, Constructive Assessment of CEFR-informed Language Teaching in Japan and Beyond
Edited by Fergus O'Dwyer, Morten Hunke, Alexander Imig, Noriko Nagai, Naoyuki Naganuma and Maria Gabriela Schmidt

The Discourse of the IELTS Speaking Test: Interactional Design and Practice
Paul Seedhouse and Fumiyo Nakatsuhara

Defining Integrated Reading-into-Writing Constructs

Evidence at the B2–C1 Interface

Sathena Chan
Centre for Research in English Language Learning and Assessment
(CRELLA), University of Bedfordshire

CAMBRIDGE UNIVERSITY PRESS

CAMBRIDGE
UNIVERSITY PRESS

University Printing House, Cambridge CB2 8BS, United Kingdom

One Liberty Plaza, 20th Floor, New York, NY 10006, USA

477 Williamstown Road, Port Melbourne, VIC 3207, Australia

314–321, 3rd Floor, Plot 3, Splendor Forum, Jasola District Centre, New Delhi – 110025, India

79 Anson Road, #06-04/06, Singapore 079906

Cambridge University Press is part of the University of Cambridge.

It furthers the University's mission by disseminating knowledge in the pursuit of education, learning and research at the highest international levels of excellence.

www.cambridge.org
Information on this title: www.cambridge.org/ 9781108442411

© Cambridge University Press 2018

This publication is in copyright. Subject to statutory exception and to the provisions of relevant collective licensing agreements, no reproduction of any part may take place without the written permission of Cambridge University Press.

First published 2018

20 19 18 17 16 15 14 13 12 11 10 9 8 7 6 5 4 3 2 1

Printed in Great Britain by CPI Group (UK) Ltd, Croydon CR0 4YY

A catalogue record for this publication is available from the British Library

ISBN 978-1-108-44241-1 Paperback

Cambridge University Press has no responsibility for the persistence or accuracy of URLs for external or third-party internet websites referred to in this publication, and does not guarantee that any content on such websites is, or will remain, accurate or appropriate. Information regarding prices, travel timetables, and other factual information given in this work is correct at the time of first printing but Cambridge University Press does not guarantee the accuracy of such information thereafter.

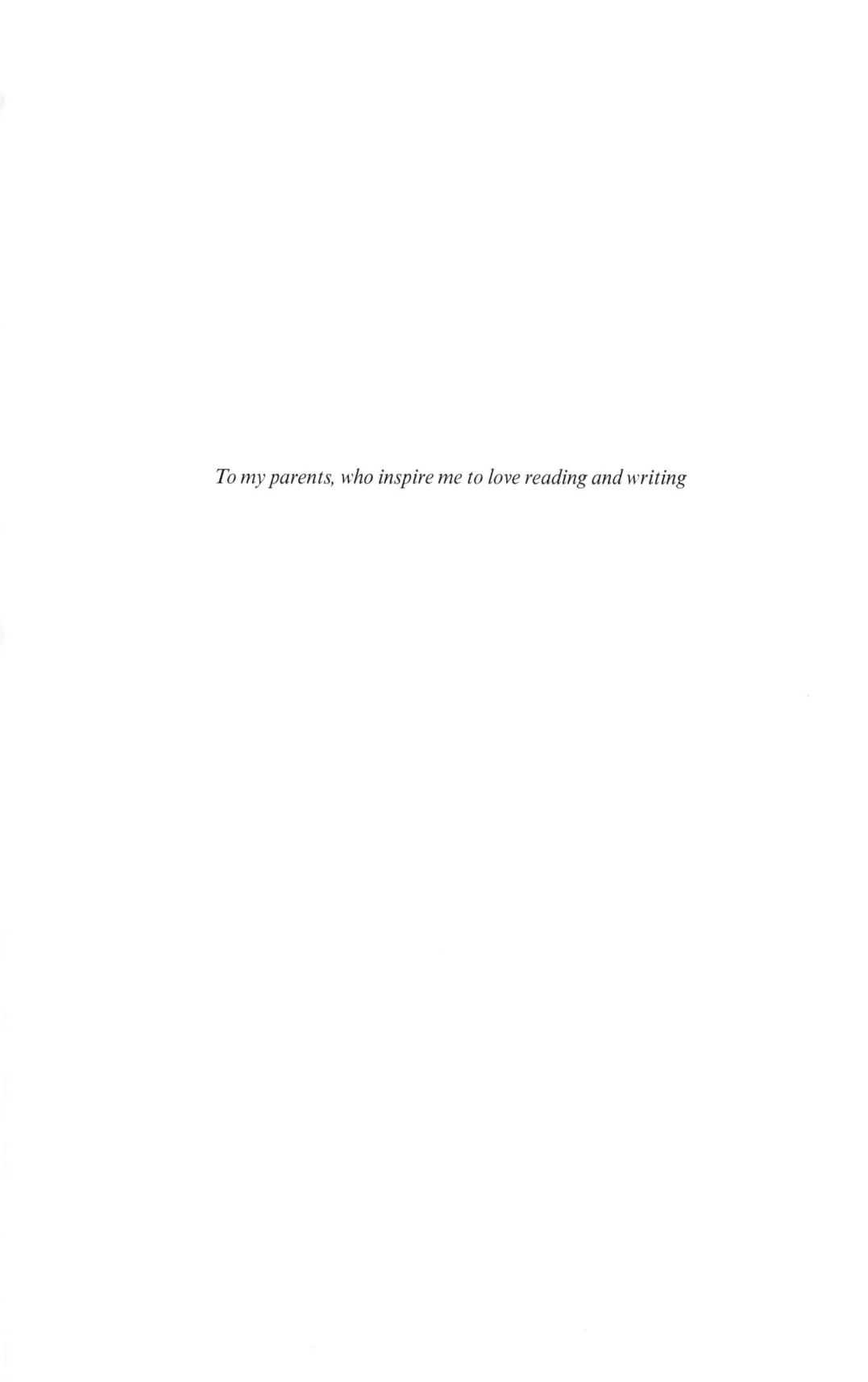

To my parents, who inspire me to love reading and writing

Contents

Acknowledgements viii
Series Editor's note ix
List of abbreviations xiii

1 Introduction   1

Section 1   Theoretical basis

2 The nature of reading-into-writing in academic contexts   15
3 A review of the use of reading-into-writing tasks in assessment   41

Section 2   Empirical evidence

4 Methodology   63
5 Contextual features of reading-into-writing tasks   84
6 Academic reading-into-writing processes   115
7 Examining the relations between tests scores and real-life
   performance   142

Section 3   Connections in English Profile

8 Conclusions and recommendations   161

References and further reading   185

Appendix 1   197
Appendix 2   203
Appendix 3   205
Appendix 4   207
Appendix 5   208
Appendix 6   213
Appendix 7   215

Author index   218
Subject index   222

Acknowledgements

I would like to express my gratitude to Fiona Barker and Nick Saville, the English Profile Studies Series Editors, for supporting my work by commissioning this volume; Stephen Bax for his invaluable feedback on the original manuscript; and John Savage for his professional editorial support throughout the production of this volume.

I am extremely grateful to Cyril Weir and Fumiyo Nakatsuhara who not only supervised my PhD studies, but who have been mentoring, helping and encouraging me on this journey. I would also like to thank David Qian and Tony Lilley for introducing me to the world of language testing. My heartfelt thanks must go to Tony Green and other colleagues at the Centre for Research in English Language Learning and Assessment (CRELLA), University of Bedfordshire, for their ongoing support, stimulating conversations and feedback on my research, from which I benefited enormously. Sincere thanks also go to the Language Training and Testing Center (LTTC), Taiwan, for funding part of the studies reported in this volume. Finally, my deepest gratitude goes to my best friend and husband, John Oyekan, and my daughter, Adelaide Oyekan, for standing by me.

Series Editor's note

The eighth volume in the English Profile Studies series, written by Sathena Chan, draws on the author's doctoral thesis, and provides much needed theoretical and empirical evidence in establishing the construct validity of *integrated reading-into-writing tasks* for L2 assessment purposes. Mastering extended writing for academic purposes is particularly difficult as students are required to retell or transform knowledge gleaned from a range of textual sources, especially textbooks and scholarly articles, in order to create new and unique pieces of discourse. They therefore need to be able to read extensively and to draw on specific information from their own domain of study in order to complete a written task. Combining reading and writing skills effectively is therefore necessary for all students, but there is an added dimension of difficulty when the target language is not the student's L1. To succeed, L2 learners require high levels of L2 proficiency in both reading and writing, as well as relevant subject knowledge and intercultural awareness within their chosen academic domain. Chan's work takes an in-depth look at the complexities of such integrated tasks and begins to unravel some of the critical factors that enable valid L2 assessments of this kind to be developed.

In keeping with the other volumes in this series, Chan relates her work to the learning and assessment of English in particular, and to the *Reference Levels* of the Common European Framework of Reference for Languages (CEFR, Council of Europe 2001) that are at the heart of the English Profile Programme. She is concerned specifically with the B2–C1 interface, as it is around this level that critical decisions are made about learners' ability to cope with a course of academic study at tertiary level.

In the introduction and Section 1 of the volume, she reviews the theoretical basis for her approach and provides a very useful overview of past and present practices in testing reading and writing. As she points out, integrated reading-into-writing tasks have a long history dating back to the early part of the 20th century, but they were later dropped by testers who focused on other constructs or struggled with the practicalities of implementing integrated tasks on a large scale. It is the practical dimension that still remains a challenge for test developers, but the availability of new technologies for language assessment is opening up opportunities and innovative approaches to address this challenge.

In Section 2, she reports on the three empirical research studies that she carried out as part of her PhD. In these studies, she covers several aspects of construct validity related to integrated task types: the task features, the mental processes of students when writing based on sources, and the relationship between test and real-life performance. Her approach is underpinned by a sociocognitive approach to construct definition as proposed by Weir (2005). These studies were carefully carried out, and the description of the methodology and outcomes should be of interest to a wide audience, especially to those who teach or test languages for academic purposes.

The good news for practitioners is that her findings show strong evidence that integrated reading-into-writing tasks can indeed be used effectively to measure academic writing from sources. Her work supports the claim that integrated essay tasks (with both verbal and non-verbal inputs) can be designed so that they have the criterial *task features* that resemble real-life writing tasks. Moreover, they can be shown to elicit the key *processes* needed for successful writing from sources, and correlate well with students' real-life writing when at university. In other words, it is possible to design integrated tasks that are both *situationally* and *interactionally authentic*, and which support the development of academic literacy in L2 learners.

In the closing Section 3, and in keeping with other volumes in this series, Chan uses her research findings to provide practical guidance for practitioners and outlines some possible directions for future research in developing integrated tasks. In doing so, she draws out the connection between her work and the English Profile Programme, and makes some recommendations for research to extend her own conclusions. For example, she suggests that a set of Can Do descriptors can be developed to describe learners' reading-into-writing abilities at the level of B2/C1, but that more evidence will be needed to determine exactly which processes would be criterial in differentiating between them. Another area for further investigation is the way that learners at different CEFR levels make use of source texts in their writing. In this respect, there is a need to understand the impact of different contextual parameters and features of input texts on the level of the task and learners' performances, including the text difficulty (e.g. as aligned to CEFR levels).

In conclusion, I believe that it is an appropriate moment to be thinking about future research on task integration. This English Profile Studies volume is being publish around the time that the Council of Europe has released a companion volume to the CEFR (Council of Europe 2018), and a key feature of this latest addition to the CEFR 'toolkit' is a focus on mediation. This concept moves us further in the direction of task integration within the sociocognitive approach to construct definition that Chan outlines.

In the CEFR (2001), mediation was introduced as one of the four modes of communication – *reception, production, interaction*, and *mediation* – in a move away from the traditional four skills (reading, writing, listening, speaking). However, mediation was not developed in the original text and there are no specific Can Do descriptors.

Series Editor's note

In the Companion Volume there is an extended treatment of mediation that opens up new avenues for language learning and assessment tasks that can be integrated in innovative ways.

Mediation is not limited to cross-linguistic mediation that involves passing on information in another language (i.e. translation and interpretation), but also covers mediation related to communication and learning. It includes transforming information from one mode to another in the *same language* (from one kind of text to another) and as such mediation is an ability that can be developed for both L1 and L2 users of a language.

The new mediation descriptors in the Companion Volume have been designed to be particularly relevant for pedagogic uses, and especially in connection to integrated, collaborative tasks. Learning tasks can be organised in such a way that learners have to share different inputs, explaining their information and working together in order to achieve a goal. The new scales for mediation are thus presented in three groups:

Mediating a text

- Relaying specific information – in speech and in writing
- *Explaining data (e.g. in graphs, diagrams, charts etc.) – in speech and in writing*
- *Processing text – in speech and in writing*
- *Translating a written text – in speech and in writing*
- *Note-taking (lectures, seminars, meetings, etc.)*
- *Expressing a personal response to creative texts (including literature)*
- Analysis and criticism of creative texts (including literature)

Mediating concepts

- Collaborating in a group
    Facilitating collaborative interaction with peers
    Collaborating to construct meaning
- Leading group work
    Managing interaction
    Encouraging conceptual talk

Mediating communication

- *Facilitating pluricultural space*
- *Acting as intermediary in informal situations (with friends and colleagues)*
- *Facilitating communication in delicate situations and disagreements*

Transforming knowledge from reading into written texts is one form of mediation that is relevant to general communication and to language learning in many contexts. In preparing learners for the use of language in academic contexts, the three groups of mediation scales can be exploited explicitly in designing learning tasks that simulate academic activities, such as seminars and workshops. For example, extensive reading could be carried out beforehand, and collaborative discussions could then take place with peers in the seminar class based on the various readings brought by each participant. Written work drawing on the sources could be produced as a follow up, either separately or in groups, and this might also lead to other kinds of output such as oral presentations.

I am sure a scenario-based approach of this kind has been used by language teachers for many years, but it has lacked the necessary theories and formalisation to enable it to be developed for high-stakes assessment purposes. Chan's work demonstrates that integrated constructs can now be defined and operationalised successfully. In the near future, it is possible to imagine how more complex types of task integration can be operationalised effectively, e.g. based on scenarios with features of mediation outlined previously. Moreover, the availability of digital technologies will enable test developers to overcome the significant practical constraints faced in the past.

Finally, I echo Chan's final conclusion that the explicit specification of academic reading-into-writing skills provided in this volume can lead to better teaching and assessment of academic writing. I also hope that this volume will inspire readers to contribute to the under-researched area of integrated language skills more generally – and I look forward to the innovative forms of integrated assessment that will be developed as a result.

Nick Saville
Cambridge
April 2018

References

Council of Europe (2001) *Common European Framework of Reference for Languages: Learning, Teaching, Assessment*, Cambridge: Cambridge University Press.
Council of Europe (2018) *Common European Framework of Reference for Languages: Learning, Teaching, Assessment. Companion Volume with New Descriptors*, Strasbourg: Council of Europe.
Weir, C J (2005) *Language Testing and Validation: An Evidence-based Approach*, Basingstoke: Palgrave Macmillan.

List of abbreviations

AWL	Academic Word List
BNC	British National Corpus
CAE	Certificate in Advanced English
CB	Computer-based
CEFR	Common European Framework of Reference for Languages
COHM	CohMetrix
CPE	Certificate of Proficiency in English
CRELLA	Centre for Research in English Language Learning and Assessment
EAP	English for Academic Purposes
EFA	Exploratory Factor Analysis
EMI	English as a Medium of Instruction
ELP	English Language Proficiency
ESP	English for Specific Purposes
ETS	Educational Testing Service
F1	Factor 1
F2	Factor 2
FYROM	Yugoslav Republic of Macedonia
GEPT	General English Proficiency Test
GSTEP	Georgia State Test of English Proficiency
IELTS	International English Language Testing System
ISE	Integrated Skills in English
KMO	Kaiser-Meyer-Olkin
LSA	Latent Semantic Analysis
LSP	Language for Specific Purposes
LTTC	Language Training and Testing Center
N.S.	No Significance
PB	Paper-based
PR	Public Relations
PTE	Pearson Test of English
RLD	Reference Level Descriptor
STD DEV	Standard Deviation
TEAP	Test of English for Academic Purposes
TEEP	Test of English for Educational Purposes
TLU	Target Language Use
TOEFL®	Test of English as a Foreign Language

TOEFL iBT	Internet-based Test of English as a Foreign Language
TTR	Type-token Ratio
UKBA	UK Border Agency
UoB	University of Bedfordshire
WPQ	Writing Process Questionnaire

1 Introduction

> This chapter gives a general overview of the volume by first explaining the research background and rationale, followed by a description of the aims and scope of the research.
>
> The aim is to orient the reader to the desire of this research to lead to better test designs to assess academic writing skills by an explicit specification of the reading-into-writing construct.
>
> The chapter covers the following areas:
> - the underrepresentation of high-level processes in L2 teaching and assessments
> - the use of integrated assessment tasks as a method to test academic writing skills
> - the insufficient attention to reading-into-writing in the English Profile
> - an overview of each chapter in the volume.

1.1 Background

The English Profile Studies series aims to expand our understanding of the way learners progress through the six levels of the Common European Framework of Reference for Languages (CEFR, Council of Europe 2001). The previous volumes have expanded our understanding of different aspects of the criterial features of L2 English at each level of the CEFR, for example, *the properties of learner language* in volume 1 (Hawkins and Filipović 2012), *language functions* in volume 2 (Green 2012), *grammar* and *vocabulary* in volume 5 (Harrison and Barker (Eds) 2015). In this volume, drawing on a comprehensive review of the literature on integrated reading-into-writing skills, we will report a range of empirical research which aimed to define learners' integrated reading-into-writing processes in academic contexts, and to identify the task variables which need to be considered for their contribution to the difficulty of integrated tasks. This volume is useful for teachers whose task is to prepare L2 students for the demands of writing from sources in academic contexts. Language test developers would also find the proposed reading-into-writing framework, which includes explicit target contextual (task) features and cognitive (learners' processes) parameters, useful as they design integrated assessment tasks at the CEFR Levels B2 and C1.

Underrepresentation of high-level processes in L2 teaching and assessments

Teaching and assessment of L2 learning of English have focused on the mastery of the 'four independent skills', i.e. reading, writing, speaking and listening. Weir, Vidaković and Galaczi (2013) conducted a comprehensive review of the practice of language assessment in the 20th century. Their findings reveal that such an approach to assessing language abilities unfortunately led to a significant underrepresentation of some, mostly high-level, processes required in the target language use (TLU) domain. For example, they observed that most standardised reading tests target lower-level processes such as *extracting factual information*, *establishing meaning at clause or sentence level*, and *inferencing the author's viewpoint*. However, high-level processes, which are essential in the academic contexts, such as *understanding ideas at textual/inter-textual levels*, and *integrating ideas from multiple sources*, are largely neglected in the reading tests they analysed. A similar issue of underrepresenting high-level processes was identified in almost all writing tests Weir, Vidaković et al (2013) surveyed. These commonly used tests mainly assessed students' abilities of writing by the knowledge telling approach (Scardamalia and Bereiter 1987), i.e. how well writers construct a written discourse from their own background knowledge on the topic. However, mastery in telling one's knowledge is hardly sufficient in real-life academic contexts where students are often expected to use the knowledge transformation approach (Scardamalia and Bereiter 1987) in which they transform or create knowledge from sources by connecting and building relationships between existing facts and ideas. Unfortunately, as noted by Weir, Vidaković et al (2013), this essential writing skill of transforming knowledge from sources has largely been neglected in L2 writing pedagogy and assessments.

The problem of underrepresentation of high-level processes was largely due to the heavy reliance on independent language tasks in L2 teaching and assessments. In the case of writing, previous research has shown that task type, among other variables such as writers' characteristics and mode of writing, has a significant impact on writers' choice of writing approach and hence the processes involved in writing (Severinson Eklundh and Kollberg 2003, Weigle 2002). In other words, independent language tasks, however well constructed, are not likely to elicit these desirable high-level processes required in the academic contexts. One obvious solution is, therefore, to use a different task type in L2 teaching and assessment.

Integrated assessment tasks as an alternative to elicit high-level processes

Based on the nature of the processing involved, language tasks can be categorised into independent and integrated tasks. Independent tasks aim to assess only one language skill, either reading, listening, speaking or writing. For example, while some reading and writing skills are usually involved in a listening task, they are not part of the construct being assessed. Writing-only tasks refer to impromptu writing tasks in which students are asked to respond to a short task prompt (instructions). One typical example of writing-only tasks is an impromptu argumentative essay task which is used extensively in large-scale academic writing tests, such as International English Language Testing System (IELTS), Test of English as a Foreign Language (TOEFL®), Aptis and Cambridge English Qualifications.

Integrated tasks, on the other hand, require students to employ more than one language skill to complete the communicative goal of the task. Integrated reading-into-writing tasks typically require students to produce a written discourse in response to some reading materials. In pedagogical context, reading-into-writing refers to those 'instructional tasks that combine reading and writing for various education purposes' (Asencion-Delaney 2008:140). Flower, Stein, Ackerman, Kantz, McCormick and Peck (1990) defined reading-into-writing as 'the process of a person who reads a relevant book, an article, a letter, knowing he or she needs to write' (1990:6). From the perspective of language testing, Weigle (2004) defines reading-into-writing as 'a test that integrates reading with writing by having examinees read and respond to one or more source texts' (2004:30).

Before we discuss our working definition of 'reading-into-writing', it is worth clarifying some related terminologies. Although some researchers use the terminology 'reading-to-write' or 'writing from sources', the term 'reading-into-writing' is usually used by large-scale testing providers as a category to refer to this task type. Due to the focus on language testing, the terminology of 'reading-into-writing' is therefore used throughout this volume. Reading-into-writing tasks are sometimes referred to as 'discourse synthesis' tasks due to the influential work conducted by Spivey (1984, 1990, 1997, Spivey and King 1989). Their work investigated how writers select, organise, and connect ideas from different reading source texts into a writing product (their findings will be discussed in detail in Section 2.3). However, this volume considers discourse synthesis tasks to be a subordinate type of the reading-into-writing tasks because apart from discourse synthesis, there are other processes, such as summarising, comparing and contrasting, and prioritising ideas, involved in different types of reading-into-writing tasks. In this volume, we define reading-into-writing as a task that requires students to write a continuous text by drawing upon single or multiple reading materials which can be verbal, non-verbal or both. Students may or may not need to find additional reading materials on their own. Common reading-into-writing tasks include, but are not limited to, summary, an essay based on multiple sources, report writing from multiple sources, case study, review, and library research paper (more details about the common reading-into-writing tasks used in academic contexts will be provided in Section 2.1).

With improved language teaching and testing literacy, there has been a renewed interest in using integrated tasks to assess language proficiency over the past decade. Integrated tasks have been introduced in the Internet-Based Test of English of a Foreign Language (TOEFL iBT), the General English Proficiency Test (GEPT) Advanced test in Taiwan, and university-wide language programmes (Plakans 2008, Weigle 2004). Based on a series of test review and redevelopment projects, Trinity College London has reinforced the role of the reading-into-writing task in its suite of Integrated Skills in English (ISE) (Chan, Inoue and Taylor 2015). The use of integrated assessment tasks as an alternative to the dominantly used independent tasks has not only generated interest in the field of language testing; researchers in relevant fields, such as L2 teaching and learning and academic literacy, have argued that integration of reading and writing skills is essential for academic success (Carson 2001, Carson and Leki 1993, Flower 1990, Grabe 2001, 2003, Johns 1993, Leki and Carson 1994, 1997, Lenski and Johns 1997). It is, therefore, important to expose L2 students, and arguably L1 students with less academic writing experience, to integrated tasks in their training.

While there is a widespread growth in popularity of integrated reading-into-writing tasks in standardised English language proficiency (ELP) tests and English for academic purposes (EAP) classrooms, researchers have complained that there is insufficient empirical validity evidence of this test task format in the literature (Asencion 2004, Esmaeili 2002, Plakans 2008, 2010, Weigle 2004). As Yu (2013) noted in a special issue of *Language Assessment Quarterly* which was dedicated to integrated reading-into-writing assessment, 'while integrated assessment has fascinated the field by its promising validity, the multidimensionality and complexity of its nature has sparked inquiries and concerns' (2013:110). Given the widespread demand of using integrated assessment, it is now time to provide a more comprehensive and consistent theoretical framework which allows us to systematically research, develop and assess integrated language assessment.

Insufficient attention to reading-into-writing in the English Profile

Due to the widespread awareness and use of the CEFR around the world today as a framework of reference for language learning, teaching and assessment, it has become desirable for test developers to bring the CEFR into the test design from the early stages of construct definition (Harsch and Rupp 2011). The CEFR describes what language learners can do at various stages of their learning. The CEFR describes language learners in relation to three groups of six broad levels of ability: the Basic User (A1 Breakthrough and A2 Waystage), the Independent User (B1 Threshold and B2 Vantage) and the Proficient User (C1 Effective Operational Proficiency and C2 Mastery). The CEFR global scale descriptors (see Table 1.1) give a useful indication of the level of skill and quality of performance that is expected of a second language user at each of the six levels. Relating test design to the CEFR is believed to facilitate stakeholders' understanding of task features and the expected student performance at each of the CEFR levels.

However, the CEFR global scale makes little reference to integrated skills, i.e. how language users at different levels can employ more than one macro skill, i.e. reading, writing, listening or speaking, to complete the communicative functions of a task. The only reference to integrated skills is at C2 level (highlighted in bold in Table 1.1). This seems to convey a message that integrated skills are evidence of a degree of language proficiency unique to the highest level.

In addition to the global scale, the CEFR provides Can Do statements to describe what learners at each level can do across four language skills: speaking (spoken interaction and spoken production), listening, reading and writing. The CEFR recognises that there are two distinct types of speaking skills in relation to the learner's speaking production, and their ability to take part in conversations and discussion where listening is involved. However, the CEFR does not distinguish the learner's ability to write from their own internal resources and their ability to write from sources where reading is involved.

Given the fact that the CEFR is designed to be language neutral, the English Profile project was funded by Cambridge University Press, Cambridge Assessment English and the European Commission (November 2009–12) as a research programme to 'help teachers and educationalists understand what the Common European Framework of Reference (CEFR) means for English' (see www.englishprofile.org). Based on data collected from real learners of English by corpus research techniques, English Profile describes what aspects of English are typically learned at each CEFR level in terms of Reference Level Descriptions (RLDs) (Council of Europe 2001, 2009). These RLDs in turn serve as a framework to classify, systematise and compare learner production of the English language. It is hoped that the framework could inform teachers, curriculum developers, coursebook authors and test writers what is suitable for learning and testing at each level.

Since its publication, the CEFR has become influential in building a shared understanding of performance levels for foreign language learners. While the CEFR distinguishes between learners' speaking production and

Table 1.1 Common Reference Levels: global scale (Council of Europe 2001:24; author's emphases)

Proficient Users	C2	Can understand with ease virtually everything heard or read. **Can summarise information from different spoken and written sources, reconstructing arguments and accounts in a coherent presentation.** Can express him/herself spontaneously, very fluently and precisely, differentiating finer shades of meaning even in more complex situations.
	C1	Can understand a wide range of demanding, longer texts, and recognise implicit meaning. Can express him/herself fluently and spontaneously without much obvious searching for expressions. Can use language flexibly and effectively for social, academic and professional purposes. Can produce clear, well-structured, detailed text on complex subjects, showing controlled use of organisational patterns, connectors and cohesive devices.
Independent Users	B2	Can understand the main ideas of complex text on both concrete and abstract topics, including technical discussions in his/her field of specialisation. Can interact with a degree of fluency and spontaneity that makes regular interaction with native speakers quite possible without strain for either party. Can produce clear, detailed text on a wide range of subjects and explain a viewpoint on a topical issue giving the advantages and disadvantages of various options.
	B1	Can understand the main points of clear standard input on familiar matters regularly encountered in work, school, leisure, etc. Can deal with most situations likely to arise whilst travelling in an area where the language is spoken. Can produce simple connected text on topics which are familiar or of personal interest. Can describe experiences and events, dreams, hopes and ambitions and briefly give reasons and explanations for opinions and plans.
Basic Users	A2	Can understand sentences and frequently used expressions related to areas of most immediate relevance (e.g. very basic personal and family information, shopping, local geography, employment). Can communicate in simple and routine tasks requiring a simple and direct exchange of information on familiar and routine matters. Can describe in simple terms aspects of his/her background, immediate environment and matters in areas of immediate need.
	A1	Can understand and use familiar everyday expressions and very basic phrases aimed at the satisfaction of needs of a concrete type. Can introduce him/herself and others and can ask and answer questions about personal details such as where he/she lives, people he/she knows and things he/she has. Can interact in a simple way provided the other person talks slowly and clearly and is prepared to help.

their ability to integrate listening and speaking when taking part in conversations and discussion as two separate skills, the writing skill focuses predominantly on learners' ability to produce written discourse from their own knowledge. There is almost no description of learners' ability to write from reading sources in the CEFR, which is the aim of this volume. The only reference to integrated reading-into-writing skills in the global scale of the CEFR is at the highest C2 level. Similarly, for the CEFR self-assessment grid, integrated skills are covered only under the category of writing at the level of C2:

'I can write summaries and reviews of professional or literary works' (Council of Europe 2009:27). Besides, these Can Do statements seem to emphasise the genre and have little reference to the integration of skills and/or the processes involved in these skills.

One could argue that the CEFR deals with learners' ability of integrating reading and writing in relation to *mediation*,[1] which is defined as follows:

> The written and/or oral activities of mediation make communication possible between persons who are unable, for whatever reason, to communicate with each other directly. Translation or interpretation, a paraphrase, summary or record, provides for a third party a (re)formulation of a source text to which this third party does not have direct access. Mediating language activities – (re)processing an existing text – occupy an important place in the normal linguistic functioning of our societies (Council of Europe 2001:14).

However, the written mediation activities referred to by the CEFR aim to serve as an intermediary between the original writer of a text and its un(intented) reader. According to the CEFR's definition, learners who engage in mediation activities are not concerned with expressing their own meanings, but with narrowing the gap of misunderstanding by, for example, paraphrasing specialised texts for lay persons. Therefore, in our view, these written mediation activities are different from the integrated reading-into-writing skills required of students in academic contexts (see Section 2.3).

While it is a general belief that integrated reading-into-writing skills involve a certain level of mastery of the individual reading (e.g. to comprehend texts) and writing skills (e.g. to produce clear, well-structured, detailed text on complex subjects), empirical evidence has revealed that integrated reading-into-writing skills are different from the ability to employ those two individual skills one after another (Asencion-Delaney 2008, Hirvela 2004). Furthermore, L1 studies which investigated younger writers' (i.e. Grade 6, 8 and 10 in US schools) abilities to write informational reports from sources found that these students' abilities to select, organise content from the sources and provide connections between ideas progressed along their grade level (Spivey and King 1989). In this case, there is a need to fill the gap in the CEFR by defining how integrated reading-into-writing skills progress across the CEFR levels with a consideration of the relevant task factors.

In addition to the underrepresentation of reading-into-writing in the global scale of the CEFR, this same issue can be found in the more detailed illustrative scales (see Table 1.2); most of the descriptors concern the use of

---

1 At the time of this volume's publication, a Companion Volume to the CEFR (Council of Europe 2018) is being prepared to extend the notion of mediation. The extended definition of mediation has more relevance to the reading-into-writing construct addressed in this volume.

Table 1.2 CEFR descriptors which are relevant to reading-into-writing constructs (Council of Europe 2001; author's emphases)

CEFR descriptors	A1	A2	B1	B2	C1	C2
Overall written production (2001:61)				Can write clear, detailed texts on a variety of subjects related to his/her field of interest, **synthesising and evaluating information and arguments from a number of sources.**		
Reports and essays (2001:62)			Can **summarise,** report and give his/her opinion about accumulated factual information on familiar routine and non-routine matters within his/her field with some confidence.	**Can synthesise information and arguments from a number of sources.**		
Overall reading comprehension (2001:69)				Can read with a large degree of independence, adapting style and speed of reading to different texts and purposes, and **using appropriate reference sources selectively.**		

Table 1.2 (continued)

| Processing text (2001:96) | Can copy out single words and short texts presented in standard printed format. | Can copy out short texts in printed or clearly handwritten format. Can pick out and reproduce key words and phrases or short sentences from a short text within the learner's limited competence and experience. | Can collate short pieces of information from several sources and summarise them for somebody else. Can paraphrase short written passages in a simple fashion, using the original text wording and ordering. | Can summarise a wide range of factual and imaginative texts, commenting on and discussing contrasting points of view and the main themes. Can summarise extracts from news items, interviews or documentaries containing opinions, argument and discussion. Can summarise the plot and sequence of events in a film or play. | Can summarise long, demanding texts. | Can summarise information from different sources, reconstructing arguments and accounts in a coherent presentation of the overall result. |

an individual language skill, reading or writing. Only four of the 12 scales which focus on reading and writing make specific reference to integrated use of skills.

As shown in Table 1.2, what is seemingly lacking is a systematic reference of the integrated reading-into-writing skills (and arguably other types of integrated skills) in the CEFR. The scale of *processing text* has the most complete description of the aspect of integrated skills involved across the levels, whereas the other three scales have occasional mentions at either B1 or B2 levels. Compared to the scales on writing (e.g. creative writing, writing correspondence, overall written interaction) and reading (e.g. reading correspondence, reading for orientation, reading for information and argument, and reading for instructions), it therefore appears that there is room to provide a more complete set of descriptors for the integrated reading-into-writing skills in the CEFR. It is hoped that the findings reported in this volume will provide the empirical basis to describe learners' integrated reading-into-writing skills in academic contexts and to identify the task variables which need to be considered for their contribution to difficulty.

1.2 Aims and scope of the empirical research reported in this volume

This volume reports on a series of three validation studies whose aim was to investigate the integrated reading-into-writing construct in academic contexts in terms of its context, cognitive and criterion-related validity.

Context validity concerns the internal task features and linguistic demands of the test task, as well as the external social and cultural contexts in which the test task is used (Weir 2005a). Cognitive validity concerns the individual language user and their cognitive or mental processing of the test (Field 2013, Weir 2005a). Criterion-related validity is concerned with the extent to which test scores correlate with a suitable external criterion of performance (Weir 2005a) (more discussion of these validity components is provided throughout the volume). As this volume mainly addresses the construct of integrated reading-into-writing skills in academic contexts, the discussion is focused on the CEFR B2 and C1 levels which are most relevant to academic language use. Specifically, the research was conducted in three strands to address each of these validity components:

1. To examine the predominant contextual features of a range of real-life academic writing tasks and reading-into-writing test tasks.
2. To investigate the cognitive processes writers employed to complete these integrated tasks.
3. To explore the relationships between reading-into-writing test scores and real-life academic writing scores.

Methods utilised include task survey, expert judgement, automated textual analysis, questionnaire and score analysis. Based upon a synthesis of relevant literature and empirical evidence from a series of studies, the volume puts forward a framework with explicit contextual and cognitive parameters to define the integrated reading-into-writing skills at the CEFR B2 and C1 levels for language teachers, test developers and researchers who intend to develop and validate reading-into-writing assessment at these levels.

To contextualise the empirical research, Chapter 2 reviews in some detail the theoretical foundations for defining the integrated reading-into-writing constructs. Particular attention is paid to theories and models that define construct in relation to task features and cognitive processes underpinning language use. Chapter 3 offers an overview of the use of reading-into-writing tasks in standardised settings, to describe some of the most widely used formats in its testing, and to discuss the benefits of using the integrated task type and some issues raised from current practice. Chapter 4 describes the methodology of the three validation studies (Study 1, Study 2 and Study 3) in detail. The findings of each of these studies are reported in Chapters 5, 6, and 7 to provide empirical evidence of the construct of reading-into-writing in relation to the three major validity components, i.e. context, cognitive and criterion-related validity. Finally, Chapter 8 summarises the main findings of the research reported in this volume, discussing the implications of the findings on teaching, assessment and English Profile, and making recommendations in relation to future test designs and research in the area.

Section 1
Theoretical basis

2 The nature of reading-into-writing in academic contexts

> This chapter builds on the general overview provided in Chapter 1 by considering the nature of reading-into-writing in academic contexts in more detail.
>
> The aim is to orient the reader through an overview of the nature of reading-into-writing and the theoretical foundations for defining the integrated reading-into-writing constructs. We pay specific attention to key theories and models that define construct in relation to task features and cognitive processes underpinning language use, so as to provide links to Chapters 5, 6 and 7 where the construct of reading-into-writing is investigated.
>
> The chapter covers the following areas:
> - common reading-into-writing tasks in academic contexts
> - task variables influencing reading-into-writing task difficulty
> - cognitive models relevant to reading-into-writing.

Reading-into-writing is essential for students' success in higher education, particularly at universities in the UK where achievement is predominantly assessed through students' written work. A sound theory of academic reading-into-writing will be essential for developing valid tasks of teaching and assessing these skills. This chapter considers the importance of developing a satisfactory understanding of academic reading-into-writing. An overview of the reading-into-writing task features is provided, followed by a discussion of how these task features may influence the reading-into-writing process and product. After that, we further explore the nature of academic writing processes and how individual processes may change at different levels of proficiency.

2.1 Common reading-into-writing tasks

The best way to understand academic reading-into-writing is perhaps to survey the types of writing that are required of students in real-life academic contexts. In recent decades, researchers have surveyed the tasks that are required of students across different academic disciplines such as linguistics, engineering, business and computing (e.g. Bridgeman and Carlson 1983,

Carson 2001, Horowitz 1986a, 1986b, Johns 1993, Leki and Carson 1994, Weir 1983).

Some of these studies were conducted with the purpose of test development, for instance, the Test of English as a Foreign Language (TOEFL) (Bridgeman and Carlson 1983, Hale, Taylor, Bridgeman, Carson, Kroll and Kantor 1996) and the Test of English for Educational Purposes (TEEP) (Weir 1983). Although the research methods and task terminologies used vary from study to study, their findings have conclusively indicated that most academic writing tasks require students to write from reading sources.

By surveying teachers in 190 academic departments across undergraduate and postgraduate levels in Canada and the USA, Bridgeman and Carlson (1983) found that two task types: a) *description and interpretation of non-verbal input* and b) *comparison and contrast plus taking a position* were perceived as the most typical by teachers. The two task types identified were adopted by the TOEFL Test of Written English and the IELTS Academic Module Writing paper. However, their study was criticised for drawing entirely upon the perceptions of teachers rather than surveying actual tasks. Other studies which surveyed actual writing tasks and/or curriculum and syllabus documents also showed that reading plays a significant role in academic writing tasks. Hale et al (1996) analysed actual writing tasks assigned in 162 undergraduate and graduate courses in several disciplines at eight universities. They found that the most common writing tasks across disciplines (social sciences group and sciences group) and levels (graduate and undergraduate) were *short task, essay based on substantial reading on a topic, summary of sources, report with interpretation* and *research paper with literature review*. Similarly, based on an analysis of writing tasks in 38 faculties, Horowitz (1986a, 1986b) reported that reading was essential in the most common academic writing task types including *synthesis of multiple sources, connection of theory and data, report, research report* and *summary*. Among these types, *synthesis of multiple sources* was most typical across the 38 faculties. More recently, Cooper and Bikowski (2007), with a pedagogical purpose for EAP, analysed 200 graduate course syllabuses from 10 academic departments with follow-up interviews at one university. Their findings similarly showed the important role of reading in the most commonly assigned writing tasks. Library research paper and project report were the most common across disciplines, while review, proposal, case study, and summary were more common in the social sciences, humanities, and arts domains. All these tasks involved some extent of integration of ideas from multiple sources. For example, the library research paper requires students to synthesise multiple bibliographic sources; project report requires students to report an original research with a critical review of previous research; summary requires students to condense information from single or multiple sources.

The findings of these studies showed that most academic writing tasks across disciplines require students to write drawing upon external materials. In other words, students have to draw purposefully on a variety of external resources, such as textbooks, journal articles, websites and lecture notes, as well as internal resources from the writer's long-term memory, such as genre knowledge, linguistic resources, topic knowledge and strategic use knowledge, during the writing process. Many of the researchers, therefore, concluded that integration across reading and writing skills is essential for academic success (e.g. Carson 2001, Grabe 2001, 2003, Johns 1993, Lenski and Johns 1997). However, when describing the task variables, most of these findings lack the level of specificity that is needed for practitioners to develop tasks for teaching or testing academic reading-into-writing skills.

When we consider the features of reading-into-writing tasks, we have to attend to important task factors which would lead to satisfactory context validity. Context validity addresses the appropriateness of the linguistic and content demands set in a language test task in comparison with the task features of those tasks in the TLU context (Shaw and Weir 2007, Weir 2005a). Bachman and Palmer (1996) defined TLU domain as 'a set of specific language use tasks that the test taker is likely to encounter beyond the test itself, and to which we want our inferences about language ability to generalise' (1996:44). The importance of developing test tasks which are representative of the TLU domain is well established in the literature (Bachman1990, Bachman and Palmer 1996, Weigle 2002, Weir 1983, 1990, 2005a). As test takers only respond to one or two writing tasks in most writing tests, researchers in the field are concerned about how the features of these chosen test tasks may reflect real-life tasks in the TLU domain, and these features should be controlled in order to simulate appropriate performance conditions at different levels. Based on the literature, we will now review task variables which are likely to have an impact on task difficulty, students' processes and performance, and therefore on context validity.

2.2 Task variables influencing task difficulty

In the last decade, a few important publications in the literature of writing tests identified the essential task variables from slightly different perspectives. Hughes (2003), in his textbook for language teachers, identified the 'minimum requirement' of writing task variables, which include operations, types of text, addressees, length of texts, topics, dialect and style. Based on Bachman and Palmer's (1996) task characteristics framework, Weigle (2002), in a book targeting a more specialised language testing readership, proposed a more detailed list of the most essential task variables. Apart from subject matter, genre, rhetorical task, pattern of exposition, specification (of audience, role, tone, and style), length and time allowance, she argued that prompt wording, stimulus material, choice of prompts, transcription mode and scoring criteria would also impact the nature and difficulty of the task.

Relating particularly to large-scale writing tests, Shaw and Weir (2007) proposed a more systematic approach to address task variables (context validity) in terms of two major components: setting (task and administration) and linguistic demands (task input and output). Setting concerns both the overall task features and administration. Administration refers to the physical testing conditions, logistics and security issues, which are important considerations for large-scale examinations. Their list of the task-setting variables echoed what have been previously identified which includes response format, purpose, knowledge of criteria, weighting, text length, time constraints and writer–reader relationship. Their discussion on the importance of specifying the linguistic demands of task input and output when developing a writing task is particularly insightful for the context of integrated tasks. Although their model does not explicitly specify the relationship between task input and output, they recognise the potential impact of task input variables on students' writing output. For integrated reading-into-writing tasks, it would be important to control the level and features of the task input students received. Another contribution of their framework is that they attempted to explain how changes in each of these task variables may influence the processes used by the test takers (cognitive validity), and in turn have an impact on their performance to be scored. For example, it is essential to specify the discourse mode of the task because, given all other features being equivalent, a task which requires a summary of the author's viewpoints is more demanding than a task which requires reporting only factual information. It is, however, equally important to specify the difficulty of the input sources. This has called for the need to research how best to control the relationship between input and output demands.

From the perspective of Language for Specific Purposes (LSP), Douglas (2000) argued for the importance of controlling task input and the expected interaction between input and response. Also, based on Bachman and Palmer's (1996) task characteristics framework, he explained thoroughly what parameters need to be specified in order to develop an 'authentic' context. A valid task prompt should specify the features of context by providing information regarding setting, participants, purpose, form, tone, language, norms and genre, and identify the problem for the writers. And input data sources need to be specified in terms of format, length and level of authenticity. The most insightful category in this framework for our discussion here is the interaction between input and response which includes the scope and directness of how writers should interact with the input materials.

The work reviewed above (i.e. Bachman and Palmer 1996, Douglas 2000,

Hughes 2003, Shaw and Weir 2007, Weigle 2004) has largely concluded the list of task features which need to be specified when developing a valid writing task. Some variables are more essential than the others depending on the nature of the task and the context in which the task is being used. However, there is insufficient discussion regarding the task features that are most essential to reading-into-writing tasks in the literature. Only a handful of studies have explored certain task features which may have a direct impact on the difficulty of integrated tasks, and hence influence the students' reading-into-writing processes and products. The literature on both reading and writing will be drawn on here to shed light on how each of these task variables might impact on the difficulty of an integrated task.

In the context of reading-into-writing tasks, it is vital to control not only the productive demands but also the receptive demands imposed on writers and the scope of interaction between input and response expected of the writers. Based on the literature, here we discuss some key task variables which are believed from the literature to be most relevant to academic writing:

- purpose of writing
- intended reader
- topic
- genre (input and output)
- interaction between input and response
- language functions
- time constraint and length
- knowledge of criteria
- complexity of the reading input (conceptual and linguistic)
- lexical
- syntactic
- degree of coherence.

It has been argued that it is vital for a writing task to present test takers with a 'clear, precise and unequivocal' *purpose of writing* which 'goes beyond a ritual display of knowledge for assessment' and information about the *intended reader* (Shaw and Weir 2007:71). Douglas (2000) similarly argued that it is important to provide test takers with a purpose for interacting with a context, which he called 'the identification of the problem'. Presenting a clear and precise purpose in the task instruction would arguably be more essential for successful completion of a reading-into-writing task. Previous studies have shown that writers plan how to make use of the reading materials based on how they perceive the task purpose and for whom they are writing (Flower et al 1990). For example, without a clear presentation of the purpose and intended readership, the notion of what constitutes a good summary or synthesis is open to the writers' own interpretation. Writers often determine what information is relevant in the sources based on their understanding of the purpose of writing and the intended readership (Van Dijk and Kintsch 1983).

Topic is another major variable shown to have significant impact on writing performance (Clapham 1996, Douglas 2000, Read 1990). In the widely adopted CEFR writing grid, topics are categorised into personal and daily life, social, academic and professional domains (Council of Europe 2001). Tasks at the lowest proficient level typically involve topics from personal and daily life, medium level in the social domain, whereas the highest level typically involves topics in the academic or professional domains. Writers in general perform better with a familiar topic than an unfamiliar one (Clapham 1996). In terms of reading, Alderson (2000:69) argued that 'topic (un)familiarity cannot be compensated for by easy vocabulary: both difficult vocabulary and low familiarity reduce comprehension, but texts with easy vocabulary do not become easier if more unfamiliar topics are used, and vice versa'. Urquhart and Weir (1998:143) suggested that text content that test takers are sufficiently familiar with can activate schemata to employ appropriate skills and strategies to comprehend the text. Therefore, a topic set for a task has a direct impact on the demands of content knowledge and lexical knowledge imposed on the writers.

Genre (the type of text to be produced and the type of text to be read), which is 'the expected form and communicative function of the written product; for example, a letter, an essay, or a laboratory report (Weigle 2002:62), is also identified as a major factor which influences the task difficulty. Generally speaking, narrative texts recount an event or a series of related events. Descriptive texts describe a person, place or thing using sensory details. Expository texts tend to give information about or an explanation of an issue, subject, method or idea.

Argumentative texts typically involve a course of reasoning. At the levels of B2 and C1, argumentative essay seems to be dominant in many large-scale writing assessments. The possibilities of input format provided in reading-into-writing tests include single or multiple verbal/non-verbal inputs.

There has been surprisingly little research on the effect of different input formats on the writing process and product. Some genres are believed to be less demanding to process and summarise than the others (Taylor 2013). For example, narratives are perceived to be easier to summarise than expository texts because the former tends to contain factual information which is organised in a linear structure whereas the latter tends to contain more complicated complex and unfamiliar ideas (Spivey and King 1989). Argumentative texts, on the other hand, would be more challenging to summarise as this requires high-level reading skills to understand the author's points of view

(Brewer 1980, Yu 2008). Weigle (1999) compared two common types of non-verbal input: table/chart and graph. The findings indicate that the table/chart prompt (making and defending a choice based on information presented in a table or chart) tends to elicit traditional five-paragraph essays, while the graph prompt (describing trends in a graph and making predictions based on the information presented in the graph) would elicit several rhetorical angles. This shows the need to investigate and control the impact of input materials on the writing process and product. Other variables of the reading materials are discussed later.

In the context of reading-into-writing, the expected *interaction between input and response* is arguably a key variable which influences the task difficulty. Therefore, we will discuss this in more detail than the other variables. Weigle (2002) is one of the few researchers who recognised the cognitive demands imposed on writers as a task variable. According to Purves, Soter, Takala and Vahapassi (1984), the three major cognitive levels are (i) reproducing facts/ideas, e.g. copying from sources, recalling from long-term memory; (ii) organising/reorganising information, e.g. retelling information, summary; and (iii) generating new ideas through processing the given ideas, e.g. applying, analysing, synthesizing, evaluating. This notion echoes Scarmadalia and Bereiter's (1987) distinction between the knowledge telling approach used typically by novice writers and the knowledge transforming approach typically used by expert writers.

Douglas (2000) argued that the cognitive demands of the interaction between input and response should be analysed in terms of the scope of the reading needing to be processed and how directly writers should draw upon the material. In other words, a task with more linguistically challenging input texts would not necessarily be more difficult than a task with easier input texts, if the former requires copying a few factual details and the latter requires a thorough evaluation of the given ideas. According to Fitzgerald and Shanahan's (2000) model of the development of reading and writing, a student's ability to handle interaction between reading and writing varies across different L1 proficiency stages from lower-level processing of mastering reading and writing as two separate skills to higher-level processing of handling multiple viewpoints in reading and writing, and constructing and reconstructing knowledge through reading and writing. Therefore, it is important to consider the cognitive demands of the reading-into-writing tasks in terms of the expected interaction between input and output texts.

Writing tasks at the lowest level require writers to retell their own prior knowledge on the topic and/or information provided in the input texts. This primarily involves a linear process of retrieving the writer's internal resources from long-term memory and/or retelling (i.e. without using the writer's own words or ideas) relevant information from the input texts in response to the communicative purpose of the writing task. Galbraith and Torrance (1999:3) described such a writing process as 'think-say' or 'what next?' writing. Writing tasks at this level do not explicitly require writers to organise or critique the information they have retrieved from long-term memory and/or have copied from the input texts. Hence, the structure of most texts produced on such tasks would largely reflect the sequences of how the writer has retrieved the content from the internal resources and/or selected the information from the external input texts. Scardamalia and Bereiter (1987) regarded such writing process as knowledge telling writing, which is an approach typically employed by immature writers. The standard test format of the impromptu writing-only task type has been criticised as being inauthentic, knowledge-telling tasks, which merely require writers to draw upon internal resources (Cumming 1997, Feak and Dobson 1996, Lumley 2005, Weigle 2002, 2004, Weir, Vidaković et al 2013).

Writing tasks at the level of reorganising content, by contrast, require writers to develop an explicit representation of the rhetorical problem of the writing task and purposefully organise the content they have retrieved from long-term memory and/or selected from the input texts to solve the rhetorical problem of the writing task. Examples include letters to inform, statements of personal views, technical descriptions, summaries and letters of advice (Purves et al 1984).

Writing tasks at the highest level – knowledge transforming (Scardamalia and Bereiter 1987) – require writers to establish an awareness of the rhetorical situation of the writing task. Writers are required to strategically organise as well as transform the content they have retrieved from long-term memory and/or selected from the input texts to fulfil writing goals. Examples include book reviews, commentaries, critical essays and reports (Purves et al 1984).

A variable related to the expected interaction between input and response is the specific *language functions* test takers are required to perform on the task. Douglas (2000) argued that these language functions, e.g. to *argue* with supporting details, to *compare and contrast* different ideas, are part of the construct definition. He argued that the functions required of writers to perform need to be identified based on context-based research and consultations with subject specialists. Shaw and Weir (2007) saw the possible relationship between the functions tested (what they called functional resources) and the Can Do statements in the CEFR (Council of Europe 2001) which aims to identify what learners are able to do across levels.

Knowledge of criteria is another task variable which often receives insufficient attention. Shaw and Weir (2007) argued that test takers should be fully aware of which criteria are to be used in the marking. Douglas (2000) commented in a similar way that evaluation criteria tend not to be well specified in task rubrics. As discussed previously, one challenge of current reading-into-writing tests is the lack of specific marking criteria. Knowledge of marking criteria is important because it affects test takers' monitoring and revising processes where differences between expert and novice writers are expected to emerge. In other words, provided with sufficient knowledge of marking criteria, skilled writers tend to monitor and revise their text based on the criteria whereas unskilled writers tend not to do so.

Time constraint is one major distinction between real-life and pedagogical/test conditions. Real-life tasks typically allow more time for completion than a practice/test task does. There is comparatively little discussion in the literature regarding how the time constraint on reading-into-writing tasks influences test takers' cognitive processes. Field (2004) argued that the difference between novice and expert writers is that the former can employ more processes with greater automaticity than the latter. Another question for reading-into-writing tasks is the proportion of time allocated for processing the reading materials. Most reading-into-writing tasks tend to allow test takers to decide upon the allocation of time themselves. *Length* of the reading materials and output is a variable related to the time allowed in the task. There is insufficient research into the how the length of reading materials impacts the difficulty of a reading-into-writing task. In reading examinations, readers are expected to read longer texts as the level of proficiency progresses. However, in the context of reading-into-writing, shorter texts, especially those which are modified from originally longer authentic texts, may well be more difficult to summarise than longer texts.

The *complexity of the reading materials* is well researched in the wider reading literature. A range of subjective textual parameters which may influence the complexity of a reading text has been identified. A few significant studies which have had impact this area of research are discussed here to aid our discussion of how reading materials might affect the difficulty of a reading-into-writing task (see a summary of other studies in Wu 2014). Bachman, Davidson, Ryan and Choi (1995) conducted a test comparability study in which they compared the complexity of reading texts used in IELTS and TOEFL. They investigated a range of text variables such as the nature of the text, length, vocabulary, grammar, cohesion, distribution of new information, type of information, topic, genre, rhetorical organisation and illocutionary acts. Alderson, Figueras, Kuijper, Nold and Takala (2006) included text source, authenticity, discourse type, domain, topic, nature of content, text length, vocabulary and grammar as relevant features for text analysis. Enright et al (2000) started to categorise these variables into three groups: grammatical/discourse, pragmatic/rhetorical and linguistic. Khalifa and Weir (2009) urged that we should take this list of text variables further by establishing how each variable might distinguish the features of reading texts at the different levels of proficiency.

These studies mainly used expert judgement to analyse the complexity of reading texts. However, with the advance of automated text analysis tools such as CohMetrix and VocabProfile, a more systematic and objective methodology for establishing the complexity of reading texts has become more popular. A series of recent studies incorporated the approach of automated textual analysis to evaluate the features of texts used in different large-scale reading tests (see Green, Ünaldi and Weir (2010) for their analysis on the IELTS Academic Reading test; Green et al (2012) on *Cambridge English: Advanced* (now known as C1 Advanced) reading texts; and Wu (2014) on the GEPT Reading test). Although these studies were conducted for reading tasks, the same method can be adapted to investigate the features of input texts of integrated tasks.

There appears to be a consensus in the literature that there are two types of text complexity: linguistic complexity and conceptual complexity (Taylor 2013). A brief review of the possible variables is provided here. *Lexical complexity* is believed to be one of the dominant factors controlling the linguistic complexity of a text. Word frequency, word length and type-token ratio (TTR) are the most commonly used lexical indices. Word frequency measures the proportion of vocabulary of a text against different wordlists such as the British National Corpus (British National Corpus 2007) and the Academic Word List (AWL) (Coxhead 2000). Word length measures the number of letters or syllables a word contains, as shorter words tend to be easier to read. TTR measures the number of different words in a text. A higher ratio indicates a higher degree of lexical variation and thus suggests increased text difficulty. As the TTR decreases, words are repeated many times within the text, which should increase the ease and speed of text processing. This measure is particularly useful if texts of similar length are compared. However, it should be noted that a limitation of TTR and other similar lexical measures is their sensitivity to the length of the text analysed (Koizumi 2012). To minimise the impact of this limitation, we controlled the length of the texts analysed (for more details, see Section 4.1).

Syntactic complexity is another major factor of the linguistic complexity of a text. Text length, average sentence length, syntactic similarity and readability formulas are syntactic-related indices commonly used to reflect the complexity of a text. Text length measures the total length of a text. The longer the text, the more difficult it tends to be. A longer text would require more information processing of word recognition, sentence parsing and propositional encoding (Grabe 2009). Average sentence length is often used to estimate syntactical complexity because short sentences tend to be syntactically simpler than long sentences.

Syntactic similarity measures how syntactically similar the sentences of a text are. It is easier to process a text with more syntactically similar sentences than with more syntactically different sentences due to a syntactic parsing effect. Readability formulas, such as Flesch Reading Ease and

Flesch-Kincaid Grade Level, measure the relative numbers of syllables, words and sentences found in a text. They are widely used to measure text difficulty, especially in the USA. Despite the widespread application of the readability formulas, researchers (e.g. Green et al 2012, Weir 2012, Weir, Vidaković et al 2013) have argued that these measures (i.e. Flesch Reading Ease and Flesch-Kincaid Grade Level) seem to come up with results which are closely aligned to individual measures of average syllables, words and sentences and therefore results from individual measures might be more useful for the purpose of development of test materials.

In addition to the lexical and syntactic complexity of a text, *degree of coherence* is also deemed important to determine the difficulty level of a text. Generally speaking, coherent texts tend to be easier to comprehend than less coherent texts (Beck, McKeown, Sinatra, and Loxterman 1991). Goldman and Rakestraw (2000) showed that cohesive devices which contribute positively to establishing textual coherence would also help readers to connect ideas. However, the effects of cohesion may not be a totally independent indicator because cohesion interacts with the readers' familiarity of the topic and their own proficiency level (Alderson 2000:68).

On the other hand, compared to linguistic complexity, there has been less attention paid to researching the *conceptual complexity* of a reading text because these variables, e.g. degree of concreteness, explicitness of textual organisation, ideas density, distribution of new information and cultural specificity, tend to be more difficult to evaluate. It is believed that a text with more abstract ideas is harder to understand than a text which contains more concrete ideas, e.g. description of real objects, events or activities. Alderson (2005) argued that the more concrete, conceivable and interesting the ideas a text contains, the more readable it is and easier to summarise. Although automated textual analysis tools, e.g. CohMetrix, claim to be able to assess such quality, Wu (2014) found that indices relating to text abstractness were of limited use. In her view, human judgement was more valid regarding the conceptual complexity of a text.

Input materials for reading-into-writing tests are usually adapted from authentic texts and their textual structure is usually simplified during such procedures. However, the *textual organisation* of the reading texts is likely to directly impact the complexity of a reading-into-writing task. In order to transform ideas from sources, high-level reading processes are needed to create a coherent representation of the reading texts at textual and intertextual levels (Britt and Sommer 2004, Hartmann 1995, Perfetti 1997, Perfetti, Rouet and Britt 1999, Spivey 1997). It is easier to process and summarise a text with an explicit structure (e.g. using cohesive markers) than one with an implicated structure.

As we can see from the review in Section 2.1, the impact of these linguistic and conceptual variables on the complexity of a reading text, and hence, the difficulty of a reading task, is well established in the literature. However, one should not automatically assume that these variables would impact the difficulty of a reading-into-writing task in exactly the same way. In this volume, we will examine the features of a range of reading-into-writing tasks in terms of these variables (for the results see Chapter 5).

To define the construct of reading-into-writing at the different CEFR levels, it is essential to identify the criterial features which are likely to impact the difficulty level of an integrated task. However, an investigation of task features on its own is insufficient for the purpose of construct definition, as Bachman (1990) criticised the deficit of many construct validation studies in that they 'examine[d] only the products of the test taking process, the test scores, and provide[d] no means for investigating the processes of test taking themselves' (1990:269). Hale et al's (1996) account of the limitations of their study further illustrates why it is important to consider students' processes in construct investigation. Initially, they planned to analyse the writing tasks in relation to four subcategories of cognitive demands (i.e. retrieve/organise/relate, apply, analyse/synthesise, and evaluate) but they later found it 'unclear from the wording of the assignment alone' (Hale et al 1996:44) to judge what processes students may use. Their solution was to categorise the cognitive demands into two broad categories: lower or higher level. Some other researchers also attempted to investigate the cognitive demands of academic writing tasks by analysing the rhetorical functions presented in the wording of the assignment. For example, Moore and Morton (1999, 2005) revealed that evaluation, description and summarisation are the three most frequently incorporated rhetorical functions. Their findings revealed, to some extent, what cognitive demands are required of students in order to complete the writing tasks. However, the cognitive processes test takers actually engage in while completing the writing tasks may not be the same as those expected of them. Therefore, effort needs to be made to investigate students' reading-into-writing processes at the different CEFR levels, even though this is 'rarely an easy matter' (Shaw and Weir 2007:35). In this volume, in addition to defining the contextual features of reading-into-writing tasks (for results, see Chapter 5), we will investigate students' reading-into-writing processes under both real-life academic and test conditions (for results, see Chapter 6). To build the theoretical foundations of our cognitive investigation, we will review models of writing, reading and discourse synthesis and discuss their relevance to reading-into-writing.

2.3 Models of writing, reading and discourse synthesis relevant to reading-into-writing

Having reviewed the list of the contextual variables which might affect the difficulty level of integrated tasks, we now turn to the theoretical basis of cognitive models of language use to establish cognitive parameters of the reading-into-writing construct at the different CEFR levels. As there is a lack of a coherent model of reading-into-writing in the literature (Hirvela 2004), we would consider the various models of writing, reading and discourse synthesis and discuss their relevance to the reading-into-writing construct.

However, before we review the literature regarding the processes of writing from sources, it is perhaps useful to clarify some key terms that are commonly used in the literature: *cognition*, *processing*, *strategy* and *metacognition*. According to Field's (2004) *Psycholinguistics: The Key Concepts*, *cognition* refers to the faculty which permits a person to think and reason and is the *process* involved in thought and reasoning. Information *processing*, which is an approach to analysing cognition developed by Donald Broadbent in the 1950s, refers to the flow of information through the mind when a task is performed. In contexts of communication, *cognitive processing* refers to the processes/operations underlying (a) the four language skills; (b) the retrieval of lexical items (decoding); and (c) the construction of meaning and discourse-level representation (Field 2004:224). The use of some low-level cognitive processes, e.g. decoding in reading, can be automatic, especially for skilled language users, and therefore may not be available to report. *Metacognition* is 'thinking about thinking'. It involves pre-planning which metacognitive process, such as macro-planning, organising, monitoring and revising, to use, and exercising control over the process or taking steps to ensure that its results are stored long term (Field 2004:61). Metacognition usually involves higher degrees of awareness and is therefore more likely to be reportable. A *strategy* is a compensatory technique '(a) to compensate for breakdowns in communication due to insufficient competence or to performance limitation and (b) to enhance the rhetorical effect of utterances (Canale 1983:10). In most second language studies, cognitive process and strategy were not made distinctive (e.g. Cohen 1984, Purpura 1997, Van Dijk and Kintsch 1983). However, it is important to differentiate these terms and concepts for the discussion in this volume. The cognitive validity of a language task concerns primarily whether the cognitive processes elicited by the tasks, through the specified task features, accurately represent those used by expert language users in real-life contexts.

A fundamental distinction of academic reading-into-writing by skilled writers from other types of writing, e.g. narrative and creative writing, is mostly due to its *knowledge transforming* nature. Following previous work (e.g. Lowenthal 1980, Murray 1978, Odell 1980), Scardamalia and Bereiter (1987) described the writing processes employed by writers at contrasting levels of writing expertise from novice writers e.g. school children and inexperienced L2 writers, to expert writers, e.g. graduates and academics in terms of 1) how knowledge is brought into the writing processes and 2) what happens to the knowledge during these processes. They found that the writing processes employed by expert writers in academic contexts involved transformation of knowledge such as synthesised facts from multiple sources or well-supported opinions on a particular topic. Expert writers have a high awareness of the conflicts between available resources (from their own memory and external materials) and the purpose of the writing task. They engage actively with the task to address the problems of 'what to write' and 'how to write' during the writing process. And they would constantly evaluate the available resources against their goals and constraints. In contrast, due to a lack of expertise in writing, novice writers tend to use a rather linear text-generating process by 'telling' existing knowledge and information available from memory which has been automatically activated by the cues provided in the writing task. When constructing a text, novice writers rely heavily on these automatic memory probes. Their primary focus is to generate enough text and hence seldom engage in goal-directed planning, monitoring, and revising processes during the composition of the task i.e. less metacognitive activity.

Bereiter and Scardamalia's (1987) influential work has differentiated the writing approaches at the two ends of writing expertise. Another contribution of their work is that they recognised the possible impact of task on a writer's approach, even though there was not much discussion about the relationship between task and process in their model. In other words, an expert writer may well choose to use a knowledge telling approach if transformation of knowledge is not required by the task. And more importantly, L2 writers can be trained to be very 'skilful' in using the knowledge telling approach to produce coherent and well-formed texts without progressing to master the knowledge transforming approach. Therefore, many researchers have argued that it is important to teach and assess academic writing using task types which elicit knowledge transformation.

As previously described, almost all academic writing tasks involve *an integration of reading and writing skills*. However, a cognitive model which accounts for the processes involved in writing from sources has yet to be fully developed, especially in relation to L2 contexts (Hirvela 2004). It is clear from previous work that academic writing, like any other reading or writing activities, involves a set of recursive multiple cognitive processes. It is beyond the scope of this volume to review the extensive literature of models of reading and those of writing (see Khalifa and Weir (2009) for a thorough review of different reading models, and Shaw and Weir (2007) for writing models), but it is useful to summarise the major components of reading and writing processes from previous models in order to shed light on the integrated nature of academic writing. Both receptive and productive language skills involve multiple cognitive phases, and each phase involves multiple processes. A major challenge for language testing is how to model these phases and processes within an overall test validation framework.

Field (2004, 2008) proposed that reading as a receptive language skill involves key cognitive phases of input decoding, lexical search, parsing, meaning construction, and discourse construction. Based on the assumption that one's short-term memory is limited, he argued that degree of automaticity of mastering these phases distinguishes differences between expert and less experienced readers. Expert readers would have high automaticity of all processes whereas less experienced readers would need to spend considerable effort in performing all or some of these processes, depending on the level of their expertise in reading.

Following Field's (2004, 2008) and Kellogg's (1996) models, Khalifa and Weir (2009) proposed a more elaborate model of reading which arranges the key reading processes in an ascending order of cognitive demands. The reading processes include *word recognition*, *lexical access*, *syntactic parsing*, *establishing propositional meaning*, *inferencing*, *building a mental model*, *creating a text-level representation* and *creating an intertextual representation*. A major contribution of Khalifa and Weir's model is that they attempted to give an account of which reading processes are tested in standardised reading tests at a range of proficiency levels based on pooled expert analysis of sample tasks. They reported that most standardised reading comprehension tests target reading at the lower end of their model, while processes at the higher end are relatively neglected. They argued there is a need to reconsider the most appropriate format to target these higher-end reading processes. Weir, Vidaković et al (2013) argued that the reading-into-writing task type would be the most authentic way to make these processes explicit. While Khalifa and Weir's model acknowledges the role of these higher-end reading processes in real-life academic contexts, they offer little discussion about how these reading processes interact with writing processes. In the context of reading-into-writing, we therefore need to consider how the reading processes interact with the writing processes when a writer writes from sources.

As mentioned previously, there is a lack of comprehensive models which include writing from sources. However, some previous research studies have investigated the 'unique' processes involved in writing from sources (i.e. the processes which are typically not involved in reading comprehension or writing from memory). Two important models proposed from this branch of work are related to summarising writing by Van Dijk and Kintsch (1983) and synthesis writing by Spivey (Spivey 1984, 1990, 1991, 1997, 2001, Spivey and King 1989). Kintsch and Van Dijk (1978) proposed that summarising writing involves three major processes: deletion of redundant propositions; substitution of a sequence of propositions by a more general one; and selection of the macro-proposition of the text, or the construction of a macro-proposition when one is not explicitly stated.

In addition, Spivey and colleagues (e.g. Mathison and Spivey 1993, Spivey and King 1989, Spivey 1990, 1997, 2001) conducted a series of studies to investigate the processes involved in different writing tasks which require the use of reading materials. This body of work is known as *discourse synthesis* which is defined as 'a process in which readers read multiple texts on a topic and synthesize them' (Spivey and King 1989:11). The findings of these studies showed that when writing from sources, a writer transforms a new representation of meaning from multiple texts to create their own text through three core processes: a) selecting relevant content from multiple texts, b) organising the content according to the writing goals, and c) connecting the content from different sources and *generating* links between these ideas. These findings indicate that reading-into-writing activities place higher cognitive demands on students than activities of reading comprehension and writing from memory.

In the L2 literature, Plakans (2008) studied 10 participants' writing processes on both reading-into-writing and writing-only tasks by the use of think-aloud protocols and interviews. The results identified two stages of reading-into-writing: *preparing-to-write* and *write*. She argued that reading plays an important role at both stages in terms of 'reading and interacting with source texts' and 'using source texts'. However, the nature of the reading process and the interaction between reading and writing were largely unexplained. In a later publication, Plakans (2009a) further explored the role of the reading process in completing the task. She identified five processes used by the participants: (a) goal-setting for reading the source texts, (b) cognitive processing, (c) global strategies, (d) metacognitive strategies, and (e) mining the source texts for use in writing. While the work provided useful insights into which reading processes writers employed when they wrote from reading materials, Plakans (2009a) did not explain how these processes fit into the reading-into-writing model she proposed earlier (2008).

Having reviewed the models of reading, we now turn to the writing literature where a considerable amount of research has been conducted in an attempt to establish the cognitive processes involved in writing and the internal and external variables that would impact on the writing processes in an educational or academic context (e.g. Field 2004, 2011, Grabe and Kaplan 1996, Hayes 1996, Hayes and Flower 1980, 1983, Kellogg 1996, Shaw and Weir 2007).

A highly influential model of writing was proposed by Hayes and Flower (1980). They investigated the writing processes of adult writers by an (at the time) innovative use of think-aloud protocols. They proposed that writing is an extended, goal-directed, problem-solving exercise which involves multiple recursions of *planning, translating* and *reviewing*. The model also explained that the writing processes interact with two other components: *task environment* and *writer's long-term memory*. Task environment is an external component which refers to task variables such as genre, topic and intended readership. Writer's long-term memory refers to the writer's internal content knowledge about the genre, topic and intended readership as well as rhetorical knowledge about how to write. Hayes and Flower's (1980) model challenged the perception of writing as a linear process and largely fixed the terminology of writing processes in the literature (Scardamalia and Bereiter 1996). However, the model has been criticised for not explaining how writing processes vary with different task types and how writing processes vary with memory constraints (Shaw and Weir 2007).

An updated version of the model (Hayes 1996) expanded the number of internal and external components which may impact on the writing processes. Internal factors include working memory, long-term memory resources and the motivation of the writers, whereas external factors include the physical environment of the task (e.g. the text read so far, the writing medium) and the social environment of the task (e.g. the audience, other texts read while writing). Regarding the writing processes, the revised model replaced the three major processes *planning, translating* and *reviewing* by more general process categories: *reflection, text production* and *text interpretation*. Planning was renamed as *reflection,* which involves problem-solving, decision-making, and inferencing processes. Writers employ general problem-solving and decision skills to achieve writing goals. At the same time, writers make inferences about audience, writing content and so forth. Translation was replaced by *text production*, which refers to a more active text-producing process guided by cues from the writing plans or text produced so far. Reviewing was no longer a separate process but became part of *text interpretation,* which involves reading and scanning graphics. The new model attempted to describe the complex interactive nature of the writing processes within and among each process category and the relationship between the writing processes and different internal and external components. It emphasised the central role of working memory in writing. However, there is apparently insufficient explanation about how various components interact with the writing processes, other than a general claim of the theoretical relationships among them.

Another important contribution of Hayes's (1996) model was its acknowledgement of 'the role of reading in writing'. Hayes (1996) highlighted three major purposes of reading in writing: reading to define the writing task, reading source texts to obtain writing content, and reading and evaluating text produced so far. However, the model did not explain in detail how the internal and external components impact on the writing processes and how the reading processes interact with the writing processes.

From a perspective of communicative language use, Grabe and Kaplan (1996) looked at cognitive processes involved in L2 writing in particular. The model consists of two major phases: the context of language use and a 'verbal working memory' unit. They proposed that goal setting, which is conducted within a task context (e.g. setting, task, text, topic), would activate three components in the 'verbal processing' unit, which are language competence, world knowledge and 'online processing assembly' (i.e. execution of the writing processes). In addition, they argued for the importance of metacognitive awareness and monitoring in the entire writing process. Although the model has drawn attention to the importance of goal setting and metacognitive processing in L2 writing, the model did not seem to distinguish adequately between the differences between resources stored in long-term memory and the processes operated by working memory (Shaw and Weir 2007:35–36).

The above models are important in shaping the current understanding of the cognitive processes involved in writing. Although these models pointed out that cognitive processes are affected by test takers' characteristics and task and social factors, they do not seem to provide enough explanation of how the cognitive processes are influenced by these factors. More recent models, which build upon psycholinguistic theory, offer a clearer account of how writing processes are influenced by internal factors, when compared to the above models. Kellogg (1996, 1999, 2001) made a strong argument for the importance of working memory in writing. He proposed that the individual processes of writing draw upon different components of working memory, rather than seeing working memory as a unitary facility. For example, planning and editing make use of spatial working memory, reading and translation make use of verbal working memory, whereas monitoring and interactions among these processes are co-ordinated by central executive working memory.

Field (2004, 2011) proposed a model which accounts for the phases that a writer goes through when they produce a text (as a productive language skill). Field's model was based upon Kellogg's (1996) model and Levelt's (1989) model of speaking. He proposed that writing, as a productive skill, involves the phases of conceptualisation, organisation, encoding (grammatical, lexical, graphic), execution and monitoring (the phases will be discussed further later in this section. Drawing upon information processing theory, Field (2004) explained how high- and low-proficiency writers tend to approach these phases differently (the term *high-proficiency writers* usually refers to writers with high proficiency of English but they may or may not have good writing skills (e.g. these writers may be able to produce a fluent written discourse but lack of summarisation skills) whereas *expert writers* usually refers to writers with expertise in writing (i.e. these writers are skilful in producing particular types of writing).

A critical issue for language teaching and testing is how to identify which phases and processes are relevant for test development and validity. Building upon Kellogg's and Field's models, Shaw and Weir (2007) considered five processes: *macro-planning, organisation, micro-planning, translation* and *monitoring and revising* to be most relevant to the discussion of the cognitive validity of writing tests. They argued that valid writing tests should elicit from test takers those core cognitive processes involved in real-life writing.

They then evaluated how these processes have been elicited by the Cambridge Assessment English (then Cambridge ESOL) Writing tests across different levels. Their approach to evaluating the cognitive validity of test tasks with a set of cognitive parameters has laid down some key principles for research in the field of language testing.

The discussion above has shown that writing from sources is not a linear act, but involves a set of multiple recursive processes, such as planning (at macro and micro levels), organising, execution/translating, monitoring and revising. Although the writer may employ particular processes at different phases, the processes are largely overlapping and looping back and forth. In addition, writing is not an isolated act but is influenced by internal variables such as working memory capacity, long-term memory sources (e.g. linguistic, discourse and content knowledge), as well as external factors, such as task variables and other social variables. The selection of individual processes and the decision as to how to employ them during the writing process is based upon conscious planning, but execution is largely controlled by working memory. Some processes, such as planning and monitoring, are largely influenced by task variables. That is why the first strand of the construct investigation reported in this volume is to identify the criterial features of a reading-into-writing task.

Based on the evidence of theoretical and empirical research into models of reading, writing and discourse synthesis, we feel that an appropriate model for EAP reading-into-writing would be multi-dimensional, considering as far as possible the global and local levels of comprehension, the key processes in discourse synthesis as well as the writing processes involved in composing different genres from various sources for various purposes. For this book, we will focus on the higher-level processes because language users in most English as a Medium of Instruction (EMI) universities are expected to be at CEFR B1 or above. Most language users at these levels would have presumably mastered high automaticity in the lower-level processes, such as decoding, lexical search, and parsing and encoding. By synthesising the models of language use reviewed earlier in this sub-section, we propose the following cognitive phases to be most relevant to our discussion of the cognitive construct of academic reading-into-writing. For each cognitive phase, we will review the findings of previous studies which investigated the sub-processes involved. This will serve as the theoretical basis of our investigation of the reading-into-writing processes in Chapter 5.

Conceptualisation (Field 2004, 2011, Kellogg 1996) is the first phase of productive skills where the writer develops an initial mental representation of a writing task. Most writers create an initial understanding of the task situation through reading the task prompt. However, Flower (1990) argued that for writers to conceptualise the task demands, interpretation is more important than reading comprehension. She defined the process of *task representation* as 'an interpretive process that translates the rhetorical situation – as the writer reads it – into an act of composing' (Flower 1990:35). Grabe and Kaplan (1996) argued that writers set goals (planning) based on their understanding of the task. When writers approach the same task, they may choose to employ different processes based on the task representation they created and hence produce very different products. Flower (1990) found that undergraduates created task representation differently for the same reading-into-writing tasks in real-life academic contexts. The students had a different understanding of the same task in terms of primary sources of ideas, features of the text, organisational structure of the text, and strategies to use. The findings showed that students with more academic writing experience tended to create a more accurate task representation than those with less academic writing experience.

Ruiz-Funes (2001) studied the processes of how 14 advanced-level L2 students produced an essay to discuss a literary text. Similar to Flower et al's study (1990), Ruiz-Funes found that the writers created task representation of the same tasks differently. Her findings also revealed that a more cognitively complex representation of rhetorical style did not always lead to a text with the most complex textual structure. Plakans (2010), as a follow-up to Plakans (2008), investigated 10 undergraduates' task representations on reading-into-writing argumentative essays through think-aloud protocols. The findings revealed that the group of students who did not have much academic writing experience believed that all source texts needed close understanding. In contrast, the group of students who were more experienced with academic writing regarded the source texts as a tool to generate ideas and tended to read the source texts quickly.

Scardamalia and Paris (1985) investigated how advanced and novice writers may create task representation differently by analysing writers' retrospective recalls of the text they produced. Their findings showed that almost 50% of the recall protocols from advanced writers reveal information other than the actual content of the text they produced. In contrast, the recall protocols of weaker writers resembled their text content closely. They argued that the additional information revealed in the protocols may reflect some of the writers' task representation. Although their method of investigating writers' task representation was indirect, their study reflected, at least to some extent, that when advanced writers approach a task they tended to generate a more complete and complex understanding of the task by considering issues such as writing goals, gist of the text (what to write) and organisational structure of the text (how to write). Task representation is therefore an important process which can distinguish skilled writers from unskilled writers.

Another important process in conceptualisation is *planning* (Hayes and Flower 1980). Field (2004) and Shaw and Weir (2007) further distinguished the planning process conducted at macro- and micro-level. Planning conducted at this phase is largely at macro-level. Shaw and Weir (2007) defined macro-planning as a process of determining what is necessary for successful task completion in terms of different aspects for consideration such as intended readership, genre, content and style.

Scardamalia and Bereiter (1987) argued that unskilled writers who use the knowledge telling approach do not seem to employ planning or goal setting at the macro level because they write a text following a process where they retrieve relevant ideas from long-term memory. On the other hand, skilled writers who use the knowledge transforming approach tend to put explicit effort into macro-planning. Field (2004) shared a similar notion that skilled writers pay a lot more attention to planning than do unskilled writers. Eysenck and Keane (2005) further argued that it is the planning process which helps to differentiate skilled from unskilled writers. Similar results showing that second language (L2) writers tend to plan less than first language (L1) writers were reported by Hyland (2002). L2 writers are also found to encounter more difficulty in setting goals. Researchers have been attempting to reveal what writers actually plan by using think-aloud protocols. The results of Burtis, Bereiter, Scardamalia and Tetroe's (1983) study showed that the planning protocols of immature writers closely resemble the ideas presented in the text they produced. In contrast, the planning protocols of advanced writers consist of 'provisional ideas, goal statements, comments, and problem-solving attempts' (Burtis et al 1983:154). The process of macro-planning is believed to be influenced by contextual features of the task (Grabe and Kaplan 1996, Shaw and Weir 2007). It is, therefore, necessary for test developers to know how the contextual features of reading-into-writing tasks impact on the test takers' macro-planning process.

In short, most writers conceptualise a task through creating a task representation and macro-planning but, as previous research shows, writers at the different proficiency levels do so differently. These processes are important in the construct of reading-into-writing as writers' understanding of the demands of a reading-into-writing task and their plan of how to fulfil these demands would directly influence the way they approach the task. Previous studies also show that writers at different proficiency levels create task representation and plan differently. In this volume, we will investigate how undergraduates conceptualise reading-into-writing tasks (see Chapter 5).

Meaning construction is a phase when the writer contextualises abstract meanings based on the contextual clues provided in the writing task and their own schematic resources (background knowledge) (Brown and Yule 1983, Field 2004). In the context of reading-into-writing, the writer constructs meaning by connecting and integrating ideas from different sources and transforming these ideas into a new representation. An obvious process is, therefore, to 'read' the sources. It is perhaps straightforward to identify when and for how long (i.e. location and length) a writer reads the sources, yet it is much more important to investigate which reading processes are involved in reading-into-writing tasks. However, such empirical evidence is seemingly very limited in the literature. Khalifa and Weir (2009), based on Weir (1983) and Urquhart and Weir (1998), identified two major types of reading: careful and expeditious reading which students perform in real-life conditions. Careful reading involves comprehension of every part of the whole text while expeditious reading means processing texts selectively, quickly and efficiently to access desired information from a text. They also identified reading processes at different levels. Higher-level processes, such as establishing propositional meaning, inferencing, building a mental model, creating a text-level representation and creating an intertextual representation, are most relevant to writing from sources.

According to Spivey (1990, 1997, Spivey and King 1989), writers establish a meaning representation by selecting and connecting information from long-term memory or sources in relation to their relevance to the writing task. The new 'meaning' generated can take the form of inferences of missing details (Kintsch 1974) or connections between present ideas from source texts and ideas stored in the mind (Seifert, Robertson and Black 1985). Scardamalia and Bereiter (1987) argued that advanced and immature writers select ideas in significantly different ways. Immature writers 'select' idea units by running a test of appropriateness, a process which is similar to what Gomulicki (1956) described as an unconscious process of ranking elements according to importance when recalling knowledge. In contrast, advanced writers select content which is relevant to the task with conscious cognitive effort. Their selecting process is guided by explicit sets of criteria regarding the writing goal, appropriateness for the intended reader, structure of text, and available linguistic resources.

According to Scardamalia and Bereiter's (1987) model, unskilled writers use a knowledge telling approach whose primary purpose is text generation. They tend not to process ideas from sources deeply nor to reconstruct relevant prior knowledge. As their focus is to generate enough text, it is not uncommon for large chunks of verbatim copying to be found in unskilled writers' texts (for details see Cumming et al 2005). In contrast, skilled writers, who use a knowledge transforming approach in writing, constantly select ideas from sources and connect them with those retrieved from memory. To construct meaning for their writing, skilled writers connect ideas from different sources to find out which ideas are most relevant or appropriate to the task context. However, these ideas from both sources are possibly repetitive or in a different order of importance according to the writers' goals. The process of organising (discussed shortly) is usually activated to solve the problem of how to express these connected ideas during text production.

As we see from the review above, the processes of meaning construction from sources is key to academic writing. In reading-into-writing, test developers should replicate the performing condition in which students are required to construct meaning by connecting and integrating ideas from single or multiple texts, and transforming these ideas into a new representation for the purpose of the task. We will investigate the extent to which these processes are elicited by reading-into-writing tasks in Chapter 5.

Organising is a phase where the writer 'provisionally organises the ideas, still in abstract form, in relation to the text as a whole and in relation to each other' (Field 2004:329). Shaw and Weir (2007) explained that the process of organising employed when writing is to order the ideas to 'determine which are central to the goals of the text and which are of secondary importance' (2007:38). Spivey (1990, 1997, Spivey and King 1989) argued that the process of organising is particularly challenging for writing which involves the use of reading materials. Field (2004) argued that there is an abstract provisional organisation of ideas in the writers' mind. For example, if a task requires the writers to describe an event, most writers would have a sequential structure in mind. If the task asks writers to compare and contrast, most writers would have an advantages-vs-disadvantages structure in mind. These structures generated in writers' minds may or may not be the same as the source texts. Therefore, when organising ideas, some writers may retain a similar global structure as one presented in a single-source text (Spivey 1984) or generate a new structure in order to incorporate different idea chunks from multi-source texts (Spivey 1991).

Scardamalia and Bereiter (1987) argued that immature writers who adopt the knowledge telling approach rely largely on a natural flow of writing without devoting much effort to organising the ideas. Their research further showed that immature writers can become very 'skilful' in 'organising' a text this way, especially when the tasks encourage retrieving ideas from memory. As knowledge telling writers aim at a smooth text generation, they are likely to put down the ideas in the same order as they were retrieved from memory (i.e. put down what appeared in mind first) or as they were presented in the source texts. In other words, this is similar to a process of 'dumping all (the) knowledge at once', which is identified as a strategy employed by writing-disabled students whose ability to organise is disrupted (cited in Cherkes-Julkowski, Sharp and Stolzenberg 1997:179). Johns and Mayes' (1990) study revealed that less proficient L2 writers tend to copy without organising the ideas they have selected from the source texts.

On the other hand, advanced writers approach a writing task as a problem-solving exercise in which they have to solve three major problems of 'what to write' created in content problem space as well as 'how to write it' and 'whom to write to' in rhetorical problem space (Graham 2006:460). When goals and constraints in one problem space interact with the other, a process of organising is activated to settle these goals (e.g. to compare A and B), constraints (e.g. lack of a structure of comparison) and resources (e.g. ideas retrieved from memory and/or selected from source texts). Most advanced writers would 'transform' available ideas into their own text by explicitly ordering them, identifying relationships between them and/or determining which are central to their writing goals and so on.

As we have seen, reading-into-writing tasks are more likely to elicit high-level organising processes beyond the level of writing down ideas in the same order as they are retrieved from memory (which is an organising process commonly reported by students while they complete a writing-only task, e.g. Chan 2011, Weir, O'Sullivan, Jin and Bax 2007). As Shaw and Weir (2007) argued that organising is an important process as it is closely related to the organisational requirements and assessment employed in most large-scale writing tests, we will investigate how students organise ideas in the reading-into-writing tasks in Chapter 5.

Translation (execution) is a phase when a writer's internal ideas are translated into linguistic forms. Shaw and Weir (2007) argued that the language translated needs to be not just lexically and syntactically appropriate but functionally appropriate as well. Field (2004) pointed out that the cognitive demand of translating for less proficient L2 writers may be so high that they would not be able to carry out other processes at the same time. Translation is an important phase in writing. However, when compared to other processes, translation seems to be more difficult to be reported reliably unless through directed verbal protocols (Field 2004). Previous studies which investigated this cognitive phase were usually conducted under experimental settings and focused on text generating at the micro level (see Kellogg (1994) for a review). This phase will not be investigated in this volume as, given our focus at the B2 and C1 levels, we are more interested in higher-level processes involved in academic writing from sources.

Monitoring and revising is a 'feedback' phase where the writer checks the quality of the text. After monitoring, a writer usually revises the unsatisfactory parts of the text (Field 2004:330). Monitoring and revising can focus on lower-level aspects of text quality such as accuracy or higher-level aspects such as argument and coherence. In the context of academic writing, writers are also typically concerned with plagiarism. For example, most writers would revise unsatisfactory parts where quotations are poorly made or where sentences are copied directly from source texts. Monitoring and revising can be employed at any point of the writing process. Fitzgerald (1987) argued that writers can revise 'a text' mentally before it has actually been composed, revise as they compose, or revise the previously composed text. But as the first type is hardly observable, we will focus on the latter two in this volume, i.e. revisions made at the current location of the text and those at a previous point in the text.

Monitoring and revising are highly demanding in terms of cognitive effect (Field 2004, Kellogg 1996, Shaw and Weir 2007). Writers, especially L2 writers, tend to focus on one aspect of the text at a time due to short-term memory constraints. With attentional constraints, many writers would set aside high-level monitoring and revising to a later stage of the production.

Many studies have compared the revising process employed by skilled and unskilled writers and found that skilled writers are better at revising than less skilled (Graham and Harris 1996, 2000, Severinson Eklundh and Kollberg 2003). Hayes and Flower (1980) found that 15% of the protocols made by skilled writers related to revising. Perl (1979) found that writers who followed the knowledge transforming model made revisions about goals and main ideas.

With the aid of keystroke-logging technology, systematic analysis of revisions is now possible. Severinson Eklundh and Kollberg (2003) used it to investigate how texts were constructed by skilled writers (a group of 10 university students) by tracking all the writers' revisions of the texts throughout the writing process. They found that these writers conducted revisions of different aspects: creating a new global content unit, revising to contrast, revising for consistency, revising for coherence, revising for clarity, explicitness, or emphasis, revising to eliminate repetition and revising to emphasise text structure. In contrast, unskilled writers tend to devote little attention to revising. They usually revise at a lower level, e.g. correcting errors and making small changes in wording (Fitzgerald 1987, Macarthur, Graham and Harris 2004). Scardamalia and Bereiter (1987) found that, provided that instruction is given, L1 unskilled writers would begin to make content-related revisions in the forms of 'changing the order of adding an introductory sentence, adding a conclusion, providing additional descriptive information, and inserting missing information' (1987:155).

In short, in our search for differentiated processes of writing from sources in academic contexts, we turned to previous models of reading, discourse synthesis and writing in the literature. As a result, we have proposed five cognitive phases which include conceptualisation, meaning construction, translation, organising, and monitoring and revising to be most useful and relevant for empirical scrutiny in Chapter 2. In addition, if EAP test task performance is to be used to support inferences about performance in the wider domain of academic real-world tasks, it is essential that both target reading-into-writing activities and test tasks be described in terms both of cognitive processes and of the contextual parameters they are performed under. A central assumption in Weir's (2005a) socio-cognitive test validation model (which will be discussed in detail in Section 3.3) is that cognitive processing always occurs within and is significantly affected by its context. Based on the literature, we have also identified a range of task features which might be important contributors to the level of task complexity and difficulty. These parameters served as the basis of a close examination of the salient task features for reading-into-writing tasks to teach and assess students' abilities in writing from sources in academic contexts. Following on from the literature review in relation to the construct of academic reading-into-writing, the next chapter first summarises the major discussions regarding the benefits and challenges of using the integrated reading-into-writing task type to assess students' abilities in writing from sources and reviews the use of different reading-into-writing tasks in standardised writing tests.

3 A review of the use of reading-into-writing tasks in assessment

> This chapter builds on the theoretical foundations for defining the construct of reading-into-writing in Chapter 2 by considering the use of reading-into-writing tasks in language assessments in detail.
>
> The aim is to orient the reader through an overview of the promises and challenges of using the integrated assessment tasks as a method to assessing academic writing skills in standardised language tests. We also aim to draw the reader's attention to the test development and validation approach which governs the direction and procedures of the three empirical studies reported in Chapters 5, 6 and 7.
>
> The chapter covers the following areas:
> - benefits and challenges of using the reading-into-writing task type
> - the use of reading-into-writing tasks in standardised writing tests
> - the approach to defining the reading-into-writing constructs.

The theoretical basis of identifying the contextual and cognitive parameters of the reading-into-writing construct was established in Chapter 2. As Yu (2013) rightly observed, while the integrated task type has recently been revitalised as a method of teaching and assessing L2 language proficiency, it continues to fascinate and trouble the different stakeholders including test developers, teachers and students. In this chapter, we discuss the benefits and challenges of using the reading-into-writing task type to teach and assess students' abilities to write from sources, followed by a review of the use of integrated reading-into-writing tasks in standardised language tests.

3.1 Benefits and challenges of using the reading-into-writing task type

From the previous chapter we learned that writing tasks in real-life academic contexts almost always involve some integration of reading materials. However, the integrated task condition seemed to be underrepresented in most standardised writing tests. Horowitz (1986a, 1986b, 1991) argued that there is a fundamental discrepancy between real-life writing tasks and test tasks regarding the use of primary or secondary reading materials during writing production.

According to studies which surveyed the task types used in writing assessments (e.g. Shaw and Weir 2007, Weigle 2002, Weir, Vidaković et al 2013), the independent writing-only task type, which does not involve any use of reading materials, has played a dominant role in most high-stakes language tests and university admission tests. Test takers are expected to produce the text by drawing solely on their internal resources, e.g. background knowledge of the topic. Among different genres, the essay task (i.e. test takers write an essay in response to a point of view, problem, or an argument provided in a single-line prompt) is found to be very common in writing assessments. IELTS Writing Task 2 is a typical example of an independent writing-only task. On the other hand, integrated reading-into-writing tasks can arguably fulfil validity considerations better than the independent writing-only tasks. This notion is well supported in the current research on writing assessments (Cumming, Grant, Mulcahy-Ernt and Powers 2004, Cumming et al 2005, Hughes 2003, Pollitt and Taylor 2006, Weigle 2002, 2004, Weir, Vidaković et al 2013). The major reasons why the reading-into-writing task type might be more appropriate in teaching and assessing academic writing are summarised in the subsequent sections.

Improved task authenticity (context validity)

Task authenticity can be achieved in terms of situational and interactional authenticity (Bachman and Palmer 1996). In more recent frameworks of test validation (e.g. Weir 2005a), situational authenticity is considered to be part of context validity whereas interactional authenticity part of cognitive validity. Shaw and Weir (2007) defined situational authenticity as 'the contextual requirements of the tasks' and interactional authenticity as 'the cognitive activities of the test taker in performing the test task' (2007:9).

Many studies which surveyed writing demands in different academic contexts have concluded that academic writing is rarely done in isolation but is overwhelmingly done in response to source texts (e.g. Bridgeman and Carlson 1983, Carson 2001, Horowitz 1986a, 1986b, 1991, Johns, 1981, 1993, Leki and Carson 1994, Weir 1983). A task is considered to be authentic if it represents the features of the task in the target language context and if it elicits processes which are similar to those which test takers have to use in the target language context. Many writing researchers have argued that as far as academic writing is concerned, writing an impromptu essay on a previously unseen topic is an inauthentic task. Specifically, Moore and Morton (1999, 2005) conducted one of the very few studies that compared test tasks and real-life tasks. They compared the IELTS Task 2 rubric with a corpus of 155 assignment tasks at both undergraduate and postgraduate levels across 79 academic departments in two Australian universities. Based on the results they argued that while the independent essay task type represented core features of the academic writing tasks, there are two key discrepancies between the test tasks and real-life academic tasks. The real-life academic tasks typically involved the use of primary sources (e.g. textbooks, journal articles, monographs) or secondary sources (e.g. a simple exhortation), either provided in tasks or collected by students. In contrast, the independent essay task type did not engage test takers with any reading materials. Test takers instead were required to compose the task based upon prior knowledge. Secondly, the most common functions identified in the real-life tasks were evaluation, description, summarisation, comparison, explanation and recommendation. The function of summarisation was not identified in their sample of IELTS Task 2. Researchers then argued that the reading-into-writing task type can better represent the 'performance conditions' of real-life academic tasks (e.g. Carson 2001, Hamp-Lyons and Kroll 1996, 1997, Johns and Mayes 1990, Johns 1981, Leki and Carson 1994, Plakans 2008, 2010, Weigle 2002, Weir 1983).

Eliciting integration of skills (cognitive validity)

While situational authenticity is related to the contextual features of the task, interactional authenticity (cognitive validity), is concerned with the cognitive processes of the writer in performing the task. The independent writing-only task type requires writers to write from long-term memory. The writer's prior knowledge of the topic inevitably plays a key role in completing the task. The process of writing from sources is, however, considerably more cognitively demanding than the process of writing from one's internal sources (Plakans 2009b). Studies of the reading-into-writing sub-processes have argued that writing from sources requires specific processes such as task representation, summarisation and discourse synthesis, which are not likely to be involved when writers write from memory (Flower 1990, Spivey 1990, 1997, Spivey and King 1989, Van Dijk and Kintsch 1983). Furthermore, most studies investigating the relationship between writing-only and reading-into-writing performance reported no significant correlation between writers' abilities to write from memory and their abilities to write from sources (e.g. Asencion-Delaney 2008, Yu 2008). Another concern of the use of independent writing-only tasks is that this task type has been shown to encourage the 'knowledge telling' rather than 'knowledge transformation' approach to writing (Scardamalia and Bereiter 1987).

One may argue that the teaching and assessing of reading abilities have been covered in reading comprehension tasks. However, Khalifa and Weir (2009) found that most standardised reading tests focused primarily on careful reading comprehension but neglected expeditious reading and intertextual reading skills. In other words, some essential reading skills for writing from sources such as identifying relevant materials, comparing and contrasting different viewpoints, and integrating ideas from different sources are insufficiently measured in current standardised reading tests. Weir, Vidaković et al (2013) suggested that when compared to the most independent reading task formats, reading-into-writing tasks would provide a more appropriate and authentic condition as a means of eliciting these integrated reading skills, especially those at the highest difficulty level.

Similar to Weir, Vidaković et al's (2013) argument that the use of independent reading and writing tasks is incomplete and ineffective as a method to assessing integrated reading-into-writing skills, Oller (1979) criticised the use of the discrete-point approach to language testing in earlier days. He argued that 'in any system where the parts interact to produce properties and qualities that do not exist in the parts separately, the whole is greater than the sum of its parts, organizational constraints themselves become crucial properties of the system which simply cannot be found in the parts separately' (1979:212). Oller's argument offers an important insight for the current discussion – teaching and testing reading ability and writing ability separately would simply not sum up adequately to the ability to write from sources.

Providing equal access to subject knowledge (test fairness)

Another issue with the independent writing-only task type raised in the literature is related to test fairness due to heavy topic effect. The task type requires test takers to write drawing upon internal resources from their long-term memory. Weigle (2004) argued that students' performances are likely to be influenced by topic effects imposed by tasks which provide no input. This has inevitably led to test fairness issues when the topic of the writing task favours some test takers or is biased against others. Brown, Hilgers and Marsella (1991) conducted a large study to investigate the impact of topic on 3,452 students' writing performances in a standardised language test. Ten topic prompt sets were used. The results showed that various topic prompts led to significant differences in the scores. The researchers thus concluded that writers' background knowledge on the topic was a variable affecting the quality of their writing performance.

Hughes (2003) argued that writing tasks in general language tests should not require the test taker to demonstrate specific topic knowledge. Douglas (2000) argued that an appropriate level of disciplinary topic knowledge should be part of the construct of the English for specific purposes (ESP) tests. However, the issue is less straightforward for English for academic purposes (EAP) tests. Although EAP tests are one type of ESP test, the majority of EAP tests are not discipline specific. The testing population of most large-scale EAP tests consists of test takers from a wide range of academic disciplines. In other words, these test takers do not share the same disciplinary background knowledge. Therefore, using independent writing-only tasks which require test takers to draw upon their background knowledge on the topic to assess their academic writing ability may not be the most appropriate method. The provision of input reading materials in reading-into-writing tasks not only reflects real-life context, but also ensures equal access to subject knowledge among test takers. Well operationalised reading-into-writing tasks could provide all test takers with equal access to the content which is sufficient for them to complete the task (Weir, Vidaković et al 2013). The potential bias of the topic effect imposed on test takers would then be minimised (see Chapter 8 for recommendations of how to ensure the appropriateness of the inputs in integrated tasks).

Positive washback

In addition to promoting test fairness, reading-into-writing tests are generally considered to have positive washback as the task type represents what students are expected to do in most academic contexts (Belcher and Hirvela 2001, Campbell 1990, Cumming et al 2004, Esmaeili 2002, Tierney and Shanahan 1991, Weigle 2004, Weir 1983). Washback broadly refers to the effect of a test on teaching and learning (see Green (2007) for a detailed discussion of washback). The importance of positive washback in language testing is emphasised in the literature (Hughes 2003). Based on the results of a student survey, Leki and Carson (1994, 1997) argued that students need practice of a range of more challenging literacy tasks that combine reading and writing. In addition, Johns (1981, 1993, Lenski and Johns 1997) made a strong argument that L2 students need to be exposed to a range of reading-into-writing tasks, so they can understand the demands of academic tasks and develop necessary corresponding skills for their undergraduate or postgraduate studies, e.g. search for relevant materials, careful comprehension, read for main ideas, build intertextual representations, summarise reading materials, express their own interpretation. His points of view have largely shaped recent developments in EAP literacy pedagogy with a focus on reading–writing relations.

In addition, writing tasks that involve integration of reading materials are regarded as having good pedagogical value for literacy development. Researchers generally regard reading–writing relations as mutually supportive in terms of literacy development (Grabe 2003). For example, Leki (1993) argued that summary writing can improve reading comprehension skills. More specifically, Armbruster, Anderson and Ostertag (1987) found that summarising instruction can facilitate higher-level reading skills, e.g. identifying the macrostructure of a text. Some argued that reading-into-writing tasks can promote the development of 'critical literacy' through high-level processes of integrating existing texts to create texts of their own (Flower et al 1990). Others have found that reading-into-writing tasks can lead to effective content learning (e.g. McCarthy and Leinhardt 1998, Perfetti, Britt and Georgi 1995, Wiley and Voss 1999).

While the reading-into-writing task type offers the above promises, it is important not to forget that the use of such a task type does not offer a simple solution to the problems found with impromptu writing tasks (Plakans 2008). To establish the reading-into-writing construct, we will now address some unique challenges of using integrated tasks to teach and assess students' reading-into-writing abilities, including defining the seemingly muddied construct of integrated skills, designing appropriate inputs, understanding of reading-into-writing performance and developing appropriate rating scales.

Muddied measurement?

Due to the under-defined role of reading and writing abilities in reading-into-writing performance, researchers have questioned the possibility of a 'muddied measurement' (Alderson, Clapham and Wall 1995, Weir 2005a:101). Their concerns are understandable because reading and writing used to be understood largely as two mutually exclusive constructs. However, as described previously, more recent studies investigating the possible overlapping constructs between reading comprehension and reading-into-writing, and between writing from memory and writing from sources, have revealed that students' performances on these tasks do not always yield a significant relationship (Asencion-Delaney 2008, Grabe 2003, Yu 2008).

It is also a common concern that poor basic comprehension skills are likely to lead to poor performance on the reading-into-writing task (Cumming et al 2004). While it is believed that basic comprehension ability is required to compose a reading-into-writing task, there is no evidence showing that test takers must be able to comprehend all reading materials in order to compose a reading-into-writing task. It is, however, important to control the level of the reading texts so that the target test takers should be able to comprehend the reading texts, an issue which will be discussed in the next section. Based on current improved understanding of the reading–writing relationship and the nature of academic literacy, it is argued that reading-into-writing tasks distinctly measure integrated language skills, such as creating a global representation at textual or intertextual level, summarising and synthesising, in an authentic manner. Weir, Vidaković et al (2013) have argued convincingly that no independent task type can possibly assess such integrated language skills.

Appropriate input

As discussed in the 'test fairness' section in Section 3.1, the provision of reading texts in a reading-into-writing task could reduce the potential bias of background knowledge imposed on test takers by providing an equal starting point. However, the task design may unintentionally hinder students from completing the task if the materials are inappropriate to the level of the task. For example, the level of the reading input texts is critical to the effectiveness of any reading-into-writing task. The difficulty of the reading materials should, therefore, be set at an appropriate level in terms of cognitive and linguistic demands appropriate to the purpose[1] of the test.

As reviewed in Section 2.2, there is a rich selection of literature on how to identify the difficulty of a reading text/test. One recent study of such was conducted by Wu (2014) who investigated the issue of the comparison of level-based test batteries by comparing two reading tests – GEPT (General English Proficiency Test, developed by the Language Training and Testing Center (LTTC) in Taiwan) and Cambridge English Qualifications – at two CEFR levels, B1 and B2. Among other results, she found that 'the Cambridge B2 level tests were significantly more difficult than the GEPT counterpart in terms of the cognitive demands made on test takers, but the Cambridge texts were significantly less complex than the GEPT in terms of contextual features' (Wu 2014:206). Test takers in her study performed significantly better on the GEPT test (higher cognitive demands on reading skills) than the Cambridge English test (higher linguistic demands on comprehending the texts) at the same CEFR B2 level. This finding is particularly relevant to our discussion for reading-into-writing tasks because it raises an interesting question of the role of linguistic demands and cognitive demands in determining the level of a test. There does not seem to be much discussion regarding this issue in the literature. This volume therefore aims to shed light on the issue by evaluating the source texts students read when composing from sources under real-life and test conditions. It is hoped that in this way the findings will reveal useful contextual parameters to differentiate different levels of reading-into-writing tasks.

Extensive copying of the input materials

Another problem that arises in reading-into-writing tasks is that the provision of reading materials might lead to significant lifting, i.e. direct copying of the input materials by students (Shi 2004). The study by Cumming et al (2005) mentioned previously found that writers at the middle range of proficiency tended to use more phrases verbatim from source texts than did their higher- or lower-proficiency counterparts. Students in Yu's (2008) study honestly admitted that they preferred the use of English summary task as a means

---

1   This volume considers the purpose of reading-into-writing tasks to be assessing academic writing skills, which involves high-level intertextual reading skills. The use of reading-into-writing tasks to assess basic reading comprehension skills is beyond the focus of this volume study.

to assess their academic writing ability because they could 'copy directly from or refer to the source texts without necessarily fully understanding the copied text or the whole text' (2008:538). Some researchers are concerned with this sort of negative impact when providing writers with reading materials. For example, Lewkowicz (1997) argued that the provision of reading materials would restrict the development of ideas as students tend to rely heavily on the source texts in terms of ideas and language.

While the above concerns are potential challenges, the problem of inappropriate lifting of sources and too much reliance on the source texts also exists in the real-life academic context, usually addressed as plagiarism. One obvious solution is that the test tasks should reflect plagiarism rules as they apply in the real-life academic context. Clear task instructions which warn test takers about the inappropriate use of source texts, in other words, could help to reduce such behaviour. For example, Weir, Vidaković et al (2013) suggested that a task should state clearly the permitted amount of direct copying from the reading input texts, e.g. no more than three words of continuous text.

It is argued that valid reading-into-writing tasks should demand some language and content transformation from sources. It is therefore vital for test developers to be able to specify how test takers are expected to interact with the source texts. However, as we currently lack a clear and coherent understanding of how writers at different proficiency levels make use of source texts when composing from sources, it is difficult for test developers to make these specifications.

Appropriate rating scale

Another challenge of using reading-into-writing tasks in large-scale writing assessments relates to a seeming lack of appropriate marking schemes. Recent studies have found that texts produced across independent writing-only and integrated reading-into-writing varied significantly. For example, Cumming et al (2005) compared the features of texts produced from six trial TOEFL iBT tasks, which included two independent essays, two reading-into-writing essays and two listening-into-writing essays. The results showed significant linguistic differences between the independent essays and the integrated essays, with regard to the aspects of lexical sophistication, syntactic complexity, argument structure, voice in source evidence, and message in source evidence. However, the rating scale of integrated reading-into-writing tasks has received much less attention than that for independent writing-only tasks. Developing specific rubrics for integrated tasks does not seem to be common practice in the field. Integrated tasks are being adopted in a number of standardised language tests, such as the General English Proficiency Test (GEPT) and Cambridge English Qualifications such as C1 Advanced and C2

Proficiency. However, most tests apply a common set of rubrics to their independent and integrated tasks.

One way to develop appropriate rating scales for integrated tasks is to understand the mental processes raters would normally go through to evaluate an integrated performance according to the construct measured. A handful of studies have investigated rater processes of assessing integrated reading-into-writing scripts and the difficulties they faced (e.g. Cumming et al 2004, Green 1998, Gebril and Plakans 2014). By using think-aloud protocols, Green (1998) investigated rater processes when rating an integrated reading-into-writing task in *Cambridge English: Advanced*, then known as Certificate in Advanced English (CAE). She categorised the processes according to scoring behaviour, text features, evaluative response, and meta-comments. Raters in her study were most commonly engaged in essay reading and rating processes related to language accuracy, language appropriateness, and task realisation/content. However, the specific focus of her work means there was little discussion of how raters handled the unique features of integrated reading-into-writing performance.

In contrast, Cumming et al's study (2004) set out to compare rater processes on the integrated and independent tasks of TOEFL iBT. Based on the think-aloud protocols of seven raters, they found that raters focused more on rhetoric and content when rating integrated tasks, whereas they focused more on language when rating independent tasks. Another validation study on the TOEFL iBT test (Lee, Kantor and Mollaun 2002) found that raters in the trial had difficulty identifying copied language versus students' own wording in the scripts. Most recently, Gebril and Plakans (2014) undertook an in-depth analysis of rater processing when rating a reading-into-writing task. Two raters were asked to rate a subset of 21 essays, representing performance at five score levels selected from a larger pool of essays. It should be noted that the design of the study deliberately did not provide the raters with guidance on how they should rate the performance. Based on think-aloud protocols and interview data, the results suggested that raters employed judgement strategies more than interpretation strategies. In more specific terms, they approached the tasks by 'locating source information', 'checking citation mechanics' and 'evaluating quality of source text'.

In a related study of rater behaviour, Chan et al (2015) reported a study of redeveloping a suite of reading-into-writing rubrics for Integrated Skills in English (ISE). The major processes which emerged from the raters' group discussion include reading the task instruction, reading the rubrics, reading the source texts, identifying relevant parts in the source texts, reading the script, assigning a score to each criterion, checking the source texts, checking the rubrics and reconsidering the assigned scores. They noted the need to investigate rater processes on reading-into-writing scales in terms of how raters create a representation of the task, how raters assign the score for each criterion, and whether different sub-categories play a different role across the CEFR levels.

Difficulties commonly associated with rating such performances are questions relating to the quality and style of source text integration, textual borrowing, time effectiveness and task specificity. Cumming et al (2004) noted that raters in their study faced a new set of demands, for instance, to distinguish how well candidates transform source materials in their writing.

Difficulties identified by the raters in the Gebril and Plakans (2014) study included distinguishing between language cited from source materials and language produced by writers, assigning a score to essays with a high incidence of quotations, the perception of inappropriate textual practices, and scoring essays that matched the profile of two adjacent levels. Chan et al (2015) interviewed raters on their experiences of applying the new suite of ISE reading-into-writing rating scales. Their findings revealed similar challenges to those mentioned above. Additionally, the raters in their study experienced difficulty in getting used to the new criterion 'Reading for Writing' which was added to the original three rating criteria – Task Fulfilment, Organisation and Language Control. In order to resolve this, the research team asked the participating raters to identify any descriptors which were ambiguous to them and discussed how they interpreted each sub-category.

We have so far discussed the four major promises of integrated assessment tasks in relation to better task authenticity, providing a better performance condition to elicit high-level academic processes from students, better test fairness by providing an equal access to topic knowledge, and promoting positive washback. We have also discussed some common challenges of using integrated tasks in teaching and assessment, including complication in construct definition, developing appropriate inputs, understanding features of integrated performance and developing an appropriate rating scale. Next, we will review the use of integrated reading-into-writing tasks in standardised language tests.

3.2 The use of reading-into-writing tasks in standardised writing tests

While the field might have concerns about using the integrated task type, these tasks are increasing in popularity and either replacing or complementing writing-only independent tasks in writing assessments (Gebril and Plakans 2014, Weigle 2002, 2004). The use of reading-into-writing tasks in language tests can be traced back as far as the early 1930s. According to Weir, Vidaković et al's (2013) volume, which reviews aspects of language testing in the past century, reading-into-writing tasks were used in large-scale language tests as early as 1931. Summary was apparently the earliest integrated reading-into-writing task type used in large-scale language tests. A summary task was used in the English Literature paper of the Certificate of Proficiency in English (CPE) (the exam has been renamed C2 Proficiency) in 1936. The task was chosen because summary writing was similar to what people did in a lot of real-life occupational and educational settings at that time, which is still true at present (for details of the use of summary in CPE, see Weir, Vidaković et al 2013:128). However, the integrated task type fell out of favour in the 1970s when the testing of separate language skills was preferred.

The communicative approach to learning, which emphasises real-life communication skills rather than language knowledge, gained popularity during the early 1980s. The integrated reading-into-writing task type was again used in standardised writing tests. For example, Part 1 in Certificate in Advanced English (CAE) (the exam has been renamed C1 Advanced), Paper 2 required test takers to write a communicative task by integrating a range of reading inputs, e.g. newspapers/magazines, letters, reports. However, the CAE Writing paper underwent a major revision in 2008 and the length of the examination was reduced from 2 hours to 90 minutes. The number of words to be written and the reading materials to be read were substantially reduced.

Apart from the Cambridge English Qualifications, integrated tasks were used in some university-based tests. For example, the Test of English for Educational Purposes (TEEP) was developed in the 1980s based on an extensive research study on the language problems of international students in the UK (Weir 1983). Task 1 of the TEEP requires test takers to produce a summary of about 200 words based on one passage and input from listening to a lecture. The TEEP was redeveloped during 1991 and 2001. The current format of the integrated writing task of the TEEP requires test takers to use their own ideas as well as ideas retrieved from the reading and listening materials (University of Reading 2013).

High-stakes examination at that time also used integrated tasks. One example was the ELTS test, which was the predecessor of IELTS (1989) and originally introduced in 1980. The writing tasks required test takers to write about the reading materials of the reading section (for details of the development of IELTS, see Davies 2008:Chapter 5). Task 1 required test takers to transfer and process non-verbal information, e.g. diagrams, tables, charts (15 minutes) whereas Task 2 required test takers to draw on information from a variety of the reading materials they read previously in the reading section in addition to using their own experience to present an argument or solve a problem (30 minutes). However, in 1995, IELTS decided to drop the integrative nature of the writing tasks by removing the thematic link between the Reading and Writing modules. This was largely due to concerns over 'muddied measurement' as discussed previously (see Charge and Taylor 1997). The post-1995 IELTS Writing Task 2 has become an independent writing-only task where test takers are required to write about their own experience to present an argument or solve a problem. As a result, the independent writing-only 'essay' task was used as the dominant task in most large-scale writing tests during the 20th century. Those integrated reading-into-writing tasks developed in the 1980s were either completely dropped from the test or downscaled to involve substantially fewer reading materials (Taylor 2013, Weir, Vidaković et al 2013).

The use of reading-into-writing tasks in large-scale writing examinations did not come back until more recently. Large-scale language tests, not only those in the UK but worldwide, have once again shown interest in incorporating different types of integrated tasks into their writing papers. For example, (Pearson Test of English) PTE Academic and Trinity College London's ISE exams in the UK, LTTC's GEPT in Taiwan, Eiken's Test of English for Academic Purposes (TEAP) in Japan, and Georgia State Test of English Proficiency (GSTEP) and TOEFL iBT by the Educational Testing Service (ETS) in the US. A summary of the features of these integrated tasks used in current standardised writing assessments at B2 or above is provided in Table 3.1.

As shown in Table 3.1, different formats of integrated tasks are adopted in different kinds of tests, including *high-stakes proficiency tests*, such as TOEFL iBT, IELTS and PTE, *level-specific proficiency tests*, such as Cambridge English Qualifications, GEPT and ISE, as well as *university in-house post-entrance tests*. We will now briefly describe some of these tests.

In the United States, following an extensive revision exercise during the early 21st century (see Cumming et al 2004, 2005), ETS added an integrated writing task which requires test takers to write on reading and listening to materials towards TOEFL (TOEFL iBT). Compared to other high-stakes international English proficiency tests, the integrated task in TOEFL iBT writing is most extensive in terms of the amount of inputs and the number of integrated skills involved. Other newer international English proficiency tests also included the integrated task type. In 2009, Pearson launched a computer-based test for academic English – PTE Academic. Part 1 of the Writing section is an integrated task which requires test takers to write a one-sentence summary (not more than 30 words) of a passage after reading a text in 10 minutes (Pearson 2010). While TOEFL iBT and PTE require students to integrate information from written materials, another high-stakes international English proficiency test, IELTS Writing (Task 2), requires students to integrate information from non-verbal inputs, e.g. graphs and tables.

Compared to these high-stakes proficiency tests which assess across the CEFR levels, integrated tasks are used more extensively in level-specific proficiency tests, such as GEPT and ISE. GEPT Advanced, developed by LTTC in Taiwan, is a level-specific test at C1 (Proficient User – Effective). The writing paper of GEPT Advanced includes two integrated reading-into-writing tasks. Task 1 requires test takers to summarise the main ideas from multiple verbal materials and express their own opinions whereas Task 2 requires test

Table 3.1 Reading-into-writing test tasks used in current standardised writing assessments at B2 or above

Test	Task	Task description	Input format	Output	Time	Marking criteria	CEFR level
Cambridge English: Proficiency *	Part 1	Write an essay summarising and evaluating the key points from two short texts	Two short written texts, up to 200 words in total	Essay (240–280 words)	1 hour 30 minutes (including another writing task)	Content Communicative achievement Organisation Language	C2
Cambridge English: Advanced **	Part 1	Read a text, and then write an essay based on points included in the text, explain which of the two points is more important, and give reasons for own opinion	One written (at the level of phrase and sentences), up to 150 words	Essay (220–260 words)	1 hour 30 mins (including another writing task)	Content Communicative achievement Organisation Language	C1
General English Proficiency Test (GEPT) Advanced	Task 1	Summarise main ideas from two passages and express opinions	Two written texts, about 400 words each	Essay (at least 250 words, including introduction, summarising the main points, stating own viewpoint, conclusion)	60 mins	Relevance and adequacy Coherence and organisation Lexical use Grammatical use	C1
	Task 2	Summarise main ideas from non-verbal input and provide recommendations	Two non-verbal (e.g. graph, table, chart or diagram)	Letter/report (at least 250 words, including introduction, summarising the main findings, discussing possible reasons, making suggestions)	45 mins		

Table 3.1 (continued)

Test	Task	Task description	Input format	Output	Time	Marking criteria	CEFR level
Integrated Skills in English (ISE) Exam III	Task 3 Reading into Writing	Use the information from four texts to write an essay	Three written texts, one non-verbal, 700 words in total	Essay or article (200–230 words, including identifying information that is relevant to the writing task and the common themes and links across multiple texts and the finer points of details, e.g. attitudes implied; paraphrase/summarise complex and demanding texts; and synthesise information to produce elaborated responses with clarity and precision)	2 hours and 30 mins (including the other three tasks)	Reading for writing Task fulfilment Organisation Language use	C1
Integrated Skills in English (ISE) Exam II	Task 3 Reading into Writing	Write an essay/article based on four short texts (including three texts with factual ideas, opinions, argument or discussion and one non-verbal text)	Three written texts, one non-verbal, 500 words in total	Essay or article (150–180 words, including identifying information that is relevant to the writing task and the common themes and links across multiple texts; paraphrasing/summarising factual ideas, opinions, argument and/or discussion; and synthesising such information to produce coherent responses to suit the purpose for writing e.g. to offer solutions to a problem and/or evaluation of the ideas)	2 hours and 30 mins (including the other three tasks)	Reading for writing Task fulfilment Organisation Language use	B2

Table 3.1 (continued)

IELTS – Academic	Task 1	Describe some visual information	Two non-verbal: graph/table/chart/diagram	Description (150 words)	20 mins	Task achievement Coherence and cohesion Lexical resource Grammatical range and accuracy	N/A
Georgia State Test of English Proficiency (GSTEP)	Integrated Reading and Writing Part 2	Read two argumentative texts and answer eight questions in Part 1, and then write an essay responding to a prompt about the passages	Two argumentative texts, 300–500 words each	Essay	45 mins (Part 2 only)	Content Organisation Language accuracy Language range and complexity	N/A
Pearson Test of English (PTE) Academic	Summarise written text	After reading a text, write a one-sentence summary of the passage	One written text (up to 300 words)	Summary (not more than 30 words)	10 mins	Content Form Grammar Vocabulary Spelling	N/A
TOEFL iBT – Writing	Integrated Writing Task: Read/Listen/Write	Write an essay based on the reading and listening texts	One reading text (230–300 words) One listening text (230–300 words)	Summary (150–225 words; summarise the main points in the listening passage, explain how these relate to the key points of the reading passage)	50 mins (including another writing task)	Content (accuracy and completeness) Appropriate use of language and sentence structure	N/A

*This exam is now known as C2 Proficiency
**This exam is now known as C1 Advanced

takers to summarise the main ideas from multiple non-verbal materials and provide solutions (Language Training and Testing Center 2012).

Trinity College London's ISE examination is another level-specific proficiency test which uses integrated tasks extensively. ISE involves integrated tasks at four proficiency levels – ISE Foundation, ISE I, ISE II and ISE III. The four levels of ISE are targeted to align with the levels of the CEFR from A2 (Basic User – Waystage), B1 (Independent User – Threshold), B2 (Independent User – Vantage) to C1 (Proficient User – Effective). ISE underwent a redevelopment phase in 2013 (Chan et al 2015). A needs analysis was conducted, and as a result, the integrated reading-into-writing task type was kept in the examinations. The new ISE consists of two modules, namely, Reading and Writing and Speaking and Listening. The Reading and Writing module includes four tasks, one of which is an integrated reading-into-writing task. The integrated task involves writing based on multiple verbal and non-verbal input reading materials (Trinity College London 2013). After the revision, ISE was officially recognised by UK Visas & Immigration (UKVI) as one of the two Secure English Language Tests (SELTs) to be used as a proof of English proficiency for entering university or employment, enrolling into a higher level of English study or further education, and/or for UK visa application purposes (UK Border Agency 2013). The other SELT is IELTS. This shows that the integrated task type is playing an even more important role in high-stakes examinations.

Integrated tasks are also used extensively in university admission or postentrance tests. GSTEP is one of the most well-documented and researched university admission tests. The integrated reading-into-writing task requires test takers to write about two passages which are also used in the Short Answer Section (Weigle 2002).

As described in Section 1.1, the integrated reading-into-writing task type has experienced its ups and downs in the past. This has resulted in a lack of thorough definition of the reading-into-writing constructs. It is encouraging to see that a range of reading-into-writing tasks are now being reinstated in standardised language tests at the levels of B2 or above. However, as shown in Table 3.1, the task setting and demands of input and output vary widely from test task to test task, and hence the cognitive processes and skills required to complete these tasks are likely to be different to some extent. Only a handful of cognitive process research has been conducted on several types of reading-into-writing task formats, which involve non-verbal materials (e.g. Bridges 2010, Yu and Lin 2014), a single verbal text (e.g. Chan 2011), and multiple verbal materials (e.g. Plakans 2009a, 2009b, 2010), but little has been done on students' processes on tasks which involve multiple verbal and non-verbal written inputs. So this requires further investigation. It is hoped that the research reported in this volume will contribute to understanding the cognitive validity of integrated reading-into-writing tasks, especially those involving multiple verbal and non-verbal written inputs.

In Chapter 2, we reviewed the literature in relation to the features of common reading-into-writing tasks and the processes involved in writing from sources. Based on a synthesis of the relevant literature, we have proposed a set of task variables and cognitive parameters as the basis for defining the construct of reading-into-writing. In this chapter, we have so far introduced the key theories of reading-into-writing, the use of reading-into-writing tasks to assess academic literacy skills in standardised language tests, and some theoretical and practical issues raised. We will now turn to discuss the approach to defining language constructs as the basis of our empirical studies reported in Chapters 5 to 7.

3.3 The approach to defining the reading-into-writing constructs

We will now review the theoretical approach we regard most suitable to defining the reading-into-writing constructs. Traditionally, validity was seen as an issue of whether a test really measures what it is supposed to measure (Lado 1961). Test validity was addressed by individual enquiries of content, construct, concurrent and predictive validities separately until the 1980s. However, Messick (1989) argued that test validity should be seen as a unified concept which integrates considerations of content, criteria and consequences into a framework. His view on unitary validity broke new ground for current understanding of validity (Weir 2005a). Now, the challenges of building a coherent validity argument are, therefore, to define which evidence is needed to demonstrate different validity arguments for a test, and so how and when to obtain such evidence, and from where.

Instead of discussing test validity abstractly, the field of language testing has moved towards an argument-based approach in test validation in which guidance for collecting validity evidence against a set of well-defined criteria is provided (for details see Fulcher 2010, Kane 2012). The criteria are set based upon the target real-life contexts. As it is impossible to replicate the entire target real-life contexts fully under test conditions, the concept of test validity is a matter of degree of representativeness (relevancy and range). In addition, instead of building validity arguments of the quality of a test itself, current understanding of validity focuses more on the quality of inferences made upon test scores (Green 2014). In other words, the inferences made based on test scores need to be supported by evidence of different validity components.

Sharing a similar view that each individual validity component combines with others to collectively demonstrate test validity, Bachman and Palmer (1996, see also Bachman 1990) argued that construct validity arguments should be built by defining the underlying trait of particular abilities or skills hypothesised on the basis of a theory of language ability. Following this notion, test developers started to make claims regarding which underlying language abilities and skills their tests are meant to measure, and what samples of language skills and structures are represented in the content of the tests in the 1990s. Bachman and Palmer's (1996) approach undoubtedly improved our awareness of test construct from a theoretical point of view. However, Hughes (2003) argued that such an approach to building validity arguments itself would not necessarily demonstrate the validity of a language test because additional empirical research is required to confirm whether 1) such language abilities or skills exist, 2) these abilities and skills can be measured, and 3) they are indeed measured in a particular test.

Following the argument-based approach to collecting evidence of test validity, Weir (1988) proposed that evidence of individual validity components should be collected before the test event as well as after the test has been administered. He stressed the need for describing the construct that a test attempts to measure at the *a priori* stage of test development and then evaluating how well the construct is operationalised in the test at the *a posteriori* stage. Weir (2005a) made a notable and influential attempt to develop an evidence-driven socio-cognitive validation framework which integrates the considerations of the underlying cognitive ability, the context of language use and the process of scoring operationalised in the language tests, and the criterion-related validity of the tests. Consequential validity (Messick 1989) was also incorporated in the framework. The framework allows test developers and researchers to conduct systematic analyses of test input and output, from both cognitive- and socio-linguistic perspectives. Unlike previous frameworks which focused on a uniform construct (content) validity, the socio-cognitive framework unpacked the abstract 'construct' of a test in terms of the cognitive and context components to provide strong evidence of construct validity.

The framework consists of five components. Context validity concerns the internal task features and linguistic demands of the test task, as well as the external social and cultural contexts in which the test task is used. Cognitive validity (which was referred to as theory-based validity in Weir 2005a) concerns the cognitive processes elicited by the test task. Linking directly to the context and cognitive validity components, scoring validity concerns the extent to which the task is objectively and reliably scored to produce reliable and valid decision-making indicators. Consequential validity addresses the social consequences of test score interpretation and the impact of the test on teaching and learning. Criterion-related validity is concerned with the extent to which test scores correlate with a suitable external criterion of performance. Three of the components were of particular interest in this volume because context and cognitive validity are the most important components of the construct validity. Criterion-related validity is essential because if a test task does not predict academic performance then its validity is in doubt.

A review of the use of reading-into-writing tasks in assessment

- Context validity – the extent to which the choice of tasks in a test is representative of the larger universe of tasks of which the test is assumed to be a sample (Weir 2005a:19)
- cognitive validity – the extent to which the chosen task 'represents the cognitive processing involved in writing contexts beyond the test itself' (Shaw and Weir 2007:34)
- criterion-related validity – the extent to which test scores correlate with a suitable external criterion of performance with established properties (Weir 2005a:35).

This socio-cognitive validation approach has led to improvements in test design and has reframed effective validity arguments (i.e. coherent evidence of different validity components supporting the interpretation of test scores) regarding the use and interpretation of test scores. Language examination boards, such as Cambridge Assessment English and Trinity College London in the UK, LTTC in Taiwan and Eiken Foundation of Japan (formerly STEP) in Japan, have used the framework to revisit the extent to which these major validity components have been operationalised in their tests of the four skills, i.e. reading, writing, listening and speaking (e.g. Chan et al 2015, Chan, Wu and Weir 2014, Geranpayeh and Taylor (Eds) 2013, Khalifa and Weir 2009, Lim 2013, Shaw and Weir 2007, Taylor (Ed) 2011, Weir, Chan and Nakatsahara 2013). However, while the socio-cognitive framework has undoubtedly made a noticeable contribution to validation in language testing since 2005, its application has been limited to language tests which assess the four skills separately. For this reason, we aim to expand the socio-cognitive framework by using it to define the construct of reading-into-writing. In order to define the construct of reading-into-writing in academic contexts, we will address three research questions in this volume:

1. What are the contextual characteristics of the academic writing tasks that students would normally encounter in real life? To what extent do two standardised reading-into-writing tests resemble these contextual features?
2. What are the cognitive processes that students would normally employ to complete the real-life academic writing tasks? To what extent do the reading-into-writing tasks elicit these cognitive processes from test takers?
3. To what extent can performances on the two reading-into-writing tests predict test takers' ability to perform on academic writing tasks in real life?

Three validation studies (Study 1, Study 2 and Study 3) were designed to answer these research questions. First of all, Study 1 aims to identify the salient task features of sampled real-life academic writing tasks and to investigate how well two reading-into-writing test formats (*essay with multiple verbal inputs* and *essay with multiple verbal and non-verbal inputs*) operationalise these task variables. Study 2 aims to identify writers' processes when they compose from sources in a real-life academic context, and to investigate if the two reading-into-writing test formats elicit the same processes from test takers. In other words, the results collected from both the real-life and test conditions are compared to provide empirical evidence of the context and cognitive validity of reading-into-writing tests in assessing academic writing abilities. Study 3 aims to investigate the extent to which performances on reading-into-writing tests predict test takers' ability to perform on real-life academic writing tasks.

We have so far argued the need to add descriptors of reading-into-writing in the English Profile to account for such skills (Chapter 1); reviewed the extent and nature of reading-into-writing activities required of students in real-life academic contexts; discussed why the integrated reading-into-writing task type could be a better tool to teach and assess these academic writing abilities at the higher CEFR levels; and established the theoretical basis of defining the construct of reading-into-writing in academic contexts in terms of contextual features and cognitive parameters (Chapter 2). We have also reviewed the use of reading-into-writing tasks in standardised language tests at CEFR Level B2 or above, and discussed the major benefits and challenges of developing and using reading-into-writing tasks in practice, and introduced the socio-cognitive approach to defining the construct of reading-into-writing (Chapter 3). We will now move on to Section 2, 'Empirical evidence', to present the research methods of the three studies (Chapter 4) and the results regarding the context (Chapter 5), cognitive (Chapter 6) and criterion-related (Chapter 7) validity of reading-into-writing.

Section 2
Empirical evidence

The integrated reading-into-writing task type was first used in standardised language tests in the UK in the 1930s because it represents what people do in real life. The integrated format then went out of favour a few times during the past century as the language testing field prioritised reliability and practicality (Weir, Vidaković et al 2013). As our understanding of academic literacy and construct validity improves, the integrated format has once again been used widely to represent more closely the ability of writing from sources. Due to an increased popularity of using the integrated task type there is an urgent need for gathering empirical evidence of the construct of reading-into-writing in the academic contexts. In Section 1, we have established the theoretical basis of establishing such a construct by reviewing the literature in relation to academic writing from sources, and past and current practice in reading and writing tests (see Chapters 2 and 3).

In this section, we now turn to the empirical evidence to define the construct of integrated reading-into-writing in academic contexts at the CEFR Level B2 or above. Three validation studies (Study 1, Study 2 and Study 3) were conducted to answer the three research questions. To recap, Question 1 investigates whether the characteristics of two reading-into-writing tests are an adequate and comprehensive representation of those that would be normally encountered in the real-life context. Question 2 investigates whether the cognitive processes required to complete the reading-into-writing test tasks sufficiently resemble the cognitive processes which a test taker would normally employ in non-test conditions, i.e. whether they are construct relevant (Messick 1989), and asks: is the range of processes elicited by the test tasks sufficiently comprehensive to be considered representative of real-world behaviour, i.e. not just a small subset of those which might then give rise to fears about construct underrepresentation? Finally, Question 3 compares writers' performances on the real-life tasks and the reading-into-writing tests to find out the extent to which performances on reading-into-writing tests predict test takers' ability to perform on real-life academic writing tasks. We will first report the methodology of these three studies in Chapter 4. In Chapters 5 to 7, we will explore three major aspects of the construct validity of the integrated reading-into-writing task type in relation to task features, students' mental processes of writing from sources, and the relationship between test and real-life performance. Chapter 8 summarises the major findings, discusses their implications and provides recommendations for future research.

4 Methodology

> This chapter builds on the theoretical foundations for defining the construct of reading-into-writing built in Chapters 2 and 3 to describe in detail the research methods of the three empirical studies reported in Chapters 5 to 8.
>
> The aim is to orient the reader to a detailed description of the design, procedures and analytical approaches of Study 1, Study 2 and Study 3 which aim to define the construct of reading-into-writing in academic contexts in relation to context, cognitive and criterion-related validity.
>
> The chapter covers the following details:
>
> - sampling of real-life and test tasks for investigation
> - characteristics of participants involved
> - development of instruments (*contextual parameter proforma* and *cognitive process questionnaire*)
> - establishing useful indices from automated textual tools
> - data collection procedures (*students' performance, expert panel judgement, automated textual analysis*)
> - data analysis procedures (*descriptive and inferential comparisons, exploratory factor analysis, correlational analysis*).

Building upon the theoretical foundations laid out in Chapters 2 and 3, this chapter describes the methodology used in the three validation studies (Study 1, Study 2 and Study 3). Firstly, we describe how the two academic writing tasks and the two reading-into-writing test tasks were selected (Section 4.1). The chapter then describes the research design with respect to the investigation of the three components of language test validity: context validity (Section 4.2), cognitive validity (Section 4.3) and criterion-related validity (Section 4.4). Each of these sub-sections presents the details of participants, instruments, data collection procedures and methods of data analysis. The chapter concludes with a summary of the methodology.

4.1 Sampling tasks

Sampling real-life tasks

The first step to understanding what makes a reading-into-writing task valid for assessing academic writing was to investigate what tasks are used in the target real-life academic context (Hamp-Lyons and Kroll 1996). This sub-section describes the real-life academic writing tasks used in this series of validation studies. Based on the literature review in Section 1, it is clear that academic writing tasks almost always involve writing from multiple sources, and that high-level knowledge transformation processes play an important role in academic success. It is beyond the scope of this book to conduct a comprehensive survey of academic tasks as previous studies have done (see Chapter 2 for a review of these studies). Nevertheless, for the purpose of the empirical validation studies reported in this volume, it was first of all necessary to sample the real-life academic writing tasks within the local context of the studies.

As reviewed in Section 2.1, the features of writing tasks that are required of students in academic contexts were well researched across recent decades (e.g. Bridgeman and Carlson 1983, Carson 2001, Horowitz 1986a, 1986b, Johns 1993, Leki and Carson 1994, Weir 1983); the primary purpose of our investigation is, therefore, not to conduct a comprehensive task survey, but to establish the construct of reading-into-writing in terms of contextual and cognitive parameters. To our knowledge, the research reported in this volume was the first to validate EAP reading-into-writing tests covering both context and cognitive validity as well as predictive power. To investigate the contextual features of real-life tasks and students' cognitive processes on the tasks, we limited our sampling to a single British university and to a single discipline. To ensure the generalisability of the results, sampling was carefully conducted based on a set of selection criteria. The University of Bedfordshire (UoB) is one of the 20 largest recruiters of international students (UK Council for International Student Affairs 2012). The business discipline was chosen for the purpose of investigation because it was the largest business school in the region with six departments, 4,000 students and over 100 teaching and research staff (University of Bedfordshire 2013). In addition, the Business School contained the highest proportion of international students in the UK (36%) (UK Council for International Student Affairs 2012).

Two authentic academic writing tasks were sampled from the UoB and two reading-into-writing test tasks were sampled from different operational tests. Sampling the predominant real-life tasks started with a survey of the writing task types assigned to students at the Business School of the UoB. All Year 1 module handbooks were collected for a 'first glance selection'. Eight of them including the module specifications and assessment plan were assessed according to the following criteria:

Methodology

- Enrolment rate of the module: The Business School offers students a choice of different selective modules to complete their programme. In order to guarantee an adequate sampling of the number of students of each module, modules which had an enrolment rate of less than 50% of the population were not considered.
- Individual writing assignments only: Group/collective assignments were sometimes used in the Business School but this volume focuses on individual writing tasks only. These tasks were therefore not considered.
- The type of input source involved: The type of input source involved in each task was examined. All tasks involved multiple input types.
- The type of response text (genre) required: Essay and report were apparently the most common genres assigned in the modules. Repeated genres were not considered.

The aim was to sample different genres and different types of input texts from the pool. As a result, two writing tasks were selected from two different modules to represent the authentic tasks in the studies reported in this volume (see Appendix 1 for the tasks).

As argued previously, it is essential to investigate the textual features and level of difficulty of input texts in the context of reading-into-writing tasks. Adapting the procedures stated in Green et al's (2010) study on undergraduate texts, the following steps were used to build a small corpus of authentic input texts involved in these two tasks:

1. 100 student scripts were collected from each of the selected real-life tasks, totalling 200 students' scripts.
2. The bibliography of each script was examined.
3. The 10 most cited source texts from each of the two real-life tasks were identified.
4. Three extracts (from the beginning, middle and end of each text) were obtained from each of the 20 selected source texts. Each extract was about 500 words long.
5. A small corpus of real-life input texts, containing 60 extracts from the 20 most cited source texts, was created.

Sampling reading-into-writing test tasks

Reading-into-writing test tasks from current large-scale language tests were collected (see Section 3.2 for a review of these reading-into-writing test tasks). The suitability of these tasks for this study was assessed. Reading-into-writing test tasks which were not for academic purposes were excluded. Preference was given to tasks which involve multiple sources as reading-into-writing involving multiple input sources has largely been neglected in the literature. Preference was also given to access to operationalised test tasks, i.e. not practice tasks, and to standardised scoring. As a result, the GEPT Advanced Writing Task 1 (hereafter Test Task A[1]) and a newly developed university in-house reading-into-writing test (hereafter Test Task B[2]) were chosen.

Test Task A, developed and administered by the LTTC, targets English learners at the CEFR C1 level (for more information about GEPT, see Language Training and Testing Center 2012). Two passages were collected from 10 testlets of Test Task A, resulting in a collection of 20 input texts. Test Task B was developed by the Centre for Research in English Language Learning and Assessment (CRELLA) to be used as part of the university's post-entrance diagnostic test. The test was set at the CEFR B2 level. As Test Task B was a newly developed test at the time of the study, only one operationalised testlet was available. The researcher obtained agreement from both test providers to supply authentic test tasks and provide standardised scoring of the scripts.

We have so far described the procedures of sampling the two real-life academic writing tasks and two reading-into-writing test tasks. These four tasks were used in the investigation of the three validation studies. We will now describe the procedures of each of the studies.

4.2 Study 1: Context validity

As mentioned, the aim of Study 1 was to analyse the features of the two sampled academic writing tasks (Real-life Task A and Real-life Task B) and the two reading-into-writing tests (Test Task A and Test Task B). Secondly, Study 1 examined the extent to which the reading-into-writing tests resembled the task features of those real-life tasks. We now describe the research methods used in Study 1.

Participants – judges

10 judges with at least five years of working experience in language testing and/or language teaching were recruited to form an expert panel to evaluate the contextual features of the real-life tasks and test tasks.

Contextual parameter proforma

A contextual parameter proforma was developed to facilitate an operationalisable analysis by the 10 judges to evaluate the features of four tasks. Two pilot studies informed the development of the proforma. The first version of the proforma was drafted based on Shaw and Weir's (2007) contextual proforma

---

1 For a sample task, see www.lttc.ntu.edu.tw/GEPT1/Advanced/writing/writing.htm
2 The copyright of the task belongs to Centre for Research in English Language Learning and Assessment (CRELLA). For a copy of the sample task, please contact the author.

for writing tests and Wu's (2014) contextual proforma for reading tests. Other materials such as Chapter 2 of Weigle's *Assessing Writing* (2002) and the CEFR grid for writing tasks (Association of Language Testers in Europe 2011) were consulted to develop the option under each category. Based on the detailed review of the literature on task variables in Section 2.2, we included the categories which are most likely to influence the difficulty of reading-into-writing tasks in the proforma. The first version included 10 categories of task features. It was piloted with 10 judges. Verbal feedback regarding the effectiveness of the proforma and their experience of the analysis was collected.

There was confusion about which part of the tasks some of the categories should be applied to, e.g. the prompt, the input texts, or the output text. It was decided that the categories would be divided into two sections: overall task setting (considering the prompt and the output) and input texts features. New categories were added to address more specifically the features of the input. In addition, some of the options which were deemed too similar were refined based on the feedback of the judges. Some judges also felt that they had difficulty in analysing the topic domain of the task. In most cases, they felt that one task fell into more than one domain. It was decided that instead of choosing one topic domain, the judges would be asked to rate the degree to which the task falls into each domain. Other amendments were made to the procedural aspect of the analysis (full procedures of the analysis will be described next). In the pilot, after completing the analysis individually, the respondents were asked to discuss their responses with the whole group. While the discussion was engaging and insightful, the discussion was sometimes dominated by a few respondents. It was therefore decided that, in the main study, the judges would be asked to discuss their individual responses in pairs and to fill in a separate proforma for their agreed responses. The judges in the pilot also recommended that the entire exercise should not take more than 3 hours to maintain the effectiveness and reliability of their judgement.

The finalised contextual parameter proforma (see Appendix 2) consists of two parts: overall task setting and input text features. Items 1 to 8 address the overall task setting which includes purpose and intended reader, time and length, topic domain, genre (response), interaction between input and response, language functions, and clarity of intended reader. Input text features (i.e. Items 9 to 17) include format and genre of the input, as well as the conceptual and linguistic complexity of the input texts. While Items 1 to 14 were analysed by human judges, the linguistic complexity (i.e. Items 15 to 17) were analysed by automated textual tools.

Automated textual analysis tools – establishing useful indices

To supplement the expert judgement analysis, the linguistic complexity of the input texts was analysed by automated textual tools. Automated textual analysis has been regarded as a more systematic way to assess textual features than the traditional expert judgement method, especially when a large number of texts are involved (Green 2012). Many researchers have used automated textual analytic tools to evaluate the features of different types of texts such as L1 students' scripts (e.g. Crossley and McNamara 2010), L2 students' scripts (e.g. Crossley and McNamara 2012), reading materials (e.g. Crossley, Louwerse, McCarthy and McNamara 2007, Green 2012), undergraduate reading texts (e.g. Green et al 2010), reading texts in language tests (e.g. Green et al 2012, Wu 2014), and L2 test takers' scripts (e.g. Weir 2012).

In this investigation, two automated textual analysis tools were chosen – CohMetrix version 2.1 (Graesser, McNamara, Louwerse and Cai 2004) and VocabProfile version 3 (Cobb 2003). CohMetrix was used in all the above-mentioned textual analysis studies. It is one of the most popular textual analysis tools in the literature. It is freely accessible online and it produces a comprehensive list of about 60 textual indices. More importantly, according to Graesser, McNamara and Kulikowich (2011), CohMetrix was designed to explore attributes of cognitive language use by measuring 'deep-level factors of textual coherence and processing' (2011:223). VocabProfile (Cobb 2003) is another popular textual analysis tool which provides a profile of texts in terms of different vocabulary frequency bands based on the British National Corpus (BNC) (2007) (e.g. the most frequent 1,000 words) and different types of vocabulary (e.g. academic words based on Coxhead 2000).

Both tools have been used in the testing literature. To name a few studies, Green et al (2010) compared IELTS reading texts and undergraduate texts at British universities, Green et al (2012) investigated reading texts targeted at different levels of the CEFR (Council of Europe 2001); Wu (2014) compared Cambridge English Qualifications and GEPT Taiwan examinations at the B1 and B2 levels; Weir (2012) investigated features of the test takers' scripts of the TEAP test in Japan; and Casey, Miller, Stockton and Justice (2016) investigated the features of 167 fourth and fifth grade children's scripts.

While CohMetrix and VocabProfile allow researchers to automate a large number of textual indices in an objective and reliable way, the results have to be interpreted with caution. Researchers have argued that not all indices produced are equally useful or interpretable. Green et al (2012), for instance, criticised the fact that some of the indices seem to overlap and attempted to identify those indices which are helpful to distinguish texts between adjacent CEFR levels.

It is seemingly important for individual researchers to establish which of the indices are helpful in their context of study. Green et al (2012) showed that 17 CohMetrix and 2 VocabProfile indices meaningfully exhibited significant differences in the reading texts across three levels of Cambridge English Qualifications: *Cambridge English: First* (B2), *Cambridge English: Advanced*

(C1) and *Cambridge English: Proficiency* (C2)[3]. Based on 25 CohMetrix indices and six VocabProfile indices, Wu (2014) compared the features of reading texts between the GEPT and Cambridge English Qualifications at B1 and B2 levels. Weir (2012) found that 12 CohMetrix indices were useful in establishing criterial differences in the L2 test takers' scripts rated at the A2 and B1 levels. Green et al (2010) compared the features of undergraduate texts and IELTS reading texts by 19 CohMetrix and five VocabProfile indices.

Drawing upon previous studies, especially those looking at reading texts (e.g. Green et al 2010, Green et al 2012, Wu 2014), the usefulness of all the CohMetrix and VocabProfile indices was carefully examined by the researcher in a pilot analysis. 30% of the real-life input texts were analysed in the pilot analysis. Some indices were excluded from the analysis in the main study for four major reasons. First, some indices overlap with other indices as they showed very similar or no difference when compared to the results of other indices. For instance, index 40 (Flesch-Kincaid grade level) and index 39 (Flesch reading ease) are already covered by index 38 (Average syllables per word) and 37 (Average words per sentence). Secondly, some indices were difficult to interpret in relation to text complexity. For example, index 23 (Ratio of pronouns to noun phrase) is affected by text type, and hence its influence on text complexity would be linear. Third, some indices were not applicable to the data collected in the study. For example, number of paragraphs was affected by the length of the text, which was controlled during sampling. Lastly, some indices produced a score which was difficult to interpret and hence they were not useful in determining the complexity of a text. For details of the list of the deleted indices, see Appendix 3. As a result, 13 CohMetrix and four VocabProfile indices were kept in the main study to analyse the features of the input texts and draw comparisons between the real-life and reading-into-writing test tasks (see Table 4.1 for a glossary of the selected indices).

As shown in Table 4.1, although our selection was similar to the indices used in previous studies, we categorised the indices in terms of lexical complexity, syntactic complexity and degree of cohesion, which are more suitable for the context of reading-into-writing, rather than categories such as vocabulary, grammar, readability, cohesion and text abstractness used in Green et al's (2010) study.

Data collection procedures

As mentioned previously, 10 judges were recruited to form a panel. They were trained prior to the panel meeting with the adapted familiarisation and specification procedures (Council of Europe 2009) as on page 71.

---

3 These qualifications have been renamed B2 First, C1 Advanced and C2 Proficiency, respectively.

Defining Integrated Reading-into-Writing Constructs

Table 4.1 Selected indices for automated textual analysis

Contextual index	Definition (extracted from the official documents of the two tools)	Automated analysis tool
Lexical complexity		
High-frequency words (K1)	The ratio of words which appear in the first most frequent 1,000 BNC (2001) wordlist to the total number of words per text	VocabProfile
High-frequency words (K2)	The ratio of words which appear in the second most frequent 1,000 BNC (2001) wordlist to the total number of words per text	VocabProfile
Academic words	The ratio of words which appear in the AWL (Coxhead 2000) to the total number of words per text	VocabProfile
Low-frequency words (Offlist)	The ratio of words that do not appear in either the most frequent 15,000 BNC wordlist to the total number of words per text	VocabProfile
Log frequent content words	The log frequency of all content words in the text	Cohm* 46
Average syllables per word	The mean number of syllables per content word, a ratio measure	Cohm 38
Type-token ratio (content words)	The number of unique words divided by the number of tokens of these words	Cohm 44
Syntactic complexity		
Average words per sentence	The mean number of words per sentence	Cohm 37
Sentence syntax similarity	The proportion of intersection syntactic tress nodes between all sentences	Cohm 56
Mean number of modifiers per noun phrase	The mean number of modifiers per noun phrase	Cohm 41
Mean number of words before the main verb	The mean number of words before the main verb of the main clause in sentences	Cohm 43
Logical operator incidence	The incidence of logical operations (i.e. connectives), such as *and*, *or*, *not*, *if*, *then*, etc.	Cohm 26
Cohesion		
Adjacent overlap argument	The proportion of adjacent sentences that share one or more arguments (i.e. noun, pronoun, noun phrase) or have a similar morphological stem as a noun	Cohm 16
Adjacent overlap stem	The proportion of adjacent sentences that share one or more word stems	Cohm 17
Adjacent overlap content word	The proportion of content words in adjacent sentences that share common content words	Cohm 58
Proportion of adjacent anaphor references	The proportion of anaphor references between adjacent sentences	Cohm 18
Adjacent semantic similarity (LSA)**	The measure of conceptual similarity between adjacent sentences	Cohm 27

*CohMetrix
**LSA=latent semantic analysis

1. The researcher explained the contextual parameter proforma (Part 1) to the judges. An explanation sheet of the analytical categories was provided. The judges sought clarification of any unclear points.
2. The judges were grouped into pairs.
3. The judges were assigned to analyse one of the four tasks (two real-life and two reading-into-writing test tasks) individually and filled in the proforma. The order of the tasks assigned to each pair was counterbalanced. After they had completed the individual analyses, they discussed their responses in pairs. They were asked to record the reasons for any disagreement. They then filled in another proforma to record their agreed responses. The judges handed in their responses (both individual and pair) to the researcher.
4. The judges analysed the other three tasks one by one following Step 3.
5. The judges completed the feedback evaluation questionnaire (see Appendix 4).

Two of the judges then participated in another panel meeting to analyse specifically the criterial features of the input texts, using Part 2 of the proforma. As described previously, a total of 44 input texts was sampled for this analysis. Following the same procedures detailed above, they analysed all the sampled texts (i.e. the 20 most-cited materials from each of the sampled authentic tasks, and two passages from 10 testlets of Test Task A and two passages from one testlet of Test Task B).

The length of the 20 input materials sampled from the authentic tasks was much longer than the input texts sampled from the test tasks. Following the procedures used in previous studies (e.g. Green et al 2010, Wu 2014), three extracts of 500 words each were obtained from the beginning, middle and end of each of the 20 real-life texts. As a result, a small corpus of 60 input text extracts was created.

The linguistic complexity of the 60 input text extracts and 22 test task input texts was then analysed by the 13 CohMetrix and four VocabProfile indices (see Table 4.1).

Data analysis

The purpose of this investigation was to investigate what criterial features are important in determining the level of a reading-into-writing task, so that the results can be used to inform decision making in task development as well as being an *a priori* validation procedure.

The expert judgement responses on the proforma regarding the overall task setting and input text features were reported. For the classification categories (i.e. Items 5 to 6, 9 to 12), results of the percentage of each option were presented. For the rating categories (i.e. Items 1, 3, 7 to 8, 13 to 14), the mean and standard deviation on the Likert scale were presented. Descriptive comparisons were made between the real-life tasks and the test tasks. Descriptive statistics instead of inferential statistics were used due to a small sample size. Graphic presentation of the data was provided for further illustration where appropriate.

Regarding the automated textual analyses of the input text features, the mean and standard deviation of the 17 selected indices were obtained. Results for each of the two test tasks were compared with the real-life tasks. As the comparisons involved non-normally distributed data, Mann-Whitney U tests were performed for inferential statistical analyses, where appropriate, between the conditions. When the sample size was smaller than 30, i.e. the minimum requirement for performing inferential statistics (Roscoe 1969), descriptive statistics were presented.

4.3 Study 2: Cognitive validity

As we argued in Chapter 2, an investigation on the contextual parameters of reading-into-writing tasks (Study 1) is insufficient. To define the construct of reading-into-writing comprehensively, we must also consider the cognitive processes elicited by the tasks. Study 2, therefore, aimed first to examine the cognitive processes which students would normally use to complete the two sampled writing tasks (Real-life Task A and Real-life Task B) in a real-life academic context, and the cognitive processes test takers used to complete two reading-into-writing tests (Test Task A and Test Task B). The study then investigated the extent to which the reading-into-writing tests elicited from test takers the cognitive processes which they use when writing from sources in real life. We now describe the research methods of this investigation.

Participants

219 Chinese students (see Table 4.2) studying on a full-time undergraduate programme at the Business School at the UoB were recruited. The impact of students' nationality and other students' characteristics on their reading-into-writing processes is an important research agenda but is beyond the scope of this volume. As the sensitivity of such impact is unknown, we took on a more conservative position in recruiting a single nationality. Chinese, which was the single nationality with the highest population at the Business School, was selected. The use of a single nationality, however, limits the generalisability of the results. They were pursuing one of five majors: Business Administration, Advertising and Marketing Communications, Human Resource Management, Marketing, and Accounting (see Table 4.3). At the time of the study, all participants had a valid IELTS score, i.e. taken within two years. Based on the IELTS scores, their English proficiency was estimated to be between CEFR B2 and C1 (see Table 4.4).

Table 4.2 Overview of the gender proportion

Gender	Frequency	Percentage
Male	110	50.2
Female	109	49.8
Total	219	100

Table 4.3 Participants' majors

Majors at the Business Department	Frequency	Percentage
Business Administration	43	19.6
Advertising and Marketing Communications	37	16.9
Human Resource Management	48	21.9
Marketing	50	22.9
Accounting	41	18.7
Total	219	100

Table 4.4 Participants' IELTS scores

	IELTS Reading	IELTS Writing
Mean	5.86	5.52
Standard Deviation	0.6	0.5
Minimum	4.5	4.5
Maximum	7.5	7

Developing and validating a writing process questionnaire

Many studies in the literature of cognitive processes of language use have employed the method of think-aloud, which involves participants thinking aloud (i.e. describing the cognitive processes) as they are completing a writing or reading-into-writing task (Hayes and Flower 1980, 1983, Plakans 2008, 2010, Spivey 1990, Spivey and King 1989). This method allows researchers to conduct an online investigation of the cognitive processes employed by the participants. Think-aloud protocols can provide comprehensive, in-depth information about the cognitive processes employed by the participants, if they are well trained (Hayes and Flower 1983). Despite its usefulness in showing the participants' cognitive processes online, however, it is not suitable for the context of this investigation, which involves a large number of L2 participants. As think-aloud is a very time-consuming method, it is usually used in studies with a small number of L1 participants. Think-aloud has also been criticised because of the reactivity and disruption imposed on the actual cognitive processes, especially with L2 participants (Smagorinsky

1994, Stratman and Hamp-Lyons 1994). In addition, the method, by its very nature, is unsuitable for use in authentic test conditions.

Many other studies instead used questionnaires as a non-intrusive method to investigate the cognitive processes employed by the participants during writing or reading-into-writing tasks (e.g. Esmaeili 2002, Weir et al 2007). The method can report the cognitive processes employed by a large number of participants in different conditions in a systematic and efficient way. Nevertheless, Purpura (1998) pointed out three suggestions regarding the use of cognitive process questionnaires. He suggested that researchers should 1) use human information processing theory as a basis for the questionnaire construct; 2) examine the psychometric characteristics of their instruments before relating them to performance; and 3) use statistical techniques to assess the underlying construct validity of the questionnaire (Purpura 1998:113).

Regarding these concerns, a writing process questionnaire (hereafter WPQ) was developed following the procedures. The theoretical framework of the questionnaire was based upon Kellogg's (1996) and Field's (2004) model of different phases of receptive and productive skills, and Shaw and Weir's (2007) model of writing processes. The questionnaire was designed to measure the processes involved in four hypothesised phases of academic writing, namely a) conceptualisation, b) meaning construction, c) organisation, and d) monitoring and revising, which are considered to be most relevant to the context of this investigation (see Chapter 2 for a detailed discussion). A number of other relevant cognitive models including Hayes and Flower's (1980, 1983) writing model, Spivey's (1984, 1990, 1991, 1997, 2001) discourse synthesis model, and Khalifa and Weir's (2009) reading model were also consulted. Eight individual processes were identified and the working definition of each is provided in Table 4.5.

Individual questionnaire items were adapted to measure these processes from a few sources, including Weir et al's (2007) WPQ, Weir et al's (2008) survey on reading behaviours, Segev-Miller's (2007) taxonomy of discourse synthesis strategies, and Esmaeili's (2002) writing strategies for integrated reading and writing tasks. The items were then reviewed for content, form and classification by a team of researchers who specialise in writing assessment or cognitive processes of language use. The questionnaire was then translated to Chinese and the translation was checked by an independent qualified English–Chinese translator. The questionnaire was then piloted prior to a trial study.

The preliminary WPQ consisted of 60 items. They were presented in a linear fashion appropriate to the usual procedures of completing a writing task: reading the task prompt then reading the input texts, before and after writing the first draft. Nevertheless, it should be noted that writing is not a linear act but a multiple overlapping and reoccurring process. The

Table 4.5 Working definition of the individual processes

Individual processes	Working definition
Task representation	Create an initial understanding of the task (e.g. the overall purpose, structure of the task, time constraints, scoring criteria word length, topic, genre and intended reader)
Macro-planning	Plan for writing goals, content and organisation of the text Identify major constraints (genre, readership, language resources)
Careful reading	Careful reading to create textual and/or intertextual representations Global/local
Scanning, skimming and search reading	Scanning: reading a text quickly in order to find specific information; skimming: reading quickly to get a general idea of meaning; search reading: select ideas which are relevant to the task
Connecting and generating ideas	Generate links between ideas from multiple sources; create new meaning by connecting ideas with own knowledge
Organising	Organise the ideas to put in the next text (e.g. prioritise ideas in terms of relevance or importance, re-order, re-combine, delete, categorise, create new structure)
Translating*	Translate abstract ideas into linguistic forms
Monitoring and revising	Higher level: meaning and coherence, impact of reader Lower level: accuracy or range of grammar, vocabulary and sentence structure, plagiarism

The process of translating was not analysed in this investigation (see page 38)

participants could score the extent to which they agree or disagree with each item's description (4=definitely agree; 3=mostly agree; 2=mostly disagree; 1=definitely disagree).

As mentioned previously, the *translation*, which is a phase when a writer's internal ideas are translated into linguistic forms (Field 2004), was not investigated in this volume. When compared to other processes, such as macro-planning and organising, university students tend to be less aware of their translation/execution processes as they presumably have acquired high automaticity in them. In the context of academic writing from sources, these processes are usually not explicitly taught or practised. Methods such as think-aloud protocols would be more appropriate for the investigation of these processes. Previous studies tended to investigate these processes at the micro level under experimental settings (see Kellogg (1994) for a review). In addition, previous studies have indicated that writing-only and reading-into-writing tasks each elicit a distinct set of processes from writers. For example, the processes of creating textual or intertextual representations are not addressed by writing-only tasks. The processes of translation, on the other hand, might not differ as much as other processes between the independent and integrated test types.

Piloting the questionnaire

The questionnaire was trialled with two Chinese students. Both participants finished the questionnaire within 15 minutes. The questionnaire was reviewed by three independent researchers. The students and the researchers were asked to identify items which were unclear to them or seemingly repetitive. As a result, the questionnaire was condensed to 54 items. The questionnaire was then trialled with 97 undergraduates[4]. The data was submitted to a series of item and reliability analyses. The subsequent changes made to the questionnaire are summarised below (for details of the changes, see Appendix 5).

Items dropped due to inadequate sampling

The sampling adequacy of each individual item, i.e. whether an item was completed by an adequate proportion of the population, was assessed by examining the anti-image correlation matrix. A value less than 0.05 indicates an inadequate sampling. One item with a value below the threshold was eliminated from the questionnaire.

The revision of items with unsatisfactory correlation with other items

An initial analysis of the correlations of individual items was then performed to investigate if any items either have no correlation to any other items or correlate too closely to other individual items (i.e. >0.70). The results showed that all items had a correlation coefficient higher than 0.30 with at least some items in the questionnaire. However, some items measuring the low-level editing processes seemed to correlate too highly to each other (i.e. >0.70). In other words, some items were perhaps redundant. As these processes contained more items than the others in the questionnaire, it was felt appropriate to revisit the items with unsatisfactorily high correlations with each other. As a result, four items were combined into two items.

Qualitative feedback

Some open space was provided at the end of each section in the questionnaire. The participants were asked to provide some qualitative feedback, e.g. to identify items that were unclear, to name any additional processes that they employed. Four items were dropped from the questionnaire because the participants thought that they were too general and were already covered by other items in the questionnaire. On the other hand, three items were added to include the processes commonly reported by the participants in the open space provided.

---

4   When deciding the size of sample in the pilot, we followed the general rule of 10 people per variable (Field 2013) (i.e. process in our study). As the questionnaire was constructed to measure four cognitive phases (see Table 4.6), we aimed to recruit a minimum of 40 participants.

Methodology

The examination of internal consistency of each cognitive phase

The questionnaire was designed to measure the writers' cognitive processes on reading-into-writing tasks. A series of reliability analyses were performed to assess the internal consistency of the questionnaire items designed to measure the processes underpinning the same cognitive phase. Overall estimated reliability of each of the cognitive phases (using Cronbach's alpha) was obtained. Item-total correlations for each item within each cognitive process were obtained. The adjusted alpha (if the item were to be deleted) was also used to inform possible changes to the questionnaire. The analysis showed good internal reliability of the categorisation of the four academic writing phases, ranging from 0.74 to 0.93. Out of the 54 individual items, only two individual items (Item 1 and Item 8) did not report satisfactory item-total correlation (i.e. 0.30 or above) in their categorisation. They were regrouped into another categorisation.

The pilot questionnaire was revised to address issues raised from these validation checks (i.e. sampling adequacy, correlations, internal consistency and qualitative feedback). The final version of the questionnaire (see Appendix 6) consisted of 48 items. Table 4.6 presents its structure.

Table 4.6 Structure of the writing process questionnaire used in Study 2 (48 items)

Cognitive phases	Items	Number of items
Conceptualisation	Q2, Q3, Q4, Q5, Q11, Q18, Q26, Q28	8
Meaning construction	Q1, Q6, Q7, Q9, Q10, Q12, Q14, Q17, Q24, Q25, Q27	11
Organising	Q8, Q13, Q15, Q16, Q19, Q20, Q21, Q22, Q23	9
Monitoring and revising	Q29, Q30, Q31, Q32, Q33, Q34, Q35, Q36, Q37, Q38, Q39, Q40, Q41, Q42, Q43, Q44, Q45, Q46, Q47, Q48	20

Data collection procedures

A total of 443 writing process questionnaires were collected from the 219 participants in two phases. The data on test tasks was collected at the beginning of the term whereas the data on real-life writing tasks was collected during the term (Table 4.7).

Test Task A and Test Task B were administered to the participants under strict test conditions during their language classes, following the instructions provided by the test providers. The writing process questionnaire was administered immediately after the participants had completed each test task. The ideal setting would be to assign all participants to do both test tasks. However, this was not achievable due to practical constraints. About 40% of the

Defining Integrated Reading-into-Writing Constructs

Table 4.7 Questionnaire data collected in Study 2

Tasks	Number	Total
Test Task A	160 (81 did both + 79 did only Test Task A)	
Test Task B	140 (81 did both + 59 did only Test Task B)	300
Real-life Task A	70	
Real-life Task B	73	143
	Total	443

participants (n = 81, from four classes) did both tasks to serve as anchor students. The order of the test administered to them was counter-balanced. Two classes did Test Task A first and the other two classes did Test Task B first. The remaining 138 students (from six classes) did either one of the test tasks. Three classes (n = 79) were assigned to do Test Task A and the other three classes Test Task B (n = 59). Independent samples t-tests were performed to confirm that there was no significant difference between the two groups' proficiency level in terms of their IELTS Reading and Writing bands (see Table 4.8).

Table 4.8 Comparisons of the proficiency of the participants who did Test Task A and Test Task B*

	Participants who did only Test Task A (n=79)		Participants who did only Test Task B (n=59)		Independent samples t-test
	Mean	Std Dev	Mean	Std Dev	
IELTS Reading	5.91	0.481	5.73	0.601	t(275)=1.901, p=0.060 (n.s.)
IELTS Writing	5.59	0.534	5.58	0.513	t(270)=1.177, p=0.860 (n.s.)

*Std Dev = Standard deviation; n.s. = no significance

Data on the real-life writing tasks was also collected during the term. The 219 participants, as other students at the Business School, were allowed to choose two to four selective tasks as their course work, depending on the structure of their programme. Seventy participants chose to complete Real-life Task A, 73 chose Real-life Task B. Although the researcher did not have any control over which real-life tasks the participants completed, it was appropriate to investigate the comparability of the level of these two groups of students. Independent samples t-tests were performed to confirm that there was no significant difference between the two groups' proficiency levels in terms of their IELTS Reading and Writing bands (see Table 4.9). Participants were asked to complete the WPQ online as soon as they had completed the task.

Methodology

Table 4.9 Comparisons of the proficiency between the participants who did Real-life Task A and Real-life Task B*

	Students who did Real-life Task A (n=70)		Students who did Real-life Task B (n=73)		Independent samples t-test
	Mean	Std Dev	Mean	Std Dev	
IELTS Reading	5.92	0.690	5.95	0.649	$t(254)=0.212$, $p=0.832$ (n.s.)
IELTS Writing	5.51	0.462	5.53	0.471	$t(210)=0.260$, $p=0.796$ (n.s.)

Std Dev = Standard deviation; n.s. = no significance

Data analysis

As mentioned earlier, the purpose of Study 2 was to examine the target cognitive constructs of academic writing ability in relation to how participants complete authentic academic writing tasks, and to investigate the extent to which these processes were measured by the reading-into-writing test tasks.

The 443 questionnaires collected from the participants on the two real-life tasks and the two reading-into-writing test tasks were computed for statistical analysis. Descriptive statistics were obtained first. The data was then submitted to exploratory factor analysis (EFA) to examine the number of distinctive cognitive processes and the underlying structure of these cognitive processes involved in the four phases of academic writing. Comparison using the Mann-Whitney U test was conducted to investigate whether the participants employed these processes differently on the two real-life tasks. Another set of Mann-Whitney U tests was conducted to examine if these EFA-generated cognitive parameters were useful in distinguishing higher-scoring and lower-scoring participants.

To examine the cognitive processes elicited by test tasks, descriptive statistics were obtained. The Wilcoxon test, which is a non-parametric-related sample test, was conducted to compare data of different groups of participants between a) Test Task A (n = 160) and the two real-life tasks (n=143), and between b) Test Task B (n = 140) and the two real-life tasks (n = 143). Finally, EFA was then performed on the Test Task A and Test Task B data separately to investigate the underlying structure of the cognitive processes involved in each of the four cognitive phases. These analyses were to reveal the extent to which the processes elicited by the two reading-into-writing test tasks resembled the target real-life cognitive constructs.

4.4 Study 3: Criterion-related validity

As mentioned, Study 1 investigated the contextual component and Study 2 the cognitive component of the construct of reading-into-writing. In Study 3, we turned the focus to the *a posteriori* component: criterion-related validity. The purpose of analysing students' performances was to investigate the extent to which the reading-into-writing tasks would demonstrate a link between test performance and real-life academic writing performance. Without such evidence, we cannot be confident that reading-into-writing tasks are a good format for assessing academic writing ability. We now describe the research methods of this investigation.

Participants

The performance of the same 219 participants who participated in Study 2 was analysed (see their profile in Section 4.3).

Data collection procedures

The primary purpose of this analysis was to investigate the relationship between the students' performance on the two sample reading-into-writing test tasks and their written academic performance in real life. It was felt that more points of reference were needed as external criteria. In addition to the real-life essay and report tasks, students' performance in the one in-class written test and one end-of-term case-study examination were collected (see Table 4.10). For the in-class test, students were required to answer four to five questions in relation to some core concepts and theories in business forecasting they learned in the module. There was no source to read. The test lasted for 1 hour and there were no specific word limits. For the end-of-term examination, students were given a case study which contained about 2,500 words and non-verbal inputs such as diagrams and tables a week in advance for preparation. During the examination, they were required to write an essay to critically analyse the issues presented in the case study, and make recommendations. The examination lasted for 2 hours and there were no specific word limits.

Students' written academic performances on the four real-life measurements were marked by the lecturers following the university's departmental marking procedures (see Appendix 1 for the marking schemes of the two real-life tasks). All scores presented later are the final standardised marks submitted to the university. Students' performances on the two reading-into-writing test tasks were marked by the test providers following their standard procedures (more details are provided later). Reliability of the test results was checked by the test providers respectively. Table 4.10 summarises the total number of scores collected.

Table 4.10 Scores collected for Study 3

Conditions	Written performance	No of scores collected
Real-life	Essay	161
	Report	136
	In-class test	145
	End-of-term examination	143
Test	Test Task A	160
	Test Task B	140

Data analysis

As noted above, the purpose of this strand of investigation was to examine the relationship between performance on the two reading-into-writing tests and written academic performance in real life. The first step was to analyse the participants' performance on individual tasks. Descriptive statistical analyses of the participants' scores were performed on individual tasks regarding the overall pattern and the score distribution across levels. Correlational analyses were then performed on scores between a) Test Task A and real-life measurements, and b) Test Task B and real-life measurements. Correlations between the performances in the real-life and test conditions as well as the percentage of variance explained were discussed. After that, using scatterplots, the patterns of the correlations between the test scores and overall real-life scores were analysed to discuss the strengths and weaknesses of the correlations, i.e. whether the test scores predicted real-life academic outcomes at some levels better than others. The findings would provide information about how well two types of reading-into-writing test tasks could predict the test takers' real-life academic performance in their degree courses.

Summary

In summary, a mixed method approach was used to establish the validity of reading-into-writing in the three validation studies (see Table 4.11 for an overview).

For context validity, both expert judgement and automated textual analysis were applied to examine the criterial features of the sampled authentic academic writing tasks and reading-into-writing test tasks in terms of overall task setting and input text features, and then to evaluate the degree of correspondence of these contextual features of the reading-into-writing test tasks to those of the academic writing tasks.

For cognitive validity, participants were asked to complete the sampled authentic academic writing tasks and reading-into-writing test tasks. A cognitive writing process questionnaire was developed to assist participants to retrospectively report the processes they engaged in during completion of the tasks. The analysis of the cognitive validity included 1) the cognitive processes involved in real-life academic writing and the underlying structure of these processes, and 2) the extent to which these processes are elicited by the reading-into-writing test tasks. A range of descriptive, inferential and factor analyses were performed on the questionnaire data.

For criterion-related validity, the participants' scores on these sampled tasks were collected for correlational analyses to investigate the relationship between the reading-into-writing test tasks and authentic academic writing tasks.

In this chapter, we have explained the research methods of Study 1 (context validity), Study 2 (cognitive validity) and Study 3 (criterion-related validity) in detail. We will present the results of the three studies in Chapters 5 to 7 to reveal the empirical evidence for establishing the construct of reading-into-writing at the CEFR Level B2 or above in academic contexts.

Table 4.11 Overview of the three validation studies

Focus	Data collection in both real-life and test conditions	Data analysis
Context validity (Study 1)	Investigated the overall task setting (four tasks) by expert judgement (n = 10) on seven categories, i.e. purpose, topic domain, genre, cognitive demands, rhetorical functions, intended reader and knowledge of criteria Investigated the input text features (42 texts) by expert judgement (n = 2) on seven categories, i.e. input format, verbal input genre, non-verbal input, discourse mode, concreteness, textual organisation and cultural specificity, and automated textual analysis (17 indices) measuring lexical complexity, syntactic complexity and degree of cohesion (60 real-life extracts and 22 test input texts)	Descriptive analyses of the expert judgement results Non-parametric independent sample tests to compare the automated textual indices between a) real-life input texts and Test Task A (with multiple verbal inputs) input texts, and b) between real-life input texts and Test Task B (with multiple verbal and non-verbal inputs) input texts
Cognitive validity (Study 2)	Investigated the cognitive processing elicited in both the real-life and test conditions by a WPQ (a total of 443 questionnaires were collected from 219 participants – 70 on Real-life Task A, 73 on Real-life Task B, 160 on reading-into-writing Test Task A, 140 on reading-into-writing Test Task B)	EFAs to show the underlying structure of the cognitive processes students used on the real-life tasks Non-parametric independent sample tests to investigate whether the cognitive parameters distinguished the processes employed by high-scoring and low-scoring participants on the real-life tasks Non-parametric-related sample tests to investigate whether the cognitive processes elicited by each of the two reading-into-writing test formats resembled the processes employed by the test takers as they did in the real-life conditions
Criterion-related validity (Study 3)	Collected the participants' performances on Real-life Task A, Real-life Task B, two other real-life tasks (i.e. question-and-answer test and case study exam) and the two reading-into-writing test tasks	Descriptive analyses of the performances on each task Analyses of the correlation between performances on the real-life tasks and Test Task A, and between the real-life tasks and Test Task B

5 Contextual features of reading-into-writing tasks

> Building upon the theoretical foundations for defining the construct of reading-into-writing in Chapters 2 and 3, and the methodology in Chapter 4, this chapter reports the outcomes of Study 1, which set out to define the range of contextual parameters appropriate for reading-into-writing tasks to assess academic writing skills.
>
> The aim is to orient the reader to an explicit definition of the construct of reading-into-writing in terms of criterial task features. It is hoped that the outcomes of Study 1 will lead to better test designs to elicit the target high-level academic reading-into-writing processes, which will be defined in Chapter 6.
>
> The chapter covers the following areas:
>
> - overall task features
> - feature and complexity of input texts.

Having described the research methods in detail in the last chapter, we turn now to reporting the results of Study 1 in relation to the salient contextual features of the two sampled real-life academic writing tasks (Real-life Task A and Real-life Task B) and the two reading-into-writing test tasks (Test Task A – *with multiple verbal inputs* and Test Task B – *with multiple verbal and non-verbal inputs*). In Chapter 2, based on a synthesis of the literature, we proposed a range of contextual parameters that are likely to influence the difficulty of a reading-into-writing task in terms of overall task setting and input text features. A contextual parameter proforma incorporating these variables was then developed to aid the investigation of this study. The overall task setting of the reading-into-writing tasks was analysed by expert judgement while the input texts were analysed by both expert judgement and automated textual tools (for details see Section 4.2). The results regarding the overall task features will be reported in Section 5.1 and for input text features in Section 5.2. With the aim to examine the context validity of the two reading-into-writing test formats, we will discuss the extent to which these two reading-into-writing test formats resemble the contextual features of the sampled real-life academic tasks in Chapter 5.3. The chapter concludes with a summary of the main results concerning the context validity of reading-into-writing tests to assess academic writing abilities.

5.1 Overall task features (real-life and test tasks)

Based on the expert panel judgement and automated textual analysis, data on each of the sampled real-life academic tasks and the two reading-into-writing tests (for the procedures of selecting these tasks, see Section 4.1) was entered into the contextual parameter proforma. Here we report the results of each parameter of the four tasks.

Genre

Regarding the response *genre* of the two real-life tasks, the judges' responses showed total agreement on their responses. For Real-life Task A, students were expected to produce an essay whereas for Real-life Task B, students were expected to produce a report (Real-life Task A hereafter will be called the essay task, Real-life Task B the report task).

There was some variation among the judges' responses regarding the response genre of the test tasks. For Test Task A, four pairs of the judges considered the genre to be 'essay' while one pair decided that it was 'essay and summary'. For Test Task B, three pairs of the judges considered the genre was 'essay' while two pairs regarded it as 'essay and summary'. Pair 1 explained that, 'although the test tasks both require the test takers to write "an essay", both tasks require the test takers to write a summary in more specific terms. Essay can be anything'. While the majority of the judges categorised the two reading-into-writing test tasks as an essay task, two pairs of the judges noted that each of the test tasks incorporated some features of genres other than an essay. They criticised that 'essay' was often used in a very loose sense in test tasks. While it is understandable that test developers want to build in features of multiple genres in a single test task, it is important to maintain the authenticity of the target genres.

Purpose

Regarding the clarity of the communicative *purpose* set in the task, i.e. 'a reason for completing the task that goes beyond a ritual display of knowledge for assessment' (Shaw and Weir 2007:71), the judges' responses fell towards the positive end of a 5-point Likert scale for all four tasks (see Figure 5.1).

However, it is interesting that Test Task A and Test Task B seemed to present a clearer purpose than the real-life tasks did. Pair 5 of the judges commented that the communicative purpose presented in the two test tasks was straightforward and unambiguous. The purpose of the essay task was perceived to be the least clear among the four. Pair 2 commented that 'there was hardly a real communicative purpose to achieve on this task, apart from following the instructions.'

Nevertheless, although the communicative purpose presented on the two

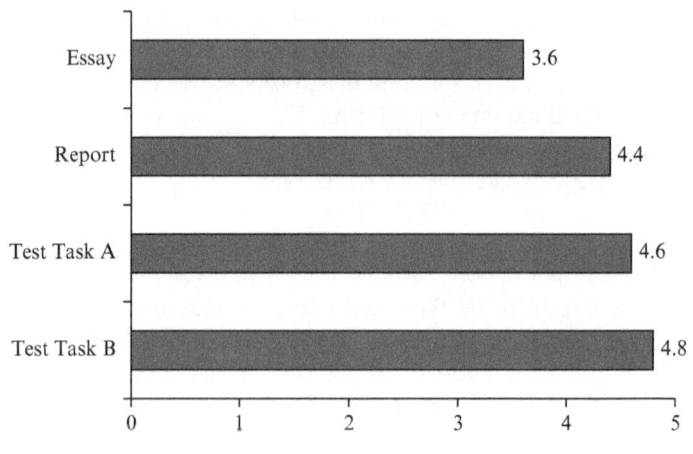

Figure 5.1 Clarity of the purpose of the tasks*

Task	Rating
Essay	3.6
Report	4.4
Test Task A	4.6
Test Task B	4.8

(1 = unclear, 5 = clear)

real-life tasks seemed to be less transparent than the test tasks, students may well receive further explanations from the lecturer. As the test takers would not receive any verbal explanation of the test task under test conditions, it is essential for the test tasks to present a clear communicative purpose. The two reading-into-writing test tasks sampled in this study did well in this regard.

Topic domain

While *topic* is regarded as one of the major contextual variables which have a significant impact on writing performance (Clapham 1996, Douglas 2000, Feak and Dobson 1996, Read 1990), it is not always straightforward to analyse the topic domain of a reading-into-writing task. The topic domain of a task can be determined intrinsically by, for instance, the context described in the prompt, the suggested title of the output text, the common theme of the input texts which typically include different perspectives of the 'topic', and the original sources of the input texts. Determining the topic domain of a task by looking at these intrinsic contextual features can be complicated enough. For example, a reading-into-writing task may have an 'academic' context (e.g. writing an academic essay), a 'professional' topic (e.g. business law) and input texts taken from a 'social' domain (e.g. newspaper and magazine articles). In addition, the topic domain can be determined extrinsically by how the writer would interpret the comparative importance among these contextual features.

In this study, as explained in Section 4.2, the judges were asked to rate the extent to which each task falls into each of the four topic domains, i.e. professional, academic, social and personal (see Figure 5.2).

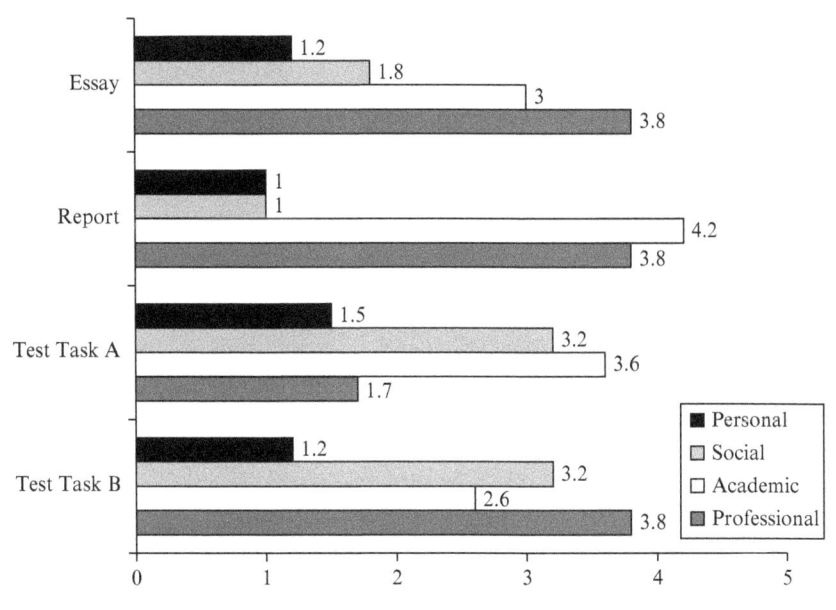

Figure 5.2 Topic domains of the tasks*

Task	Personal	Social	Academic	Professional
Essay	1.2	1.8	3	3.8
Report	1	1	4.2	3.8
Test Task A	1.5	3.2	3.6	1.7
Test Task B	1.2	3.2	2.6	3.8

(1 = not at all, 5 = definitely)

Based on the judges' response, the topic domain of the essay task was judged as largely professional (i.e. business) in the context of the study, but also, to a slightly lesser degree, academic. The topic domain of the report task was regarded as primarily academic, followed by professional. Both the real-life tasks were predominantly in the professional and academic domains. Agreeing with the literature (Khalifa and Weir 2009), the personal and social domains did not play an important role in the academic writing context. Tasks are seen to be in the academic domain when they are concerned with the teaching/learning sectors. The topic in the academic domain can be related to a particular discipline or field of study which may have no practical purpose or use. The professional domain refers to the occupational contexts. The topic is usually related to the specialised knowledge of a profession. According to the judges' responses, both of the real-life tasks fell into the academic and professional domains but the essay task was more 'professional' while the report task was more 'academic'.

The two test tasks also possessed multiple topic domains. However, based on the judges' responses, the topic domain of Test Task A was academic and social, and Test Task B fell into the professional and social domains. The social domain refers to the contexts connected with general social interaction in a public domain, one usually adopted in language tests of general proficiency. The topic of Test Task A was about whether it is worth saving endangered languages, whereas the topic of Test Task B was about the causes of work-related stress and its solutions. The judges felt that although the topic of Test Task A was academic and Test Task B was set in a professional context, both test tasks' input texts contained rather general content, which would usually appear in the social domain. This reflects one of the challenges in developing integrated assessment tasks. While the topic of a task could be in one domain, selection/manipulation of input materials could lead the task in a different domain, which might or might not be intentional. In either case, guidance on how to develop reading inputs aligned with the specified topic domain needs to be provided for item writers. Some recommendations will be provided in Section 8.3.

Scope of interaction between input and output

The *scope of interaction* between input and response is a key variable which may impact on the difficulty of a reading-into-writing task. The judges were asked to determine the scope of interaction by considering the nature of the cognitive processes required and in what way writers should draw upon the input texts. The findings show that none of the real-life tasks or the reading-into-writing test tasks were regarded as knowledge-telling tasks (see Figure 5.3). According to the judges, the two real-life tasks and the reading-into-writing test tasks were mapped towards the knowledge transforming end of the continuum (Scardamalia and Bereiter 1987). As shown in Figure 5.3, the report task scored an average of 3 and the essay task an average of 2.8. On the other hand, Test Task A scored an average of 2.2, and Test Task B an average of 2.6. The results showed that the real-life tasks were certainly towards the highest level of transforming content, whereas the two reading-into-writing tasks were deemed to be more towards the level of organising/reorganising content.

In other words, the real-life academic writing tasks were regarded as knowledge transforming tasks. In order to complete a knowledge transforming task, writers are expected to employ the high-level processes mentioned above, such as planning rhetorical goals, integrating ideas from different sources and transforming ideas (the actual processes reported by the writers on the tasks are discussed in Chapter 6).

The two reading-into-writing test tasks were apparently easier than the real-life tasks in terms of the expected scope of interaction between input and output. Both required the test takers to transform the ideas by selecting, organising and summarising relevant ideas from the input sources as well as evaluating different points of view. However, the test tasks might not require test takers to interpret, evaluate, and apply ideas in context to the extent that the real-life tasks did. Perhaps this is not surprising given the constraints on an exam essay as compared to the wider possibilities of transformational activity in university writing tasks.

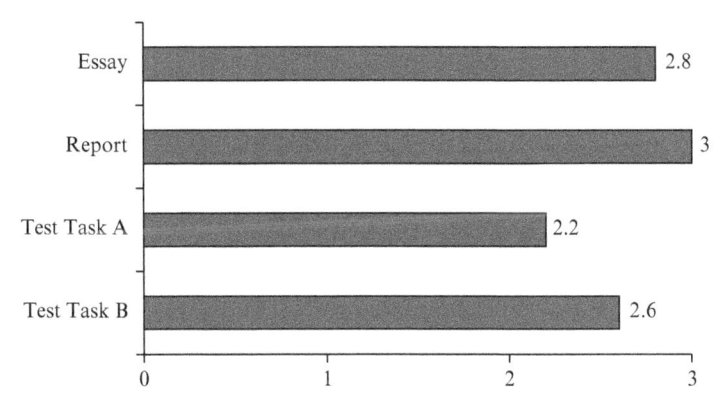

Figure 5.3 Scope of interaction between input and output*

Task	Value
Essay	2.8
Report	3
Test Task A	2.2
Test Task B	2.6

(1 = retelling information, 2 = reorganising information, 3 = transforming information)

Language functions

The judges were also asked to analyse the *language functions* that the writers are expected to perform on the four tasks. The judges' evaluations of the language functions varied the most among all categories in the exercise. They felt that it was comparatively subjective to determine what language functions are expected from a task because different people might approach the task differently. The findings showed that, according to the judges, the real-life report task required students to perform more language functions than the essay task and the two test tasks.

The judges deemed that the most important functions in completing the report task included describing, defining, reasoning, illustrating visuals and citing sources, followed by evaluating, predicting, recommending, synthesising and expressing personal views. The most important language functions elicited by the essay task were deemed to be reasoning, expressing personal view and citing sources, followed by evaluating, persuading and synthesising. Three pairs of the judges regarded describing and summarising to be also necessary (see Figure 5.4; the darker shade refers to categories agreed by two or more pairs of judges).

According to the judges, Test Task A apparently required fewer language functions. Only two language functions, i.e. expressing personal views and summarising, were determined by five pairs of the judges as necessary and one function, i.e. citing sources, by four pairs. Two or more pairs of judges identified evaluating, recommending, reasoning, synthesising and describing. One pair of judges identified persuading, predicting and defining.

The judges deemed that Test Task B required test takers to perform, mostly necessarily, reasoning, summarising and expressing personal viewpoints,

Defining Integrated Reading-into-Writing Constructs

followed by evaluating, recommending, synthesising and illustrating visuals. It is worth noting that these core functions were also considered to be those expected in Test Task A by at least two of the pairs of judges. These core language functions, apart from *citing sources,* were considered essential in Test Task B by at least three pairs of the judges.

The finding shows that some language functions, e.g. synthesising, evaluating, reasoning, expressing personal views, and citing sources, were deemed to be important for both real-life tasks. If students are expected to perform these language functions in academic writing, it is important that we teach and assess them. As we can see from the results, a wider range of language functions were required by the sampled real-life tasks than the test tasks. It is perhaps unrealistic to expect a test task to elicit language functions as widely as a real-life academic writing task does due to the stricter time constraints. This, however, indicates a need for identifying the 'core' language functions from the TLU domain and operationalising them in task design (for more recommendations, see Section 8.3).

Figure 5.4 Language functions

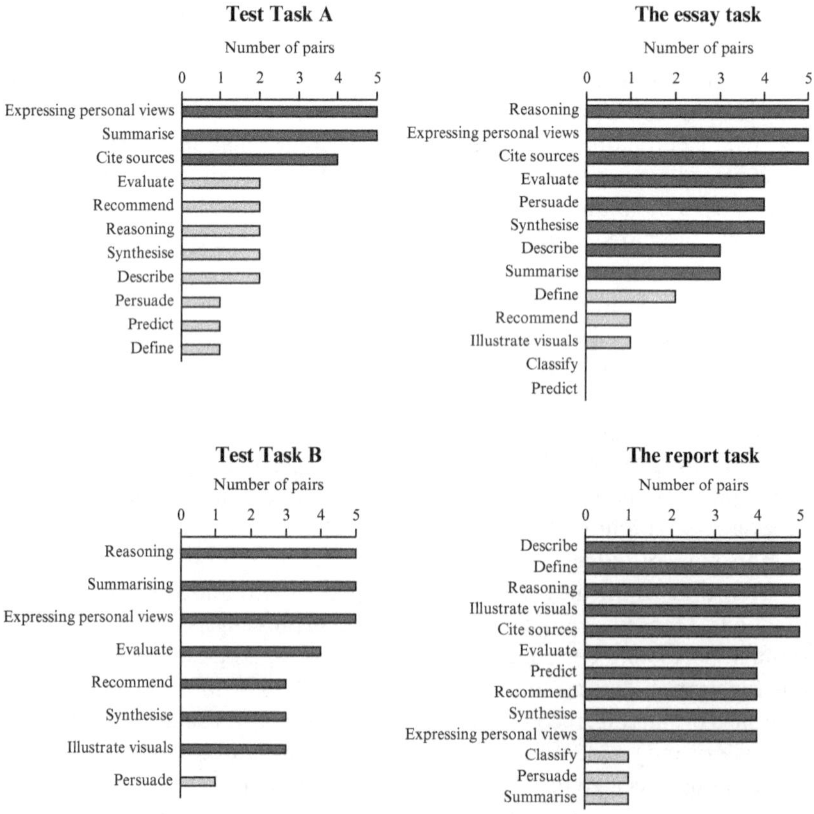

Test Task A — Number of pairs

- Expressing personal views: 5
- Summarise: 5
- Cite sources: 5
- Evaluate: 2
- Recommend: 2
- Reasoning: 2
- Synthesise: 2
- Describe: 2
- Persuade: 1
- Predict: 1
- Define: 1

The essay task — Number of pairs

- Reasoning: 5
- Expressing personal views: 5
- Cite sources: 5
- Evaluate: 4
- Persuade: 4
- Synthesise: 4
- Describe: 3
- Summarise: 3
- Define: 2
- Recommend: 1
- Illustrate visuals: 1
- Classify: 0
- Predict: 0

Test Task B — Number of pairs

- Reasoning: 5
- Summarising: 5
- Expressing personal views: 5
- Evaluate: 4
- Recommend: 3
- Synthesise: 3
- Illustrate visuals: 2
- Persuade: 1

The report task — Number of pairs

- Describe: 5
- Define: 5
- Reasoning: 5
- Illustrate visuals: 5
- Cite sources: 5
- Evaluate: 4
- Predict: 4
- Recommend: 4
- Synthesise: 4
- Expressing personal views: 4
- Classify: 1
- Persuade: 1
- Summarise: 1

Clarity of intended reader

With respect to *the clarity of intended reader*, the judges considered that both real-life tasks did not perform satisfactorily (see Figure 5.5). Pair 5 commented that while it might be obvious to the students that the 'real' intended reader of the real-life tasks were the lecturers, both tasks did not provide any information about the intended reader. Mature writers would consider the needs of the reader while they plan, write and edit their text (Scardamalia and Bereiter 1987). A valid writing task should always clearly present the intended reader, e.g. self, well-known other, distant other (Shaw and Weir 2007). The judges gave an average of 3.2 out of 5 for the Test Task A. However, there was some obvious disagreement in the focus group meeting (the rating ranged from 2 to 5). The context of the task was a national essay contest. While some judges considered the implied reader was clear, i.e. the judges of the writing contest, other judges thought that no actual information was provided regarding the intended reader. It was unclear to them whether the reader would be a single judge, a group of judges, or even a bigger community which could get access to the writing contest. Test Task B received the highest rating (4.3 out of a score of 5) regarding its clarity of the intended reader among the tasks. Test Task B required the test takers to write to a single lecturer. The judges believed that the relationship between test takers and the intended reader was made clear.

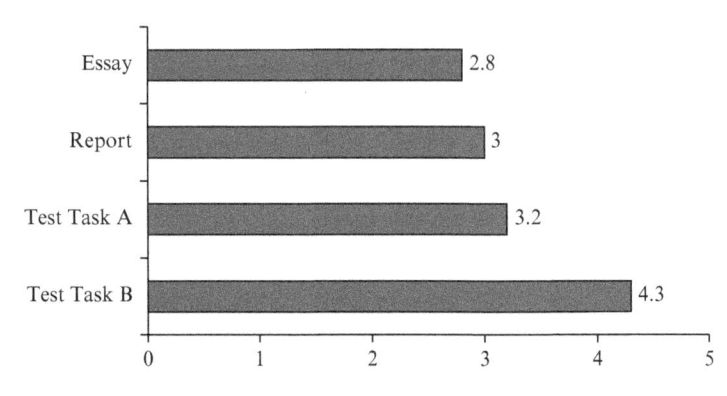

Figure 5.5 Clarity of intended reader of the task*

Task	Rating
Essay	2.8
Report	3
Test Task A	3.2
Test Task B	4.3

(1 = unclear, 5 = clear)

Knowledge of criteria

The judges felt that both real-life tasks provided students with very clear and detailed *marking criteria* (see Figure 5.6). On the other hand, the judges gave an average rating of 3.8 out of 5 for Test Task A. The task stated that test takers' performance would be scored according to four criteria: a) relevance and adequacy, b) coherence and organisation, c) lexical use and d) grammatical use. However, most judges reported that some more specific descriptions of the criteria would be helpful. Regarding Test Task B, the judges thought that although the descriptions of the marking criteria were much less detailed than those provided on the real-life tasks, the criteria were clear and precise enough in a test situation (4.6 out of 5).

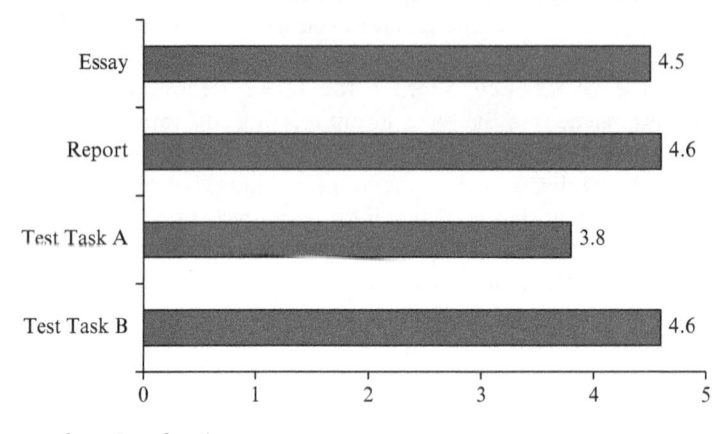

Figure 5.6 Provision of the knowledge of criteria*

Task	Rating
Essay	4.5
Report	4.6
Test Task A	3.8
Test Task B	4.6

(1 = unclear, 5 = clear)

We have so far discussed the overall task setting of the two real-life tasks and the two reading-into-writing test tasks as evaluated by the expert panel. We now look at the results regarding input text features of the tasks.

5.2 Input text features and linguistic complexity (real-life and test tasks)

As described in Section 4.2, 10 sample texts from each of the real-life tasks, 20 from 10 testlets of Test Task A and two from one testlet of Test Task B were analysed. Here we present the results of the second panel judgement exercise in which two judges individually analysed all the pooled input texts using part 2 of the proforma template. Although the sample size was small, the exercise demonstrated the practicality of a thorough manual analysis of the complexity of source texts.

Input format

For the two real-life tasks, verbal input was more dominant on the essay task while the combination of verbal and non-verbal input was more dominant on the report task. None of the input texts contained solely non-verbal input. This supports the use of both verbal and non-verbal materials in reading-into-writing tasks. The input format of the two reading-into-writing test tasks was standardised. Test Task A contained two verbal passages while Test Task B contained two passages with a non-verbal input in each.

Input genres

Regarding input genres, the real-life tasks consisted of a wider range of materials than the test tasks. Writers most frequently cited news/magazine articles, journal articles, reports and reviews on the essay task. Non-verbal materials included diagrams and pictures. Most-cited genres on the report task were book chapters, journal articles, case studies, news/magazine articles and reports. Non-verbal materials included were predominantly tables and graphs. It should be noted that only the 10 most frequently cited texts on each task were sampled in this investigation, which means an even wider range of genres were likely involved in the completion of the authentic tasks.

In contrast, the genres involved in the test tasks were narrowly controlled. Each Test Task A contained two input texts. All input texts from the 10 testlets collected in this study seemed to belong to a rather non-specific text created specifically for the exam, perhaps a simplified version of the essay genre. For Test Task B, only one testlet was available at the time of the study. Test Task B contained two input texts, of which one was identified by the judges as a news/magazine article and the other as a report. Both included a diagram. Nevertheless, the judges felt the input texts in Test Task B did not appear totally authentic. This raises an issue of how to develop or modify texts for teaching or test purposes. Recommendations for reading-into-writing task design will be provided in Chapter 8.

Discourse mode

In the context of reading-into-writing, writers are expected to actively interact with the input texts, and hence the discourse mode of these materials would have a direct impact on the task difficulty. Both real-life tasks involved the reading of expository and argumentative texts. The report task contained more expository texts (70%) than argumentative texts (30%) while the essay task contained more argumentative texts (60%) than expository texts (40%). In contrast, the input texts on the test tasks were dominated by single discourse mode. All texts in Test Task A were identified as argumentative texts (100%) while all texts in Test Task B contained only expository texts.

Concreteness of ideas

Based on the specificity of the main ideas in the texts (for the procedures, see Section 4.2), the ideas of the input texts in the test tasks were considered by the judges more concrete than those in the real-life input texts (see Figure 5.7). In other words, the input texts of the test tasks contained ideas which were more concrete (i.e. less knowledge specific). For example, the input texts of one testlet of the real-life essay task were related to the phenomenon of feminisation in the public relations (PR) industry; another testlet related to the advertisement strategies of a department store to focus on core family values. The input texts of one testlet of the real-life report task were related to business-specific knowledge such as different techniques to predict the uncertain nature of business trends and graphics useful for modelling and forecasting time series.

On the other hand, the input texts of the two test tasks are much less knowledge specific. For example, one testlet of Test Task A was about the reasons why saving the disappearing languages is important (e.g. every language has unique characteristics) as well as the reasons why people should not be concerned about saving disappearing languages (e.g. resources need to be allocated to more important concerns such as education, health and jobs). The input texts of Test Task B were about different methods of handling work-related stress. This is appropriate given the fact that these test tasks are not used to assess writers' abilities in English for specific purposes.

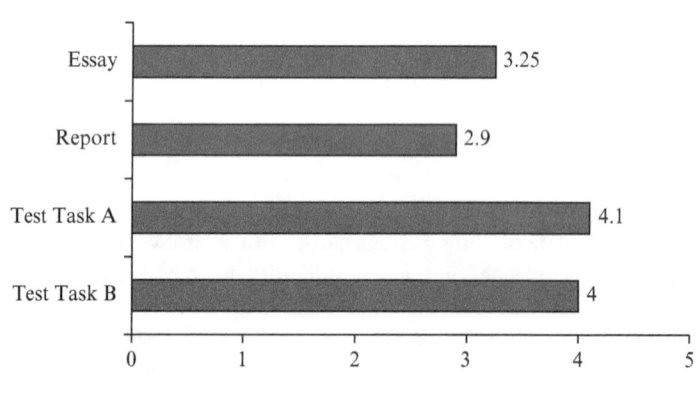

Figure 5.7 Concreteness of ideas*

Task	Value
Essay	3.25
Report	2.9
Test Task A	4.1
Test Task B	4

(1 = abstract, 5 = concrete)

Explicitness of the textual organisation

As expected, the input texts of the test tasks were more explicitly organised than the real-life input texts (see Figure 5.8). Most of the test task input texts were organised mechanically into three to five paragraphs, each containing a main idea. The judges felt that these paragraphs were sometimes too explicitly linked with the use of formulaic markers such as *firstly*, *in addition* and *lastly*. These formulaic markers were found to be less frequent in real-life input texts. The real-life tasks imposed a higher demand for the writer to figure out how each paragraph relates to the others, and to the whole text.

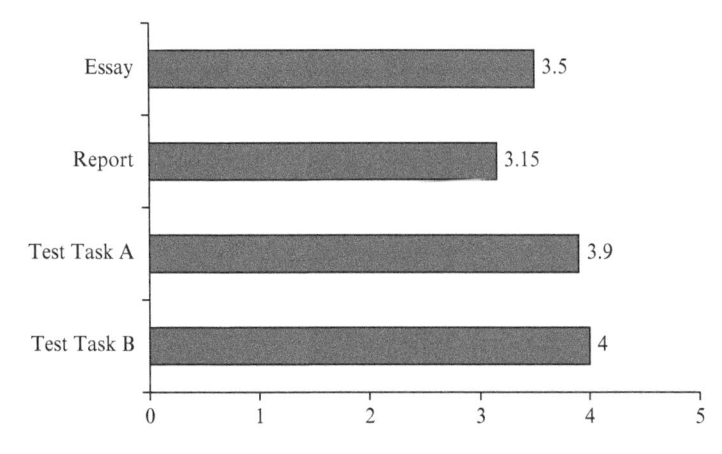

Figure 5.8 Explicitness of textual organisation*

Task	Rating
Essay	3.5
Report	3.15
Test Task A	3.9
Test Task B	4

(1 = inexplicit, 5 = explicit)

Feedback from judges

To evaluate how confident the judges felt when evaluating the contextual features of the tasks using the contextual parameter proforma (see Appendix 2), an evaluation questionnaire was developed to collect feedback of their experience. Overall, the judges reported that they were confident when responding to the items of the proforma on a scale out of four (4 = very confident; 3 = confident; 2 = not confident; 1 = not confident at all) (see Table 5.1).

The mean rating of the 10 judges for each category ranged from 2.6 to 4.0. The only category rated lower than 3.0 was topic domain. They were comparatively least confident when evaluating this because, as explained in Chapter 4.2, the decision might be influenced by a range of task features, such as the context described in the prompt, the suggested title of the output text, the common theme of the input texts, and the original sources of the input texts. This reflects the complexity in designing reading-into-writing tasks, and hence indicates the need to provide a clear specification on these variables (further recommendations will be provided in Section 8.3).

Defining Integrated Reading-into-Writing Constructs

Table 5.1 Feedback from judges

	Mean	Standard Deviation
Part 1 (Number of judges: 10)		
Purpose	3.8	0.42
Topic domain	2.6	0.52
Genre	4.0	0.00
Cognitive demands	3.3	0.48
Language functions	3.5	0.71
Clarity of intended reader	3.6	0.52
Clarity of knowledge of criteria	3.6	0.70
Part 2 (Number of judges: 2)		
Input format	4.0	0.0
Verbal input genre	4.0	0.0
Non-verbal input	4.0	0.0
Discourse mode	3.5	0.71
Concreteness of ideas	3.5	0.71
Explicitness of textual organisation	3.0	0.0
Cultural specificity	3.5	0.71

Having discussed the results regarding the features of the four tasks evaluated by human judges, we turn now to the results of the automated textual analysis in relation to the level of difficulty of the input texts.

In addition to the expert panel judgement, the 60 input text extracts and 22 test task input texts (for details of the procedures, see Section 4.2) were subjected to automated textual analysis. The two real-life tasks have been analysed and discussed separately so far, but the 60 sample extracts collected from the two tasks will be treated together in this analysis. The purpose of the automated textual analysis was to determine the difficulty level of the input texts in terms of lexical complexity, syntactic complexity and degree of cohesion. It was felt more beneficial to analyse all the real-life input texts as a whole group, so that the results will provide a more generalisable picture of the appropriate difficulty level of the input texts. Table 5.2 presents the results.

Lexical complexity refers to the richness of the lexicon in a text (Knoch, Macqueen and O'Hagan 2014). In a recent meta-analysis study to synthesise research on the relationship between task complexity and features of L2 writing, Johnson (2017) argued that lexical complexity could be measured by (a) text-internal measures such as lexical diversity (the proportion of unique words to total words) and lexical density (the proportion of content words to total words), and (b) text-external measures such as lexical sophistication (the proportion of frequency/infrequency words to total words). These measures have long been used to determine the difficulty level of reading texts in the second language learning context (Green et al 2010). In the context of reading-into-writing, the lexical complexity of the input texts could impact the

Contextual features of reading-into-writing tasks

Table 5.2 Input text features – linguistic complexity (real-life texts)

	Authentic input texts (n = 60 extracts)			
	Mean	Std Dev	Minimum	Maximum
Lexical complexity				
1. High-frequency words (K1)	77.20	4.60	68.96	85.94
2. High-frequency words (K1+K2)	87.76	2.98	82.06	93.63
3. Academic words	10.37	3.79	2.62	19.83
4. Low-frequency words (Offlist)	2.41	1.85	0.00	6.87
5. Frequency log – content words	2.10	0.15	1.83	2.38
6. Average syllables per content word	1.70	0.11	1.46	1.93
7. Type-token ratio (TTR) (content words)	0.69	0.08	0.47	0.85
Syntactic complexity				
8. Average words per sentence	21.38	3.27	15.32	28.56
9. Logical operator incidence score	45.12	12.97	16.17	77.28
10. Mean number of modifiers per noun phrase	1.03	0.17	0.67	1.38
11. Mean number of words before the main verb of the main clause in sentences	5.50	1.46	2.62	10.65
12. Sentence syntax similarity	0.08	0.02	0.05	0.11
Degree of coherence				
13. Adjacent overlap argument	0.55	0.18	0.17	0.89
14. Adjacent overlap stem	0.58	0.19	0.09	0.83
15. Adjacent overlap content word	0.10	0.04	0.04	0.22
16. Proportion of adjacent anaphor references	0.25	0.18	0.03	0.74
17. Adjacent semantic similarity (LSA)	0.23	0.09	0.09	0.49

difficulty of the task. For example, a text with a higher proportion of unique and infrequent content words would be more difficult to summarise than a text with a lower proportion of these words.

In terms of lexical sophistication, the proportion of different frequency words of the BNC corpus[1] was measured. The results show that 77.2% of the vocabulary in the authentic input texts were found within the first 1,000 frequent words of the BNC corpus (Index 1) and 87.76% the first 2,000 (Index 2) (see Table 5.2). The input texts only contained 2.41% of low-frequency words (Index 4) (i.e. those not included in the frequency list of 15,000 on the BNC) and some input texts contained no low-frequency words at all. The real-life input texts on average included 10.37% *academic words* (Index 3). However, it was surprising that the percentage ranged from 2.62% to 19.83% – to complete the real-life tasks, students integrated ideas from inputs of a range of genres,

---

1 The BNC was used because it is the largest corpus of its kind, with a 100-million-word collection of samples of written (90%) and spoken (10%) language from a wide range of sources from the late 20th century (for more details about BNC, see www.natcorp.ox.ac.uk/corpus/index.xml).

such as news/magazine articles. These texts contained a lower proportion of academic words than the other academic genres, such as research articles.

When we consider how easy or difficult it is to summarise a text, it is important to consider lexical density, which is typically measured by the proportion of the content words (e.g. nouns, main verbs, adjectives and adverbs) which contain conceptual meaning in a text (Johansson 2008). Index 5 (Frequency log) in Table 5.2, ranging from 0 to 6, indicates the *frequency level of content words* by computing the log frequency of all content words in a text. The lower the score is, the less frequent the content word is. The mean score of the frequency level of the content words in the authentic input texts was 2.10. The figure on its own might not be directly interpretable but it could be useful when used to compare the lexical density across texts.

Index 6 in Table 5.2 measures *the average syllables per content word*. Content words with more syllables are probably more difficult to process because decoding multisyllabic words takes more time and cognitive effort than decoding a monosyllabic one (Rayner and Pollatsek 1989). This index therefore partly reflects the decoding demand of the input texts. The content words in the authentic input texts on average contained 1.70 syllables, ranging from 1.46 to 1.93. Index 7 measures *the type-token ratio (TTR) of all content words*. The ratio reflects the proportion of unique content words which need to be decoded. The higher the ratio is, the more unique content words there are in the real-life texts. A TTR of 1 means that all words of the text occur only once. The sampled authentic texts on average had a TTR ratio of 0.69.

Syntactic complexity is believed to be an important indicator of the difficulty of a text (Crossley, Greenfield and McNamara 2008). In the context of reading-into-writing, the more complex sentence structures a text contains, the more difficult it would be for writers to summarise the text. Syntactic complexity is particularly important in determining the difficulty of a reading-into-writing task in which higher-level reading processing (such as creating textual and intertextual representations) rather than low-level lexical decoding is targeted. Although syntactic complexity was traditionally examined by measure of subordination, researchers have recommended the use of multiple measures of syntactic complexity, especially those that measure the features of complexity at phrase level, in research of text complexity in academic prose (Biber, Conrad and Cortes 2004, Bulté and Housen 2012, Norris and Ortega 2009).

Index 8 in Table 5.2 measures *the average number of words per sentence*. Generally speaking, the longer a sentence is the more complex it is because the sentence might contain more phrases and clauses. A text with many complex sentences is demanding to process and integrate because the reader needs to build and reorganise elaborate syntactic structures. Processing longer sentences is demanding also because it requires more working memory while the reader is building the syntactic structure (Graesser, Cai, Louwerse and Daniel 2006). Such a process of building and analysing the syntactic pattern in a string of words is known as parsing (Rayner and Pollatsek 1989). The sampled real-life input texts on average contained 21.38 words per sentence, with a wide range between 15.32 and 28.56.

The next syntactic measure (Index 9) indicates *the density of logical operators* (connectives). Logical operators, e.g. *and* and *or*, are used to explicitly express the relations among the ideas in a text, and therefore, texts with a high density of logical operators are difficult (McNamara, Louwerse, Cai and Graesser 2005). One would normally expect a wider range of connectives in academic texts. However, when considering the difficulty level of a reading-into-writing task, students might find it more challenging to process an advanced text with few logical connectives. Building textual and intertextual representations from the input texts is an important part of the reading-into-writing construct. A lack of connectives in advanced texts means that it is harder for the reader to build the relationships between the ideas within a text or across texts (Brown and Yule 1983). Therefore, we side with Brown and Yule that, in the case of advanced academic texts, the lower the mean logical operator incidence score is, the more difficult it would be for students to build textual representations. Real-life input texts had a mean logical operator incidence score of 45.12, with a wide range from 16.17 to 77.28. However, as CohMetrix did not provide sufficient information concerning how the incidence was computed, the meaning of the index can only be interpreted indirectly as a direction that the lower the score is, the fewer logical operators (connectives) a text contains. Although we can only infer the meaning of this index (i.e. it is not as transparent as measures such as average sentence length), it serves as a useful reference. When developing input texts in integrated tasks, it is important to maintain a similar level of the mean logical operator incidence of those real-life input texts in the TLU domain.

The next two syntactic indices – 10 and 11 (*mean number of modifiers per noun phrase* and *mean number of words before the main verb of the main clause in sentences*) – concern the noun phrases and main clauses of the texts. They measure the mean number of modifiers per noun phrase and the mean number of words before the main verbs of the main clauses respectively. Noun phrases and main verbs in a text are believed to carry the key meaning of a text. Modifiers, e.g. adjectives, adverbs, or determiners, are used to describe the property of the head of a noun phrase or the main verb. They indicate the difficulty of building the syntactic structures in a text. The more modifiers or words the reader has to read before getting to the head nouns or the main verbs, the more demanding it is to build the syntactic structures. The indices also reflect the complexity of the ideas in the text. The more modifiers before the head nouns and more words before the main verbs mean the more qualities these key ideas possess. One important aspect of academic writing ability is to synthesise, i.e. select, connect and organise, the ideas from the input texts based on the writing purpose. The more qualities the ideas in the input texts possess, the more demanding it is to synthesise these ideas. The mean number of modifiers per noun phrase in real-life input texts was 1.03, ranging from 0.67 to 1.38. The mean number of words before the main verbs of the main clauses in the real-life input texts was 5.5, ranging from 2.62 to 10.65.

Index 12 (syntax similarity index) measures how syntactically similar the sentences are, by calculating the proportion of nodes in the two syntactic tree structures that are intersecting nodes between all sentences and across paragraphs. It is easier to process a text with more syntactically similar sentences than with more syntactically different sentences due to a syntactic parsing effect. The parsing effect is used to describe the high possibility that a speaker would produce an utterance with a structure similar to the previous utterance he or she produced (Pickering and Branigan 1998). Ledoux, Traxler and Saab (2007) found that the syntactic parsing effect was also present in reading processes. The syntax similarity index between all sentences of the authentic input texts was 0.08, which means 8% of the nodes in the two syntactic tree structures are intersecting nodes between all sentences and across paragraphs.

Measurement of coherence is used less frequently to determine the difficulty level of a text than the measurements of lexical and syntactic complexity. One reason is because the coherence of a text may not be reflected directly by the occurrence of cohesive devices. Kennedy and Thorp (2007) argued that, especially concerning a more advanced level, an overt occurrence of cohesive devices does not necessarily improve the cohesion of a text. Therefore, the results have to be interpreted with caution. Taking this into consideration, the degree of coherence of the input texts is particularly relevant to the discussion of the reading-into-writing tasks. The more coherent a text is, the easier it would be for the reader to build the textual representation because a cohesive text contains 'explicit features, words, phrases or sentences that guide the reader in interpreting the substantive ideas in the text, in connecting ideas with other ideas and in connecting ideas to higher-level global units, e.g. topics and themes' (Graesser et al 2004:193). Previous research has shown that students engaged in coherence-enhancing processes during reading create the level of coherence required by the task (Kaakinen and Hyönä 2005). For example, it is more essential for a reader to create a coherent representation of the texts when reading textbooks for study than when reading newspapers for pleasure. In reading-into-writing activities, the level of coherence a reader needs to maintain is higher than tasks that involve merely reading comprehension. With a more coherent and cohesive text it would be easier for students to create a textual representation of the ideas and to integrate them for the writing purposes.

The first three coherence indices in Table 5.2 (Index 13 – *adjacent overlap argument*, Index 14 – *adjacent overlap stem* and Index 15 – *adjacent overlap content word*) measure the proportion of adjacent sentences sharing one or more arguments (i.e. nouns, pronouns and noun phrases), stems and content words, respectively. The occurrence of repeated arguments, stems or content

Contextual features of reading-into-writing tasks

words would make the text more cohesive and hence easier to be processed (Crossley, Clevinger and Kim 2014). These previously occurring ideas would ease the demand on the reader to process new ideas. The authentic input texts had a mean adjacent argument overlap score of 0.55, a mean adjacent stem overlap score of 0.58, and a mean adjacent content word overlap score of 0.10. In other words, about 50% of the adjacent sentences shared one or more argument and word stems, and 10% of the content words in adjacent sentences shared one or more common content words.

Index 16 (*anaphor reference adjacent*) measures the proportion of anaphor references between adjacent sentences. It is easier for the reader to resolve the anaphor reference when the referent is in an adjacent sentence, rather than at a distance of a few sentences. The authentic input texts showed a mean adjacent anaphor reference score of 0.25. In other words, 25% of the anaphor references in the texts referred to their referents in an adjacent sentence. The last index (17 – *adjacent semantic similarity*) measures how conceptually similar each sentence is to the following sentence by comparing the latent semantic analysis (LSA) dimensions of their lexical items. The score can vary from 0 (low cohesion) to 1 (high cohesion). The higher the score, the more conceptually similar the adjacent sentences are with each other. The sampled real-life input texts have a mean adjacent semantic similarity score of 0.23.

In short, the degree of coherence of input texts would impact on the difficulty of a reading-into-writing task. For example, as shown in previous research, a less coherent text would require more cognitive effort from the reader to refresh text information in working memory that could then be incorporated in text representation (Kaakinen and Hyönä 2005) or in order to resolve a coherence break introduced by incoherent sentences (Kaakinen, Olkoniemi, Kinnari and Hyönä 2014). The five coherence measures (Index 13 to 17) we reported give an indication of the degree of coherence in the real-life input texts students used to complete academic writing tasks. When developing input texts into integrated tasks, it is important to ensure that the input texts are of a similar degree of coherence as those texts students are expected to integrate in real-life academic writing.

Having established the complexity level of the real-life input texts sampled in this study in relation to lexical complexity, syntactic complexity and degree of coherence, we now turn to the analysis of the input texts of the test tasks. The reported indices (see Table 5.2) will be used as a reference to examine the extent to which the input texts in the two reading-into-writing test tasks were set at a comparable level.

The textual features of the real-life input texts have been discussed so far. In order to further discuss the level of difficulty of the input texts which the participants in this study integrated in their writing assignments, the textual features of the undergraduate course texts reported in Green et al (2010) are compared in Table 5.3 as a reference. They computed the values from 42 passages extracted from 14 undergraduate textbooks at a British university. Their results were compared descriptively to the results obtained from the real-life input texts in this study to explore if there was a difference in the difficulty level between undergraduate coursebook texts collected in Green et al's study and those sampled in this study.

Regarding the lexical complexity, as shown in Table 5.3, the real-life input texts sample in this study showed similar figures to the undergraduate course texts analysed in Green et al (2010) in terms of the frequency level of the content words, average syllables per content word and the TTR of all content words. Nevertheless, the real-life input texts had a slightly lower percentage of academic words than the undergraduate texts, though the difference was small. In addition, there were more frequent words (the first 1,000 and the first 2,000) and fewer low-frequency words in the real-life input texts than the undergraduate course texts. This implies that the real-life input texts were easier than the undergraduate coursebook texts in terms of the proportion of word frequency bands.

With regard to the five indices related to the syntactic features of the texts, the difficulty levels of the real-life input texts collected in this study and the undergraduate coursebook texts collected by Green et al (2010) were largely comparable (see Table 5.3). They contained almost the same average length of sentences (average words per sentence). In addition, the range of sentence structures (sentence syntax similarity) and the average number of modifiers per noun phrase were very close between the real-life input texts and the undergraduate coursebook texts. However, the real-life input texts contained a slightly higher number of words before the main verbs of the main clauses than the undergraduate texts, and had a slightly lower logical operator incidence score than the undergraduate texts. The results indicate that it might be slightly more demanding to work out the meaning and syntactic structure embedded in the main clauses in the real-life input texts, and slightly more demanding to build the textual representation of the real-life input texts.

Based on the five indices which indicate the degree of coherence of the texts, the real-life input texts and undergraduate coursebook texts appear to be comparable (see Table 5.2). The only difference was that the real-life input texts had a slightly lower adjacent semantic similarity score than the undergraduate coursebook texts. In other words, adjacent sentences in the real-life input texts seemed to be less conceptually similar than those in the undergraduate coursebook texts. Nevertheless, the difficulty level of the real-life input texts sampled from a single discipline (i.e. from the Business School) in this study was very close to those undergraduate coursebook texts sampled from multiple disciplines in Green et al's (2010) study. This gives us confidence that the complexity features of our sample of the real-life input texts are generalisable to the wider academic writing contexts. We will now turn to examine the extent to which the input texts in the two reading-into-writing tests were comparable to the real-life input texts.

Table 5.3 Descriptive comparisons with Green et al (2010) findings

	Real-life input texts (60 extracts from 20 texts) Mean	Coursebook texts (Green et al 2010) (40 extracts) Mean	Descriptive comparison of the difficulty level between real-life input texts and undergraduate coursebook texts
Lexical features			
High-frequency words (K1)	77.20	74.00	The real-life input texts had more first 1,000 frequency words in proportion to the coursebook texts.
High-frequency words (K1 + K2)	87.76	85.89	The real-life input texts had more first 2,000 frequency words in proportion to the coursebook texts.
Academic words	10.37	10.51	The real-life input texts had slightly fewer academic words in proportion to the coursebook texts.
Low-frequency words (Offlist)	2.41	4.33	The real-life input texts had fewer low-frequency words in proportion to the coursebook texts.
Log frequent content words	2.10	2.14	The real-life input texts had a similar frequency level of the content words to the coursebook texts.
Average syllables per content word	1.70	1.72	The real-life input texts had a similar number of syllables per word to the coursebook texts.
Type-token ratio (TTR) (content words)	0.69	0.65	The real-life input texts had a similar TTR as the coursebook texts.
Syntactic features			
Average words per sentence	21.38	21.47	The real-life input texts had a similar average sentence length as the coursebook texts.
Sentence syntax similarity	0.08	0.07	The range of sentence structures used in the real-life input texts was very close to the coursebook texts.
Mean number of modifiers per noun phrase	1.03	0.95	The real-life input texts had a similar number of modifiers per noun phrase to the coursebook texts.
Mean number of words before the main verb	5.50	4.59	The real-life input texts had more words before the main verb per verb phrase than the coursebook texts.
Logical operator incidence	45.12	46.14	The real-life input texts had a slightly lower proportion of connectives than the coursebook texts.

Table 5.3 (continued)

Cohesion	Real-life input texts (60 extracts from 20 texts) Mean	Coursebook texts (Green et al 2010) (40 extracts) Mean	Descriptive comparison of the difficulty level between real-life input texts and undergraduate coursebook texts
Adjacent overlap argument	0.55	0.56	The real-life input texts had a similar percentage of the adjacent sentences that shared one or more arguments (i.e. nouns, pronouns, noun phrases) to the coursebook texts.
Adjacent overlap stem	0.58	0.58	The real-life input texts had almost the same percentage of the adjacent sentences that shared one or more word stems as the coursebook texts.
Adjacent overlap content word	0.10	0.10	The real-life input texts had almost the same percentage of the adjacent sentences that shared one or more content words as the coursebook texts.
Proportion of adjacent anaphor references	0.25	0.24	The real-life input texts had a similar percentage of the adjacent sentences that shared one or more argument to the coursebook texts.
Adjacent semantic similarity (LSA)	0.23	0.26	The real-life input texts were conceptually less similar across the text than the coursebook texts.

5.3 Comparison between the real-life and test task input texts

Having established the generalisability of our sampled real-life texts, we will now report findings regarding the extent to which the input texts in the two reading-into-writing tests were comparable to the real-life input texts. As described in Section 4.2, the difference between the sampled real-life and Test Task A input texts was analysed by the Mann-Whitney U test, as the data was non-parametric. The differences between the real-life and Test Task B input texts were compared descriptively only, due to the small sample size of the Test Task B input texts.

Overall, the difficulty level of sampled Test Task A input texts was comparable to the level of the authentic input texts (see Table 5.4). The differences in 14 out of the 17 indices obtained between the two conditions were non-significant. In the remaining three indices, with the exception of *low-frequency words (Offlist)*, the differences obtained were slight.

With regard to lexical complexity, Test Task A input texts contained a similar proportion of high-frequency words (K1 and K1 + K2) as the real-life input texts. However, they contained slightly fewer academic words (though the difference was not significant). Interestingly Test Task A contained significantly (z=-6.545, p<0.01) more *low-frequency* words than the real-life input texts and the mean difference was as large as 8% (real-life: M=2.41%, Test Task A: M=10.41%). The *low-frequency* words on the Test Task A input texts were mainly proper names of places and organisations. For the remaining lexical indices concerning the content words, there was not much difference in terms of the frequency of content words and the average syllables per word. Test Task A input texts had a slightly higher TTR but the difference was not significant.

Regarding the syntactic complexity, there was no significant difference in three syntactic indices (average words per sentence, mean number of words before the main verb and logical operator incidence) between the Test Task A and real-life input texts. However, Test Task A input texts had a significantly higher sentence syntax similarity index, and significantly fewer modifiers per noun phrase than the real-life input texts. This suggests that the Test Task A texts might be less complex to process than the real-life input texts in terms of syntactic complexity, although the actual mean differences were very small.

The degree of text cohesion in Test Task A and the real-life input texts was similar. There was no significant difference in all cohesion indices obtained between Test Task A and the real-life input texts (see Table 5.4).

Having reported the findings of Test Task A's input texts, we now report the results of Test Task B. At the time of the study, only one set of operationalised Test Task B was available. Due to a limited sample size, only descriptive statistics of the textual indices of the two Test Task B input texts are presented

Table 5.4 Linguistic complexity between Test Task A and real-life source texts

	Real-life tasks (60 extracts from 20 texts) mean	Median	Test Task A (20 texts) mean	Median	Mann-Whitney U test	Wilcoxon W	z	Asymp. Sig. (2-tailed)
Lexical features								
High-frequency words (K1)	77.20	77.48	76.54	76.50	556.0	766.0	-.489	0.63
High-frequency words (K1 + K2)	87.76	87.76	87.69	87.53	600.0	810.0	.000	1.00
Academic words	10.37	10.73	8.84	8.54	437.0	647.0	-1.811	0.07
Low-frequency words (Offlist)	2.41	2.02	10.41	10.80	11.0	1841.0	-6.545	**0.00**
Log frequent content words	2.10	2.07	2.05	2.06	508.0	718.0	-1.022	0.31
Average syllables per content word	1.70	1.70	1.72	1.70	591.000	2421.0	-.100	0.92
Type-token ratio (TTR) (content words)	0.69	0.70	0.72	0.73	448.0	2278.0	-1.689	0.09
Syntactic features								
Average words per sentence	21.38	21.53	20.49	20.90	514.0	724.0	-.956	0.34
Sentence syntax similarity	0.08	0.08	0.09	0.09	401.5	2231.5	-2.206	**0.03**
Mean number of modifiers per noun phrase	1.03	1.05	0.91	0.91	336.0	546.0	-2.933	**0.00**
Mean number of words before the main verb	5.50	5.20	5.76	5.40	493.5	2323.5	-1.183	0.24
Logical operator incidence	45.12	44.21	43.76	43.97	560.5	770.5	-.439	0.66
Cohesion								
Adjacent overlap argument	0.55	0.55	0.60	0.59	520.5	2350.5	-.884	0.38
Adjacent overlap stem	0.58	0.58	0.65	0.63	500.5	2330.5	-1.106	0.27
Adjacent overlap content word	0.10	0.07	0.09	0.08	490.5	700.5	-1.217	0.22
Proportion of adjacent anaphor references	0.25	0.19	0.28	0.27	457.0	2287.0	-1.589	0.11
Adjacent semantic similarity (LSA)	0.23	0.21	0.25	0.25	488.0	2318.0	-1.245	0.21

here (see Table 5.4). The indices obtained from the authentic input texts are provided in the table for a descriptive comparison. For the 17 textual indices, larger descriptive discrepancies were found in six indices (two lexical, one syntactic and three coherence indices) between the Test Task B input texts and the authentic input texts.

According to Table 5.5, Test Task B input texts seemed to be slightly easier than the authentic input texts in terms of lexical complexity due to a higher proportion of the first 1,000 and 2,000 frequency words. However, larger discrepancies were obtained in other indices (academic words and low-frequency words). Text Task B input texts contained more academic words (14.46% vs 10.37%) and low-frequency words (6.63% vs 2.41%) than the authentic input texts. In addition, Text Task B input texts had a slightly higher TTR of the content words than the authentic input texts. There was not much difference between the Test Task B input texts and the authentic input texts in terms of the frequency level of the content words and the number of syllables per word. Therefore, while containing a slightly higher proportion of high-frequency words, Test Task B input texts could be more difficult to process than the real-life input texts, due to a higher proportion of academic words and low-frequency words, and a higher proportion of unique content words (TTR).

Regarding the syntactic features (see Table 5.5), Test Task B had a much lower proportion of connectives (logical operator incidence score) and a slightly more modifiers per noun phrase than the real-life input texts. This could indicate a higher demand to process the noun phrases and to sort out the logical connections between ideas in the Test Task B input texts than in the real-life texts. On the other hand, Test Task B input texts contained a lower average number of words per sentence, a higher sentence syntax similarity score, and a lower number of words before the main verbs in verb phrases, but the actual differences were very small. Therefore, the results seemed to suggest that Test Task B input texts were more syntactically challenging than the real-life input texts due to a noticeably lower proportion of connectives in the texts.

As shown in Table 5.5, regarding the degree of text cohesion, the Test Task B input texts had a lower proportion of adjacent anaphor references than the sampled real-life input texts. This indicates a more demanding process of resolving the anaphor references in the Test Task B input texts and the real-life input texts. However, the other four text cohesion indices seemed to suggest that Test Task B input texts had a better cohesion than the authentic texts, and hence were less challenging. Test Task B input texts had higher proportions of adjacent sentences sharing one or more arguments (i.e. nouns, pronouns, noun phrases), word stems and content words than the real-life texts. This means it would be easier to process the main themes in Test Task B input texts than in the real-life texts. Test Task B input texts also had a higher

Table 5.5 Linguistic complexity between Test Task B and real-life source texts

	Real-life tasks (60 extracts from 20 texts)	Test Task B (two texts)	Descriptive comparison of the difficulty level between real-life and Test Task B input texts
Lexical features	Mean	Mean	
High-frequency words (K1)	77.20	81.9	The Test Task B input texts had slightly more first 1,000 frequency words in proportion to the authentic input texts.
High-frequency words (K1 + K2)	87.76	91.99	The Test Task B input texts had slightly more first 2,000 frequency words in proportion to the authentic input texts.
Academic words	10.37	14.46	The Test Task B input texts had more academic words in proportion to the authentic input texts.
Low-frequency words (Offlist)	2.41	6.63	The Test Task B input texts had more low-frequency words in proportion to the authentic input texts.
Log frequent content words	2.10	2.11	The Test Task B input texts had almost the same frequency level of the content words as the authentic input texts.
Average syllables per content word	1.70	1.79	The Test Task B input texts had almost the same number of syllables per word as the authentic input texts.
Type-token ratio (TTR) (content words)	0.69	0.77	The Test Task B input texts had a slightly higher type-token ratio than the authentic input texts.
Syntactic features			
Average words per sentence	21.38	20.32	The Test Task B input texts had a slightly shorter average sentence length than the authentic input texts.
Sentence syntax similarity	0.08	0.10	The sentence structures used in the Test Task B input texts were slightly more similar to each other than those in the authentic input texts.
Mean number of modifiers per noun phrase	1.03	1.41	The Test Task B input texts had slightly more modifiers per noun phrase than the authentic input texts.
Mean number of words before the main verb	5.50	4.75	The Test Task B input texts had fewer words before the main verb per verb phrase than the authentic input texts.
Logical operator incidence	45.12	28.16	The Test Task B input texts had a much lower proportion of connectives than the authentic input texts.
Cohesion			
Adjacent overlap argument	0.55	0.73	The Test Task B input texts had a higher percentage of the adjacent sentences that shared one or more arguments (i.e. nouns, pronouns, noun phrases) than the authentic input texts.
Adjacent overlap stem	0.58	0.73	The Test Task B input texts had a higher percentage of the adjacent sentences that shared one or more word stems than the authentic input texts.
Adjacent overlap content word	0.10	0.80	The Test Task B input texts had a higher percentage of the adjacent sentences that shared one or more content words than the authentic input texts.
Proportion of adjacent anaphor references	0.25	0.18	The Test Task B input texts had a lower proportion of adjacent anaphor references than the authentic input texts.
Adjacent semantic similarity (LSA)	0.23	0.28	The Test Task B input texts were slightly more conceptually similar across the text than the authentic input texts.

adjacent semantic similarity score than the authentic texts, which indicates that the adjacent sentences in the Test Task B input texts were more conceptually similar than those in the real-life input texts.

In short, when compared descriptively to real-life input texts, Test Task B input texts were more demanding in terms of lexical complexity (more academic words and more low-frequency words) and syntactic complexity (lower proportion of connectives), but less demanding in terms of text cohesion (higher proportions of shared arguments, words stems and content words). However, given the fact that Test Task B is a post-university entrance test and targets fresh undergraduates, it seems that the lexical complexity and syntactic complexity of its input texts could be adjusted. In particular, the proportion of academic words and uncommon words could be reduced slightly to a similar level as those of the sampled real-life texts. In addition, as reported previously, the real-life input texts had many more logical connectives proportionally than the Test Task B input texts. This means that there would be a greater cognitive demand for students to build the relations between ideas on Test Task B input texts and real-life input texts. Nevertheless, due to the small number of testlets available for Test Task B, it was not possible to generate any inferential statistics on the textual indices between Test Task B and real-life input texts. The descriptive results reported above are only suggestive.

5.4 Summary

It is well established that the difficulty level of a test task is largely determined by its contextual features, but very few studies in the literature to date systematically provide detailed information of the contextual features of academic reading-into-writing tasks. Using a chosen set of criterial task variables drawn from the literature, the purpose of Study 1 reported in this chapter was to describe the key features of two common reading-into-writing tasks which students would normally encounter in the UK academic setting, and to investigate the extent to which these features are represented in two reading-into-writing test formats (essay with multiple verbal inputs and essay with multiple verbal and non-verbal inputs). Task variables examined included eight parameters of overall task setting, six parameters of input texts' features and 17 automated textual indices of textual complexity.

The results regarding the overall task setting are summarised in Table 5.6. Based on the expert judgement analysis, the two reading-into-writing test tasks resembled the overall task setting of the real-life tasks in a number of important ways.

Both reading-into-writing test tasks (Test Task A and Test Task B) required an output of an essay, which was one of the most common genres required in the real-life academic context. Nevertheless, it was observed that

Table 5.6 Summary of overall task features

Overall task setting	Real-life Task A	Real-life Task B	Test Task A	Test Task B
Target level	Undergraduate Year 1	Undergraduate Year 1	C1	B2
Brief instruction	Summarise salient issues from the sources and discuss the issues with justified personal views	Describe the business of a company based on the data provided; discuss and justify ways of analysis; make recommendations	Summarise the main ideas from the input texts and stating own viewpoints	Summarise the main ideas from both verbal inputs and non-verbal inputs and express opinions
Time and length	5,000 words	2,000 words	At least 250 words in 60 minutes	180–220 words in 60 minutes
Genre (response)	Essay	Report	Essay	Essay
Purpose*	3.6	4.4	4.6	4.8
Topic domain**	Professional (3.8) Academic (3.0) Social (1.8) Personal (1.2)	Professional (3.8) Academic (4.2) Social (1) Personal (1)	Professional (1.7) Academic (3.6) Social (3.2) Personal (1.5)	Professional (3.8) Academic (2.6) Social (3.2) Personal (1.2)
Scope of interaction between input and output**	2.8	3.0	2.2	2.6
Language functions to perform (numbers indicate the number of pairs of judges chosen)	Classify (0) Cite sources (5) Describe (3) Define (2) Evaluate (4) Persuade (4) Predict (0) Recommend (1) Reason (5) Summarise (3) Synthesise (4) Express personal views (5) Illustrate visuals (0)	Classify (1) Cite sources (5) Describe (5) Define (5) Evaluate (4) Persuade (1) Predict (4) Recommend (4) Reason (5) Summarise (1) Synthesise (4) Express personal views (4) Illustrate visuals (5)	Classify (0) Cite sources (5) Describe (2) Define (1) Evaluate (2) Persuade (1) Predict (1) Recommend (2) Reason (2) Summarise (5) Synthesise (2) Express personal views (5) Illustrate visuals (0)	Classify (0) Cite sources (0) Describe (0) Define (0) Evaluate (4) Persuade (1) Predict (0) Recommend (3) Reason (5) Summarise (5) Synthesise (3) Express personal views (5) Illustrate visuals (3)
Clarity of intended reader*	2.8	3.0	3.2	4.3
Knowledge of criteria*	4.6	4.5	3.8	4.6

* *(1 = unclear, 5 = clear)*
** *(1 = not at all, 5 = definitely)*
*** *(1 = limited transformation, 2 = some transformation, 3 = much transformation)*

the 'essay' required in the test tasks was somehow modified for the purpose of assessment, and thus was not entirely authentic. Hyland (2002), in his book on genre, argued that genre represents 'how writers typically use language to respond to recurring situations' (2002:4). It is important for writers to be able to identify the genre when they approach a task because their 'choices of grammar, vocabulary, content, and organisation depend on the situations in which they are writing' (2002:9). It might be problematic if test takers are required to produce a combined form of different genres that only exist in the test conditions.

Agreeing with the literature, the *academic* and *professional* domains were dominant in the sampled real-life tasks. A rather surprising finding was that both test tasks were seen to be, at least partly, associated with the social domain. Test Task A was considered to be in the *academic* and *social* domains while Test Task B fell into the *professional* and *social* domains. As both test tasks serve in academic contexts, the social domain does not seem to be entirely appropriate from this perspective. Test Task A serves as a means of measuring the English language ability of Taiwanese applicants who wish to pursue further studies overseas (Language Training and Testing Center 2012). Test Task B is a university diagnostic test which aims to differentiate the new international students who would need to receive support in writing, and diagnosing the weaknesses in their academic writing ability. However, it is understandable why both reading-into-writing test tasks did not contain very specific content. As argued in Chapter 3, one advantage of reading-into-writing tasks is that they can provide an equal access of background knowledge of the topic to prevent bias against test takers. If the content provided in the input texts is too specific, it may impose a background effect on test takers (Ackerman 1990, Clapham 1996, Kellogg 1987). Unlike ESP tasks, EAP writing tasks do not usually require a high level of specific knowledge (Douglas 2000).

As expected from the literature, both real-life tasks were knowledge transforming tasks which required a high level of interaction between input and output. The tasks require from the students a contribution of transformed or new knowledge through the activation of high-level processes, such as defining the rhetorical situation of the writing tasks, integration of (contradictory) content from multiple internal and external sources as well as interpreting, elaborating, evaluating, and modifying ideas to satisfy rhetorical goals. Flower (1990), therefore, argued that these academic writing tasks promote the development of critical literacy.

It is encouraging that the two reading-into-writing test tasks also required from students a certain level of interaction between input and output, even though the degree of knowledge transformation required was apparently lower than the real-life tasks. Both were seen to require the students to transform the ideas by selecting, organising and summarising relevant ideas from the input sources as well as evaluating different points of view. Nevertheless,

Defining Integrated Reading-into-Writing Constructs

the test tasks might not require test takers to interpret, evaluate and apply ideas in context to the extent that the real-life tasks did.

The two test tasks required a wide range of language functions, such as reasoning, expressing personal views, evaluating, synthesising and citing sources, which were also deemed to be important for the real-life tasks. This indicates the need for these 'core' language functions to be taught or tested in academic writing tasks. Although the two test tasks did not seem to require these language functions as widely as the real-life tasks, the core language functions were also considered to be expected in the test tasks. The judges' evaluations of the language functions varied the most among all categories in the investigation. This indicates that when developing reading-into-writing tasks, item writers would probably need some training and support to determine which language functions to target.

The judges thought that both real-life tasks did not do very well with respect to the presentation of a clear intended readership but they stressed that it was more important for test tasks to do so. Test Task B received a higher rating than the real-life tasks while Test Task A received a similar rating to the real-life tasks. The judges felt that Test Task A could explicitly mention the intended reader rather than only imply it in the context.

Regarding the knowledge of criteria, the judges felt that both real-life tasks provided students with very clear and detailed marking criteria. For Test Task A, most judges considered that the criteria were presented clearly but some additional descriptions of the criteria might be helpful. For Test Task B, the judges thought that although the descriptions of the marking criteria were much less detailed than those provided on the real-life tasks, the criteria were clear and precise enough in the test conditions.

Having summarised the results regarding the overall task features, we now summarise the results regarding the input text features analysed by expert judgement (see Table 5.7). The features of the input texts provided on Test Task A and Test Task B were largely comparable to the real-life input texts with some discrepancies.

Both real-life tasks required students to write about multiple external reading resources. The real-life input texts contained a variety of genres, such as *news/magazine articles*, *journal articles* and *book chapters*. This supports the need to assess students' ability to write from multiple sources in reading-into-writing tests. Test Task A replicated the context by requiring the test takers to write about two passages. Test Task B replicated the real-life context by requiring the test takers to write about two passages containing non-verbal information. While the two test tasks did well to include multiple sources, the genre of their input texts was comparatively limited. All input texts on Test Task A were regarded as belonging to a simplified version of the *essay* genre. Test Task B, on the other hand, contained texts belonging to simplified versions of the *report* and *news/magazine article* genre. While we appreciate the

Table 5.7 Summary of input text features

	Real-life Task A (n = 10 most frequently used texts)	Real-life Task B (n = 10 most frequently used texts)	Test Task A (n = 20 texts from 10 testlets)	Test Task B (n = 2 texts from 1 testlet)
Input text features				
Input format	Verbal passage (80%) Passage with non-verbal information (20%)	Verbal passage (30%) Passage with non-verbal information (70%)	Verbal passage (100%)	Passage with non-verbal information (100%)
Genre (input)	News article (50%) Journal article (30%) Review (10%) Report (10%)	Book chapter (60%) Report (10%) Journal article (10%) News article (10%) Case study (10%)	Essay (100%)	Report (50%) News article (50%)
Non-verbal input	Pictures (50%) Diagrams (50%)	Graphs (71%) Tables (29%)	N/A	Diagrams (100%)
Conceptual complexity				
Discourse mode	Argumentative (60%) Expository (40%)	Expository (70%) Argumentative (30%)	Argumentative (100%)	Expository (100%)
Concreteness of ideas	3.3	2.9	4.1	4
Explicitness of textual organisation	3.5	3.15	3.9	4

reasons for standardising the genre of the input texts in the reading-into-writing tests, test developers may consider using a wider range of different input genres to better represent what students would encounter in their studies.

In terms of discourse mode, most of the real-life input texts were expository and argumentative. Brewer (1980) argues that the cognitive demands of processing different discourse modes vary. Argumentative and expository texts are believed to be more demanding than narrative and descriptive texts. Descriptive texts usually require the reader to build a visual and spatial cognitive structure; narrative texts require creating a mental representation of a series of occurring events; expository texts would require the cognitive processes of constructing induction, classification and comparison; and argumentative texts would require a reader to establish the author's position, reasons, supporting evidence and/or counterarguments. It was good that the reading-into-writing test tasks also targeted at the expository and argumentative texts. However, the test tasks seemed to have limited their input texts to only one discourse mode. Test Task A required test takers to process argumentative texts while Test Task B required test takers to process expository texts. As students are required to work with both expository and argumentative texts in their academic tasks in the TLU domain, it is desirable for the test tasks to operationalise both types in their input texts.

Lastly, the ideas in the test task input texts were considered slightly more concrete than those in the real-life input texts, and the textual organisation of the test task input texts was more explicitly organised than the real-life input texts. This means the reading-into-writing test input texts are likely to be easier to process than the real-life input texts. This is nevertheless considered reasonable because the test conditions impose a time pressure on students to process these sources, whereas in real life time pressure is much more lenient. In other words, the features of the input texts provided on Test Task A and Test Task B to a large extent matched up with those of the real-life input texts. However, for a number of variables, including input genre, discourse and language functions, the test tasks appeared to have a narrower range of representation. If this is the case due to the need for standardising the test tasks, we need a better understanding of the impact of these variables on the level of task difficulty. Recommendations for future test design are provided in Section 8.3.

Having established the contextual features of reading-into-writing tasks in the academic contexts and discussed the results of Study 1 in this chapter, we turn now to consider the cognitive aspects of these tasks. In Chapter 6, we will report the findings of Study 2 in relation to students' cognitive processes on the sample reading-into-writing test under the real-life and test conditions. It is hoped that the findings will demonstrate the range of cognitive parameters appropriate for the construct of reading-into-writing in academic contexts at the CEFR Levels B2 or above.

6 Academic reading-into-writing processes

> Building upon the theoretical foundations for defining the construct of reading-into-writing in Chapters 2 and 3, and the methodology in Chapter 4, this chapter reports the outcomes of Study 2, which set out to define the range of cognitive parameters appropriate for reading-into-writing tasks to assess academic writing skills.
>
> The aim is to orient the reader to an explicit definition of the construct of reading-into-writing in terms of the cognitive processes needed to perform academic writing tasks. It is hoped that the outcomes of Study 2 will lead to a more complete representation of these target high-level academic reading-into-writing processes in future test tasks to assess academic writing skills
>
> The chapter covers the following cognitive processes:
>
> - conceptualisation (task representation, macro-planning)
> - meaning construction (careful reading, discourse synthesis)
> - organising ideas
> - monitoring and revising.

In order to establish a correspondence between test takers' performance on a language test and their ability to use the language in the target language use (TLU) domain, e.g. academic context, the characteristics of a test task should reflect the features of those which students are expected to encounter in the TLU in real life (Bachman and Palmer 1996:23). To establish this link between reading-into-writing tasks and real-life academic writing tasks, we analysed the contextual features of the two sampled real-life academic writing tasks (Real-life Task A and Real-life Task B) and the two reading-into-writing test tasks (Test Task A – *with multiple verbal inputs* and Test Task B – *with multiple verbal and non-verbal inputs*) using both expert judgement and automated tools in Study 1. In Chapter 5, we reported the results of Study 1 in relation to a set of salient contextual features, which are likely to affect the difficulty level of reading-into-writing tasks (as reviewed in Section 2.3), and discussed the extent to which these two reading-into-writing test formats resemble the contextual features of the writing tasks in the real-life academic context.

Having established the context validity of reading-into-writing, we

Defining Integrated Reading-into-Writing Constructs

address the cognitive aspects of the construct of reading-into-writing next. Previous studies, as reviewed in Section 2.2, found that language users tend to employ different processes when they read and write for different purposes (Spivey 1990, Urquhart and Weir 1998). For example, when they read to fill in some factual details, they tend to scan the source text quickly to locate the relevant information. On the other hand, when they read to summarise, they tend to read carefully at the global level. When defining the construct of reading-into-writing in academic contexts, it is essential to obtain evidence on students' cognitive processes on the academic writing tasks in real life. Weir (2005a) argued that any valid test task should, as far as possible, operationalise the cognitive processes which students would normally use when completing similar tasks in real life. To achieve this, we examined participants' cognitive processes when they composed Real-life Task A and Real-life Task B, and investigated the extent to which these target cognitive processes were elicited by each of the two reading-into-writing test formats (Test Task A – with multiple verbal inputs and Test Task B – with multiple verbal and non-verbal inputs) in Study 2. In this chapter, we will report the results of Study 2 in order to define the cognitive component of the reading-into-writing construct. We will first report the findings of the underlying structure of reading-into-writing processes in the real-life academic context identified in this study, followed by the results in relation to any differences in processes observed between the two real-life task genres (report and essay) and between two levels of students' performance (high-scoring and low-scoring) on the tasks. After that, we will compare the processes used by high-scoring and low-scoring test takers on each of the test tasks, and the processes they used between the real-life and test conditions. This is in order to establish the cognitive validity of the two reading-into-writing test formats.

6.1 How do undergraduates compose from sources in real life?

As described in Section 4.3, the cognitive processes employed by the participants when they completed the two real-life tasks (Real-life Task A – essay and Real-life Task B – report) were measured by the writing process questionnaire (WPQ) (see Appendix 6). The questionnaire consisted of 48 items, measuring writers' processes of several major cognitive phases (i.e. *conceptualisation, meaning and discourse construction, organising, low-level monitoring and revising,* and *high-level monitoring and revising*) when writing from sources (a glossary was presented in Table 4.1 in Chapter 4). A total of 143 questionnaires were collected on the two real-life tasks: essay and report. Seventy participants who completed the real-life essay task and 73 who completed the report task filled out the cognitive process questionnaire. We now present the findings of how the participants completed these two real-life tasks.

The underlying structure of reading-into-writing processes (real-life)

First of all, a series of EFAs were conducted to investigate the number of distinct cognitive processes within each of the four cognitive phases. Pre-requisite analyses of EFA, which include the Kaiser-Meyer-Olkin (KMO) measure of sampling adequacy and Bartlett's test of sphericity, were performed to test the data's appropriateness for factor analysis. In addition, the data was tested by a Kolmogorov-Smirnov test with regard to its normal distribution and the results indicated a non-normal distribution ($p<0.01$). Following Fabrigar, Wegener, MacCallum and Strahan's (1999) recommendation, the Principal Axis Factor Method was performed to extract the initial factors.

For an initial indication of the possible number of factors extracted by the data, the eigenvalues and scree plot were examined. Rotated solutions of the factor loadings, which avoid maximising the variance accounted by the first factor, were obtained by an oblique promax rotation. This rotation method is often used in social science and language studies because it allows the factors to be correlated. To determine the ultimate number of underlying factors to be extracted, the possibilities were interpreted and evaluated based on both statistical results and theoretical rationale. The findings then provided statistical evidence of 1) how many distinct cognitive processes loaded on each academic writing phase, and 2) the extent to which each distinct cognitive process loaded on each cognitive phase.

The conceptualisation phase (real-life)

The conceptualisation phase was measured by eight questionnaire items. The initial factor extraction and the scree plot supported a one- or two-factor solution (see Appendix 7). The two-factor was accepted as it provided additional information in relation to which processes were distinct from the more basic planning and task representation processes. The rotated two-factor loadings and the interacted correlations of the factors are presented in Table 6.1. The percentage in brackets indicates the extent to which each factor accounts for the variance.

According to the matrix (Table 6.1), six sub-processes are associated with Factor 1. The macro-planning process in relation to the relevance and adequacy of content to be written (Item 2) had the highest loading of 0.806. Two other macro-planning processes regarding the purpose of writing and reader representations (Items 5 and 3) were also associated with Factor 1. The other three sub-processes loaded on Factor 1 were processes of constructing task representation, and reviewing the representation during source text reading and writing.

Factor 1 was named *Planning and constructing task representation*. The results seemed to indicate an overall interplay between the processes of

Defining Integrated Reading-into-Writing Constructs

Table 6.1 Pattern and interfactor correlations matrix for the conceptualisation phase (real-life)*

		F1 Planning and constructing task representation (34%)	F2 Reconstructing writing plans (19.09%)
2	I thought about what I might need to write to make my text relevant and adequate to the task.	0.806	
5	I thought about the purpose of writing.	0.688	
4	I understood the instructions for this writing task very well.	0.588	
3	I thought about how my text would suit the expectations of the intended reader.	0.519	
26	I read the task requirements again while writing.	0.449	
11	I read the task requirements again while reading the source texts.	0.445	
18	I changed my writing plans while reading the source texts.		0.804
28	I changed my writing plans while writing.		0.583
Interfactor correlations matrix			
Factor 1		1.000	
Factor 2		0.061	1.000

F1 = Factor 1; F2 = Factor 2

Academic reading-into-writing processes

macro-planning and creating the author's representation of the task in the real-life academic context.

On the other hand, only two sub-processes – *reconstructing the initial writing plans* as a result of interaction with the reading sources and *generating texts* – loaded on Factor 2. The factor was named *Reconstructing writing plans*. This supports Kellogg's (2001) hypothesis that more advanced writers, i.e. university students in this case, are able to hold in mind the author's plan, and review it in response to the interaction with reading materials and to the text being generated. These processes are arguably more demanding than the processes of initial task representation and planning because the writer must hold these initial representations and plans active in the working memory and allocate regular attention to them while reading new materials and generating texts (Gernsbacher 1990).

Based on the fact that the Factor 1 and Factor 2 correlated weakly (r=0.06), the results also seemed to indicate that the more demanding process of revising macro plans loaded on Factor 2 were apparently an academic writing construct distinctive from the more basic processes of planning and creating a task representation loaded on Factor 1.

The meaning construction phase (real-life)

The meaning construction phase was measured by 11 questionnaire items. The initial factor extraction and the scree plot indicated possibilities of a one- or three-factor solution (see Appendix 7). The three-factor solution was accepted as it reviewed a clear distinction between the factors (see Table 6.2). Items 1 and 27 loaded on both Factor 1 and Factor 2 in the initial rotated solution, and hence were dropped from the analysis.

Integrated tasks require writers to demonstrate source use skills, which are typically not required in impromptu writing tasks. The results here suggested that such skills involve three distinct yet correlated cognitive processes. As shown in Table 6.2, Factor 1 (named *Connecting and generating ideas*) included four sub-processes in relation to sorting connections between new ideas and background knowledge, and between ideas from multiple sources, and to building a deeper understanding of the topic. Three reading sub-processes which are purposeful and selective loaded on Factor 2 (named *Search reading*). Through these processes, the university students determined the importance of source text ideas according to the writing goals, and decided how they would use these ideas in the writing. Factor 3 set apart another type of reading skill – *careful reading*.

To successfully integrate source ideas into their own writing, students needed to understand the materials thoroughly and to fill in gaps such as inferring the author's intention when necessary through slow and careful reading. The reading and discourse synthesis processes included in the

Defining Integrated Reading-into-Writing Constructs

Table 6.2 Pattern and interfactor correlations matrix for the meaning construction phase (real-life)*

		F1 Connecting and generating ideas (33.27%)	F2 Search reading (12.53%)	F3 Careful reading (9.57%)
17	I developed a better understanding of the topic while I was reading the source texts.	0.665		
14	I linked the important ideas in the source texts to what I know already.	0.528		
24	I developed new ideas while writing.	0.514		
25	I made further connections across the source texts while writing.	0.274		
10	I read part(s) of the texts which are relevant to the task.		0.767	
12	I took notes on or underlined the important ideas in the source texts.		0.715	
9	I searched quickly for part(s) of the texts which might help complete the task.		0.383	
6	I read through the whole of each source text slowly and carefully.			0.846
7	I read the whole of each source text more than once.			0.509
Interfactor correlations matrix				
Factor 1		1.000		
Factor 2		0.595	1.000	
Factor 3		0.377	0.223	1.000

F1 = Factor 1; F2 = Factor 2; F3 = Factor 3

questionnaire were by no means exclusive but the findings showed that students made use of these three types of reading processes when writing from source in an authentic academic context.

The organising phase (real-life)

The organising phase was measured by nine questionnaire items. The initial factor extraction and the scree plot suggested a one-, two- or three-factor solution (see Appendix 7). The three-factor solution was rejected because Factor 3 was difficult to interpret. The two-factor solution, on the other hand, revealed a new dimension of how students organised ideas in the context of reading-into-writing (see Table 6.3). Item 22 did not load on either of Factor 1 and Factor 2 in the initial rotated two-factor solution, and hence was dropped from the analysis.

Academic reading-into-writing processes

After the meaning construction phase where writers select and connect relevant ideas from reading sources and background knowledge, writers would typically organise these ideas in some way. The findings here revealed that Factor 1 (*organising intertextual relationships between ideas*) involved four sub-processes of organising intertextual relationships between ideas. Through these processes, the students would add layers of meaning to the sources based on their prior knowledge, understanding and writing goals. The representation created as a result may be drawn upon later on when writers formulate their own text.

Four other organising sub-processes loaded on Factor 2 (*organising ideas in a textual structure*). When generating texts, the students shaped their contents into a logical and coherent structure. In interaction with the text produced so far, they sometimes removed some ideas from the initial writing plans, recombined or reordered ideas, filled in information or made clear transitions so that their text would be effectively organised to achieve its communicative purpose.

The ability to organise ideas in writing is well recognised as part of good academic writing skills. The results showed that the construct of organising intertextual relationships between ideas is distinctive from that of organising ideas into a textual structure, and university students used both when they composed from sources.

Table 6.3 Pattern and interfactor correlations matrix for the organising phase (real-life)*

	F1 Organising intertextual relationships between ideas (34.73%)	F2 Organising ideas in a textual structure (16.60%)
16 I organised the main ideas across the source texts based on how they relate to each other.	0.984	
15 I organised the main ideas in each source based on how they relate to each other.	0.761	
13 I prioritised the ideas in relation to their importance to the task.	0.564	
8 I used my knowledge of how articles like these are organised to find parts to focus on.	0.437	
21 I removed some ideas I planned to write.		0.691
20 I recombined or reordered some ideas to fit the structure of my writing.		0.627
19 I structured my ideas before starting to write.		0.441
23 I sometimes paused to organise my ideas while writing.		0.314
Interfactor correlations matrix		
Factor 1	1.000	
Factor 2	0.533	1.000

*F1 = Factor 1; F2 = Factor 2

The monitoring and revising phase (real-life)

Monitoring and revising problems and inadequacies of one's writing is an essential part of writing (see Hayes and Flower 1980, Kellogg 1996, Shaw and Weir 2007). Broadly speaking, writers monitor and revise at two levels (Bereiter and Scardamalia 1987). Monitoring and revising at the low level tend to be conventional, rule governed and language bound. When writers monitor and revise at this level, they would predominantly evaluate the quality of their text in relation to linguistic accuracy, for instance, in spelling, grammar and forms of expression (Fitzgerald 1987, Flower, Hayes, Carey, Schriver and Stratman 1986). In contrast, monitoring and revising processes at the high level tend to be driven by an awareness of the writing goal and hence meaning bound. When writers monitor and revise at this level, they would concentrate on global text content, for example, clarity and appropriateness of ideas, coherence of arguments, and possible effect on reader. Revision process researchers like Lindgren and Sullivan (2006) cautioned that not all writers' monitoring and revising processes would lead to a change in the text, which then become directly accessible in the end-product. Therefore, we should investigate writers' internal monitoring and revising processes when defining the construct of reading-into-writing.

In Study 2, participants' monitoring and revising processes were measured by eight (those at lower level) and 12 (those at higher level) questionnaire items. The initial factor extractions and the screen plots indicated a two-factor solution (see Appendix 7). The final matrixes (see Table 6.4 and 6.5 on pages 123 and 124) reviewed a clear distinction between the monitoring and revising processes which took place after text production (Factor 1) and during text production (Factor 2). This supports the literature that students' monitoring and revising processes after text production play an important role in academic writing.

Text generating, like other processes, requires the use of working memory. However, one's working memory is of limited capacity. Increased cognitive effort devoted to monitoring and revising is believed to lead to a decrease in the remaining available resources (Field 2004). As a result, writers, especially L2 writers, tend to focus on one aspect of the text at a time due to linguistic constraints. Therefore, they would tend to set aside the monitoring and revising processes to a later stage of the production (Chan 2017, Stevenson, Schoonen and de Glopper 2006). The results here confirm this notion that students' monitoring and revising processes took place not only during the text-generating phase, but also in a final review phase where they could devote more cognitive effort to making the necessary changes.

We have so far presented the results of the underlying structure of the cognitive processes in each of the cognitive writing phases when the students composed from sources in an authentic academic context. EFA proved invaluable in providing empirical information about the clustering of the individual processes within each writing phase. The results showed that the hypothesised academic

Academic reading-into-writing processes

Table 6.4 Pattern and interfactor correlations matrix for monitoring and revising at lower level (real life)*

	F1 Lower-level monitoring and revising after text production (47.70%)	F2 Lower-level monitoring and revising during text production (23.9%)
44 I checked that the quotations were properly made after writing.	0.898	
45 I checked that I had put the ideas of the source texts into my own words after writing.	0.872	
47 I checked the accuracy and range of the sentence structures after writing.	0.848	
48 I checked the appropriateness and range of vocabulary after writing.	0.847	
38 I checked the appropriateness and range of vocabulary while writing.		0.908
37 I checked the accuracy and range of the sentence structures while writing.		0.783
34 I checked that the quotations were properly made while writing.		0.515
35 I checked that I had put the ideas of the source texts into my own words while writing.		0.488
Interfactor correlations matrix		
Factor 1	1.000	
Factor 2	0.347	1.000

*F1 = Factor 1; F2 = Factor 2

writing phases arising from the literature review were largely supported by the statistical analysis of the questionnaire data collected in this study.

Altogether the participants in this study utilised 11 distinct yet correlated processes of academic reading-into-writing (see Table 6.6 on page 125 for a summary). While we have identified 11 processes involved in the four cognitive phases elicited by the real-life academic writing tasks, the results indicated that the variance of each cognitive phase was not fully accounted for. Future studies should examine the other cognitive processes involved in each phase, preferably with an alternative research method, such as keystroke logging or stimulated recall.

Difference in processes between tasks (real-life)

Here we examine whether the participants employed these 11 core cognitive processes differently while composing Real-life Task A and Real-life Task B, i.e. essay and report. The mean of the average rating (*4=definitely agree; 3=mostly agree; 2=mostly disagree; 1=definitely disagree*) of each cognitive process is presented in Table 6.7 on page 126.

Defining Integrated Reading-into-Writing Constructs

Table 6.5 Pattern and interfactor correlations matrix for monitoring and revising at higher level (real life)*

		F1	F2
		Higher-level monitoring and revising after text production (42.92%)	Higher-level monitoring and revising during text production (24.35%)
41	I checked that my text was coherent after writing.	0.903	
40	I checked that my text was well organised after writing.	0.880	
43	I checked that I included my own viewpoint on the topic after writing.	0.877	
39	I checked that the content was relevant after writing.	0.865	
42	I checked that I included all appropriate main ideas from the source texts after writing.	0.797	
46	I checked the possible effect of my writing on the intended reader after writing.	0.748	
31	I checked that my text was coherent while writing.		0.747
29	I checked that the content was relevant while writing.		0.618
30	I checked that my text was well organised while writing.		0.613
32	I checked that I included all appropriate main ideas from the source texts while writing.		0.581
33	I checked that I included my own viewpoint on the topic while writing.		0.575
36	I checked the possible effect of my writing on the intended reader while writing.		0.446
Interfactor correlations matrix			
Factor 1		1.000	
Factor 2		0.208	1.000

F1 = Factor 1; F2 = Factor 2

Overall, the participants reported the processes in a very comparable way between the two writing tasks with minimal differences. The students reported employing six processes: *planning and constructing task representation, reconstructing writing plans, careful reading, search reading, connecting and generating ideas,* and *high-level monitoring and revising during text production* slightly more on the report task than on the essay task. As previously presented in Chapter 5, the expert judgement on the overall task setting showed that the report task presented the students with a clearer purpose and a clear intended reader. The belief that a writing task with a clear communicative purpose and intended reader would encourage better macro-planning is supported by the results here. Besides, according to the information provided in the questionnaire, for the report task, students made use of a wider range of additional materials which included textbook chapters, journal articles, notes from a lecturer, and relevant

Academic reading-into-writing processes

Table 6.6 A summary of the underlying structure of reading-into-writing processes (real-life)*

Cognitive phases	Sub-processes
Conceptualisation	F1: Planning and constructing task representation (34%)
	F2: Reconstructing writing plans (19.09%)
Discourse construction	F1: Connecting and generating ideas (33.27%)
	F2: Search reading (12.53%)
	F3: Careful reading (9.57%)
Organisation	F1: Organising intertextual relationships between ideas (34.73%)
	F2: Organising ideas in a textual structure (16.60%)
Monitoring and revising	F1: Lower-level monitoring and revising after text production (47.70%)
	F2: Lower-level monitoring and revising during text production (23.9%)
	F1: Higher-level monitoring and revising after text production (42.92%)
	F2: Higher-level monitoring and revising during text production (24.35%)

*F1 = Factor 1; F2 = Factor 2; F3 = Factor 3

information searched from the internet. On the other hand, for the essay task, most students referred closely to the single article provided by the task while some read a few other similar articles. The fact that the report task involved more reading materials than the essay task may well explain why the students engaged more in the reading and connecting ideas in the former task.

Nevertheless, none of the difference was significant (p>0.05), as indicated by the Mann-Whitney U test. This is not to say that the considerable difference in contextual features reported in Chapter 5 do not have an impact on how students compose the tasks. This only suggests that in relation to these 11 core processes, more similarities than differences were observed. It is anticipated that the difference in processes would be reflected in the individual sub-processes, including those captured by or beyond the questionnaire used in this study, associated with each of the core processes. In future studies, to examine such differences, the use of qualitative research methods might be more effective. Future studies which aim to explore in detail how individual contextual features might impact on the use of cognitive processes should also consider other variables.

While differences were small, a few similarities between the two real-life tasks are worth noticing. Participants reported employing search reading more than careful reading on both tasks in real life. This has an important implication for teaching and assessing students' reading-into-writing skills in academic contexts. Explicit pedagogical attention would therefore be needed to teach students how to read expeditiously, e.g. scan for relevant information, for the purpose of writing. Second, the students reported organising

Table 6.7 Comparison of the cognitive processes employed between the two real-life tasks

	Report (n=73)			Essay (n=70)			Mann-Whitney U	Wilcoxon W	Z	Asymp. Sig. (2-tailed)
	Mean	Std Dev	Mean rank	Mean	Std Dev	Mean rank				
Planning and constructing task representation	3.25	0.52	73.65	3.20	0.47	70.28	2348.5	4833.5	−0.839	0.401
Reconstructing writing plans	2.83	0.68	76.95	2.71	0.74	66.84	2325.5	4810.5	−0.949	0.342
Careful reading	2.97	0.73	74.41	2.90	0.65	69.49	2379.0	4864.0	−0.728	0.467
Search reading	3.28	0.58	77.01	3.18	0.54	66.77	2189.0	4674.0	−1.507	0.132
Connecting and generating ideas	3.21	0.57	74.18	3.20	0.44	69.73	2396.0	4881.0	−0.647	0.518
Organising intertextual relationships between ideas	2.92	0.55	74.03	2.93	0.43	69.89	2407.0	4892.0	−0.601	0.548
Organising ideas in a textual structure	3.10	0.57	70.32	3.17	0.45	73.76	2432.0	5133.0	−0.502	0.616
Low-level monitoring and revising during text production	3.07	0.65	69.57	3.18	0.56	74.54	2377.5	5078.5	−0.729	0.466
Low-level monitoring and revising after text production	2.78	0.88	69.34	2.85	0.93	74.78	2360.5	5061.5	−0.793	0.428
High-level monitoring and revising during text production	3.17	0.59	73.94	3.15	0.49	69.98	2413.500	4898.500	−0.574	0.566
High-level monitoring and revising after text production	2.74	0.89	68.10	2.85	0.95	76.07	2270.000	4971.000	−1.158	0.247

ideas in a textual structure more than they organised ideas at the intertextual level on both real-life tasks. Lastly, the students reported monitoring and revising (at both low and high levels) more during text production than at the final stage. Generally speaking, L2 writers tend not to make major changes to their writing as they write, because their text generation processes are not automatic and hence require conscious cognitive efforts, which means little cognitive capacity would be left available for conducting high-level revisions (Field 2004). However, the results in Table 6.7 showed that the students in this study made more revisions during writing than after writing when they completed their academic assignments. This could be because they were not under tight time pressure, as compared to test conditions, when composing the real-life tasks. They were able to monitor and make changes as they wrote. However, there was also a possibility that these students were not fully aware of the importance of final revisions in academic writing.

Difference in processes between levels of performance (real-life)

As mentioned, the purpose of Study 2 was to define the cognitive parameters which are appropriate for reading-into-writing tests for academic literacy skills. The results of EFA reported so far have defined the 11 cognitive processes which students employed to complete the real-life academic writing tasks. A further step was to investigate whether these defined cognitive parameters can to some extent distinguish between the higher-scoring and lower-scoring students.

The 143 participants who completed either one of the real-life tasks were ranked according to their scores. Each performance can be scored from 0 to 16 (details are provided in Chapter 7). They were divided into four groups (i.e. high, higher middle, lower middle and low) representing roughly 25% of the population of participants who completed the tasks (i.e. the exact number of participants in each group varies). As a result, 40 participants were classified as the high-scoring group (a score of 12 or above) and 39 participants were classified as the low-scoring group (a score of 7.5 or below). The means and standard deviations of the average rating (4=definitely agree, 3=mostly agree, 2=mostly disagree, 1=definitely disagree) of the 11 processes reported by the high-scoring and low-scoring groups are presented in Table 6.8.

As shown in Table 6.8, the high-scoring students reported employing eight processes out of the 11 more than the low-scoring group. According to the Wilcoxon test, the difference in six of these processes between the groups was significant, i.e. $p<0.05$. While the low-scoring group reported using three processes, including *reconstructing writing plans* and *monitoring and revising after text production* at both high and low levels, more than the high-scoring group, the difference in their mean rating was minimal.

Table 6.8 Comparisons between high-scoring and low-scoring participants (real-life)

	High-scoring (n=40)			Low-scoring (n=39)			Mann-Whitney U	Wilcoxon W	Z	Asymp. Sig. (2-tailed)
	Mean	Std Dev	Mean rank	Mean	Std Dev	Mean rank				
Planning and constructing task representation	3.29	0.442	44.86	3.09	0.474	35.01	585.5	1365.5	−1.917	0.055
Reconstructing writing plans	2.78	0.847	39.18	2.80	0.713	40.85	747.0	1567.0	−0.330	0.741
Careful reading	3.09	0.823	43.52	2.91	0.648	36.40	639.5	1419.5	−1.412	0.158
Search reading	3.47	0.488	47.64	3.10	0.525	32.17	474.5	1254.5	−3.058	0.002
Connecting and generating ideas	3.35	0.432	43.80	3.12	0.487	36.10	553.5	1333.5	−2.243	0.025
Organising intertextual relationships between ideas	3.03	0.443	46.46	2.86	0.399	33.37	521.5	1301.5	−2.552	0.011
Organising ideas in a textual structure	3.28	0.507	45.95	3.01	0.503	33.90	542.0	1322.0	−2.360	0.018
Low-level monitoring and revising during text production	3.36	0.543	46.44	3.00	0.691	33.40	522.5	1302.5	−2.578	0.010
Low-level monitoring and revising after text production	2.83	0.866	39.19	2.84	0.920	40.83	747.5	1567.5	−0.322	0.747
High-level monitoring and revising during text production	3.30	0.467	45.66	3.01	0.540	34.19	553.5	1333.5	−2.233	0.026
High-level monitoring and revising after text production	2.82	0.857	39.23	2.84	0.915	40.79	749.0	1569.0	−0.306	0.760

The high-scoring participants employed *planning and constructing task representation* more than the low-scoring participants, though the difference was not significant. There was not much difference in the extent to which they reported *reconstructing writing plans*. According to Scardamalia and Bereiter's (1987) continuum of writing expertise, skilled writers are cautious about the rhetorical situation of the writing task and therefore actively establish writing goals to fulfil the communicative purpose of the task. In contrast, most unskilled writers might not be able to establish a complete representation the writing task (e.g. communicative purpose, intended readership, genre, content and style) and therefore would not establish comprehensive macro plans before they start to write. The results here seem to support this notion. Another challenge for less proficient L2 writers is that they may not be able to hold their task representation and macro-plan in working memory while they are executing their plan (Field 2013, Kellogg 2001).

The high-scoring participants reported all three reading processes and two organising processes more than the lower-scoring group (see Table 6.8). Field's model of receptive skills (2004) argued that meaning construction in reading is more cognitively demanding than decoding, lexical searching and parsing. Less proficient L2 students would focus on the lower processes while the proficient language users would have high automaticity in executing these processes and hence be able to focus on constructing meaning. Khalifa and Weir's (2007) model of reading skills similarly argued that lower proficiency L2 readers would focus on establishing understanding at local level (words, phrases, sentences) while high-proficiency readers would be able to establish understanding at global textual and intertextual level. It is also argued that skilled readers are able to connect ideas between their background knowledge and reading sources and link these connections to the context of writing task (Scardamalia and Bereiter 1987, Spivey 1991) The results here support the notion that these higher-level reading processes at textual and intertextual levels and organising processes are important as higher-skilled students transform knowledge from reading sources to their own writing. Therefore, it is important that these processes are targeted in academic writing.

The high-scoring participants also reported monitoring and revising processes during text production (both at high and low levels) significantly more than the low-scoring group. There was almost no difference in the extent to which they reported these processes after text production. Field (2004) argued that monitoring and revising during text production are highly cognitively demanding, particularly for L2 writers. While monitoring and revising can be employed at any time during the writing process, most writers can only focus on one aspect of the editing at one time (e.g. grammatical accuracy at low level, or argument coherence at high level). Therefore, less proficient writers who have not acquired high automaticity in the executing processes tend not to be able to spare attention on monitoring and revising during text production.

In this sub-section, we reported the findings of a set of EFAs which revealed the 11 underlying processes of the core cognitive phases employed by the undergraduates when they composed a report and an essay from sources. The students reported using these processes in a very comparable way between the two real-life writing tasks. There were only some descriptive differences in the way students employed these processes between the two real-life tasks. For example, the report task, which was regarded by the judges to have clearer information about communicative purpose and intended reader than the essay task, seemed to have engaged the participants in macro-planning slightly more than the essay task. The report task, which required the use of more extensive reading materials than the essay task, also seemed to have engaged the participants in both careful and search reading more than the essay task.

A few similar patterns were observed between the two real-life tasks which include: (i) the students reported more search reading than careful reading; (ii) the participants reported organising ideas in a textual structure more than organising intertextual relationships between ideas, and (iii) the participants reported employing editing (at both low and high level) during writing more than after writing.

These 11 cognitive processes identified, to some extent, accounted for the difference in scores they received. The high-scoring students employed eight of the 11 cognitive processes significantly more than the low-scoring group. This argues strongly for the need to have cognitively valid academic writing tests which assess the same cognitive processes that are required in real-life conditions.

In the next section, we report the results in relation to the extent that the two reading-into-writing test formats (Test Task A with multiple verbal inputs and Test Task B with multiple verbal and non-verbal inputs) elicited these 11 cognitive processes from the test takers.

6.2 To what extent can the two reading-into-writing tests elicit the target processes?

Study 2 aimed to examine the extent to which the two types of reading-into-writing test tasks (Test Task A with multiple verbal inputs and Test Task B with multiple verbal and non-verbal inputs) elicited the same cognitive processes as the real-life writing tasks did. Therefore, having identified the cognitive constructs elicited in real-life academic conditions, we will now examine the cognitive processes that the participants used when they completed the two reading-into-writing tests (for details of the tests, see Section 4.1). As described in Section 4.3, the test takers' cognitive processes on the two reading-into-writing tests were measured by the WPQ (see Appendix 6). Test Task A was completed by 160 participants (essay with multiple verbal inputs) and

Academic reading-into-writing processes

140 participants completed Test Task B (essay with multiple verbal and non-verbal inputs). Immediately after they had completed each of the test tasks, the participants filled out the questionnaire. First, we will report whether there was any difference in the way the high-scoring and low-scoring test takers employed the 11 target processes when they completed each of the reading-into-writing tests, followed by a comparison of the processes used by test takers at different performing levels between real-life and test conditions.

Difference in processes between levels of performance (test tasks)

As previously reported, results on the real-life tasks showed that high-scoring participants reported employing eight of the 11 cognitive processes more than low-scoring students, and six of the differences were significant. Here we report if these cognitive parameters distinguished the high-scoring and low-scoring test takers in the same way. The 160 participants who completed Test Task A and the 140 participants who completed Test Task B were ranked according to their scores (their scores will be discussed in more detail in Chapter 7). Based on the ranking, the participants were divided into four groups (i.e. high, higher middle, lower middle and low scoring) representing roughly 25% of the population each.

As a result, on Test Task A, 36 participants were classified as high scoring (with a score of 10.5 or above out of 20) and 34 participants were classified as low scoring (with a score of 7.5 or below). On Test Task B, 27 participants were classified as the high-scoring group (with a score of 7 or above out of 9), and 34 were classified as the low-scoring group (with a score of 3 or below). (There is a noticeable disparity between the cut-off scores of different levels of achievement on the two test tasks because Test Task A is a level-specific criterion-referenced test whereas Test Task B is a university diagnostic test.) The comparisons between how the high-scoring and low-scoring participants employed the cognitive processes on Test Task A are shown in Table 6.9, and the comparisons for Test Task B are shown in Table 6.10.

As shown in Table 6.9, it is somewhat surprising that the results showed no significant difference in the extent to which high-scoring and low-scoring participants employed the 11 processes on Test Task A. However, it should be noted that Test Task A was a level-specific test targeting C2 level while most of the participants in this study were at B2 level. In addition, the range of the participants' performances on Test Task A was the narrowest when compared to Test Task B and the two real-life tasks (the participants' performances on all tasks will be discussed in detail in Chapter 7). Therefore, the range of performances elicited on Test Task A in this study might have limited the difference which can be obtained in the use of cognitive processes between high-scoring and low-scoring participants.

Table 6.9 Comparisons between high-scoring and low-scoring participants (Test Task A)

	High-scoring (n=36)			Low-scoring (n=34)			Mann-Whitney U	Wilcoxon W	Z	Asymp. Sig. (2-tailed)
	Mean	Std Dev	Mean rank	Mean	Std Dev	Mean rank				
Planning and constructing task representation	3.04	0.54	35.43	3.06	0.54	35.57	609.5	1275.5	−0.030	0.976
Reconstructing writing plans	2.56	0.59	36.22	2.53	0.82	34.74	586.0	1181.0	−0.313	0.754
Careful reading	2.74	0.91	31.32	3.16	0.59	39.93	461.5	1127.5	−1.813	0.070
Search reading	3.51	0.44	37.35	3.33	0.70	33.54	545.5	1140.5	−0.803	0.422
Connecting and generating ideas	2.92	0.65	34.86	2.95	0.68	36.18	589.0	1255.0	−0.273	0.785
Organising intertextual relationships between ideas	3.07	0.46	35.15	3.08	0.53	35.87	599.5	1265.5	−0.148	0.882
Organising ideas in a textual structure	3.20	0.68	38.33	3.00	0.69	32.50	510.0	1105.0	−1.235	0.217
Low-level monitoring and revising during text production	3.02	0.67	37.83	2.82	0.78	33.03	528.0	1123.0	−0.994	0.320
Low-level monitoring and revising after text production	2.43	0.90	3.13	2.23	1.15	33.78	553.5	1148.5	−0.698	0.485
High-level monitoring and revising during text production	3.02	0.68	35.61	3.06	0.55	35.38	608.0	1203.0	−0.047	0.962
High-level monitoring and revising after text production	2.56	1.09	38.71	2.20	1.11	3.10	496.5	1091.5	−1.381	0.167

Table 6.10 Comparisons between high-scoring and low-scoring participants (Test Task B)

	High-scoring (n=27)			Low-scoring (n=34)			Mann-Whitney U	Wilcoxon W	Z	Asymp. Sig. (2-tailed)
	Mean	Std Dev	Mean rank	Mean	Std Dev	Mean rank				
Planning and constructing task representation	3.31	0.39	36.89	3.04	0.50	26.32	300.0	895.0	−2.331	0.020
Reconstructing writing plans	2.28	0.92	23.00	2.94	0.56	37.35	243.0	621.0	−3.199	0.001
Careful reading	3.20	0.76	32.94	3.10	0.66	29.46	406.5	1001.5	−0.784	0.433
Search reading	3.69	0.31	40.54	3.17	0.56	23.43	201.5	796.5	−3.840	0.000
Connecting and generating ideas	3.00	0.80	31.35	3.00	0.60	30.72	441.5	1036.5	−0.257	0.797
Organising intertextual relationships between ideas	3.44	0.48	39.85	2.98	0.46	23.97	220.0	815.0	−3.499	0.000
Organising ideas in a textual structure	3.16	0.55	32.33	3.10	0.58	29.94	423.0	1018.0	−0.546	0.585
Low-level monitoring and revising during text production	3.28	0.64	37.65	2.80	0.74	25.72	279.5	874.5	−2.633	0.008
Low-level monitoring and revising after text production	2.84	1.14	38.70	2.01	0.99	24.88	251.0	846.0	−3.097	0.002
High-level monitoring and revising during text production	3.37	0.47	38.76	2.92	0.63	24.84	249.5	844.5	−3.063	0.002
High-level monitoring and revising after text production	2.88	1.10	39.91	2.00	0.89	23.93	218.5	813.5	−3.555	0.000

Defining Integrated Reading-into-Writing Constructs

While the difference obtained between the groups was non-significant, the high-scoring participants reported employing six of the processes, which include *reconstructing writing plans, search reading, organising ideas in a textual structure, low-level monitoring and revising during text production, low-level monitoring and revising after text production* and *high-level monitoring and revising after text production*, more than the low-scoring group.

The greatest discrepancy observed in terms of mean rating between the two groups was in the process of *careful reading*. The low-scoring group reported more careful reading than the high-scoring group, indicating a possibility that they have relied too much on careful reading under the test conditions.

The results of the comparison of the cognitive processes employed by the high- and low-scoring groups on Test Task B are presented in Table 6.10. The high-scoring participants reported employing nine of the cognitive processes more than the low-scoring group (see Table 6.10). The differences of seven processes (which include *planning and constructing task representation, search reading, organising intertextual relationships between ideas, low-level monitoring and revising during text production, low-level monitoring and revising after text production, high-level monitoring and revising during text production* and *high-level monitoring and revising after text production*) between the two groups were significant ($p<0.05$).

The results largely resemble the results of the same analysis on the real-life tasks. In addition, similar to the results reported on the real-life tasks, the low-scoring group reported that they reconstructed writing plans more than the high-scoring group. This is probably because the low-scoring group was less capable of establishing a complete representation of the writing task (e.g. communicative purpose, intended readership, genre, content and style) and hence planned their writing more effectively than the high-scoring group.

Comparisons between real-life tasks and Test Task A

Valid cognitive parameters should sufficiently resemble the processes which a test taker would normally employ in non-test conditions. We now examine how students with different levels of performance employed the 11 core cognitive processes in academic writing between the test and real-life conditions. The data is presented in three groups of performance level:

- high-scoring group – the participants who were identified as high-scoring on both the test task and the real-life tasks
- medium-scoring group – the participants who were identified as either higher-medium or lower-medium on both the test task and the real-life tasks

Academic reading-into-writing processes

- low-scoring group – the participants who were identified as low-scoring on both the test task and the real-life tasks.

As shown in Table 6.11, the high-scoring participants, those whose performances were ranked in the top 25% on both Test Task A and the real-life tasks, reported employing all cognitive processes similarly in test and real-life conditions. All differences obtained were not significant. The high-scoring group seemed to be able to utilise the processes under both conditions. This suggests that provided that the test takers were proficient in academic writing, Test Task A was able to elicit the same processes from test takers to a similar extent as they employed them on the real-life tasks.

The low-scoring group (those whose performances were ranked in the bottom 25% on both Test Task A and the real-life tasks) reported employing most of the cognitive processes similarly in both conditions. However, they reported monitoring and revising after writing significantly more on the real-life tasks than on Test Task A. They barely monitored and revised after text production under the test conditions. This was probably because the low-scoring test takers simply did not have the processing capacity to deal with these processes as less was available for this activity than in the case of the higher proficiency group.

In comparison to the other two groups, the middle-scoring group showed a greater discrepancy in how the students employed the processes between the conditions (see Table 6.11). This is probably because they were in a transitional state of developing their academic writing skills and perhaps more affected by the performance conditions, e.g. stricter time allowance. There was no significant difference in the extent to which they reported the five reading and organising processes. However, they reported reconstructing their writing plans and the four monitoring and revising processes significantly more in the real-life than test conditions.

Considering the three groups together, it is encouraging that all reported using the five reading and organising processes with no significant difference between the conditions. This evidence supports the literature that the integrated task type encourages higher-level discourse synthesis and knowledge transformation, which are believed to play an important role in academic literacy (Flower et al 1990, Spivey 1984, 2001, Spivey and King 1989).

Comparisons between real-life tasks and Test Task B

As shown in Table 5.12, the high-scoring students (those whose performances were ranked in the top 25% on both Test Task B and real-life tasks) reported eight of the 11 cognitive processes between the conditions with no significant difference. However, they appeared to reconstruct writing plans, organise intertextual relationships between ideas, and monitor and revise at low level

Table 6.11 Comparison of processes between Test Task A and real-life tasks

	High-scoring						Middle-scoring						Low-scoring					
	Test Task A (n=14)		Real-life tasks (n=14)		Z	Sig.	Test Task A (n=85)		Real-life tasks (n=85)		Z	Sig.	Test Task A (n=13)		Real-life tasks (n=13)		Z	Sig.
	Median	Std Dev	Median	Std Dev			Median	Std Dev	Median	Std Dev			Median	Std Dev	Median	Std Dev		
Planning and constructing task representation	3.30	0.58	3.17	0.47	-.566	0.572	3.00	0.64	3.17	0.525	-2.005	0.045	3.00	0.56	3.00	0.28	-0.039	0.969
Reconstructing writing plans	2.50	0.59	2.75	0.80	-1.650	0.099	2.30	0.75	2.59	0.90	-2.248	0.025	2.50	0.74	3.00	0.64	-1.08	0.280
Careful reading	2.50	1.17	3.25	1.07	-1.767	0.077	3.00	0.65	3.00	0.65	-0.947	0.344	3.50	0.51	3.00	0.63	-1.218	0.223
Search reading	3.67	0.36	3.67	0.53	-.654	0.513	3.67	0.82	3.00	0.55	-1.031	0.303	3.33	0.58	3.00	0.67	-1.620	0.105
Connecting and generating ideas	3.00	0.74	3.33	0.44	-1.446	0.148	3.00	0.68	3.00	0.53	-1.261	0.207	3.00	0.47	3.00	0.46	-0.356	0.722
Organising intertextual relationships between ideas	3.30	0.62	3.00	0.46	-.594	0.552	3.00	0.60	3.00	0.49	-0.705	0.481	3.20	0.39	2.83	0.46	-1.505	0.132
Organising ideas in a textual structure	3.00	0.62	3.50	0.51	-1.259	0.208	3.00	0.65	3.25	0.53	-1.732	0.083	3.00	0.52	2.75	0.33	-0.768	0.443
Low-level monitoring and revising during text production	3.25	0.82	3.25	0.55	-.595	0.552	2.75	0.72	3.00	0.59	-3.262	0.001	2.25	0.62	3.00	0.67	-0.994	0.320
Low-level monitoring and revising after text production	3.25	1.01	3.00	0.95	-.971	0.331	2.50	1.01	3.00	0.90	-3.140	0.002	1.00	0.92	3.00	1.06	-2.558	0.011
High-level monitoring and revising during text production	2.50	0.79	3.17	0.51	-.118	0.906	2.83	0.65	3.17	0.54	-3.904	0.000	3.17	0.53	3.00	0.38	-0.223	0.823
High-level monitoring and revising after text production	3.50	1.25	3.00	1.00	-.070	0.940	2.67	1.02	3.00	0.92	-2.69	0.010	1.00	1.04	3.00	1.02	-2.572	0.010

during text production significantly more under real-life than test conditions. One participant in the high-scoring group commented on the questionnaire that 'I planned the writing following closely the instructions did not make much change'. The fact that all key points are listed in the task prompt of Test Task B might have offered too much help to the high-scoring participants. This should not be a big concern in terms of cognitive validity because, as described in Section 4.1, Test Task B is a university in-house test which aims to distinguish students who are in need of academic literacy support. The test is set at the level of CEFR B2, so it is understandable that the highest scoring students on this task would find the task not challenging enough. In addition, the discussion below will show that the other two groups reported that they reconstructed writing plans similarly between the real-life and test conditions.

The low-scoring group (those whose performances were ranked the bottom 25% on both Test Task B and real-life tasks) reported employing most cognitive processes similarly between the two conditions. The only significant difference was found in the processes of monitoring and revising at low level after text production. They monitored and revised at the final stage significantly more under real-life than test conditions.

Again, the middle-scoring group showed most discrepancy in how they composed between the two conditions. As argued previously, the middle group was perhaps more affected by the different performance conditions. Under a stricter time allowance performance condition, they reported connecting and generating ideas, monitoring and revising after text production at both levels on Test Task B significantly less than the extent to which they did under the real-life conditions which provided a much longer time allowance. However, they apparently reported careful reading significantly more under the test than real-life conditions. Some students commented that as the input texts on Test Task B were comparatively short, they read them a few times to avoid missing any important points. It seems that the length of the sources might have contributed to an apparent over-eliciting of careful reading processes for this group of students.

It is encouraging that the two sample reading-into-writing test tasks examined in this investigation were able to elicit from high-scoring and low-scoring students most of the 11 cognitive processes to a similar extent as they would normally use when composing from sources in real life. The middle group showed a greater discrepancy in how they employed these processes between the test and real-life conditions. They tended to employ the processes less in the test conditions than in real life. This group of students might not be able to employ all processes with full automaticity as they were at the transitional stage of developing their academic writing ability. Due to limited cognitive capacity, they may need more time to utilise these processes. Many participants in this group commented on the questionnaire that they did not have sufficient time to 'read the passages and understand better', 'proofread the

Table 6.12 Comparison of processes between Test Task B and real-life tasks

	High-scoring group						Middle-scoring						Low-scoring group					
	Test Task B (n=11)		Real-life tasks (n=11)		Z	Sig.	Test Task B (n=65)		Real-life tasks (n=63)		Z	Sig.	Test Task B (n=13)		Real-life tasks (n=13)		Z	Sig.
	Median	Std Dev	Median	Std Dev			Median	Std Dev	Median	Std Dev			Median	Std Dev	Median	Std Dev		
Planning and constructing task representation	3.20	0.31	3.17	0.45	−1.782	0.075	3.20	0.54	3.17	0.55	−0.642	0.521	2.80	0.518	3.00	0.35	−0.035	0.972
Reconstructing writing plans	1.50	0.60	2.50	1.01	−2.102	0.036	2.50	0.90	3.00	0.49	−0.259	0.796	3.00	0.77	3.00	0.66	−0.815	0.415
Careful reading	3.00	0.61	2.50	1.12	−0.850	0.396	3.50	0.59	3.00	0.65	−2.769	0.006	3.00	0.47	3.00	0.81	−0.171	0.864
Search reading	3.67	0.33	3.67	0.51	−0.680	0.497	3.33	0.52	3.00	0.62	−0.959	0.338	3.33	0.64	3.33	0.43	−0.738	0.461
Connecting and generating ideas	3.00	0.95	3.33	0.42	−0.045	0.964	3.00	0.58	3.33	0.57	−3.539	0.000	3.00	0.516	3.00	0.51	−0.275	0.783
Organising intertextual relationships between ideas	3.60	0.50	3.00	0.44	−2.762	0.006	3.00	0.54	2.83	0.56	−1.947	0.052	3.00	0.45	2.83	0.36	−1.434	0.152
Organising ideas in a textual structure	3.00	0.50	2.75	0.68	−0.106	0.916	3.00	0.69	3.00	0.54	−0.485	0.628	3.00	0.40	3.00	0.59	−0.677	0.498
Low-level monitoring and revising during text production	3.00	0.75	3.00	0.79	−2.081	0.037	3.00	0.78	3.00	0.67	−0.872	0.383	2.75	0.56	3.00	0.49	−1.740	0.082
Low-level monitoring and revising after text production	3.00	1.15	2.75	1.06	−0.340	0.734	2.50	1.14	3.00	0.90	−2.996	0.003	2.00	0.927	3.00	0.92	−2.336	0.019
High-level monitoring and revising during text production	3.33	0.54	3.00	0.57	−1.137	0.256	3.00	0.70	3.17	0.61	−1.683	0.092	2.83	0.45	3.00	0.515	−0.666	0.505
High-level monitoring and revising after text production	3.00	1.12	3.33	1.12	−0.422	0.673	2.67	1.14	3.00	0.94	−2.695	0.007	2.50	0.95	3.00	0.88	−1.887	0.059

mistakes', 'improve the writing' and 'think more carefully'. It would be interesting in future research to consider why, under test conditions, the middle-achieving participants employed some of the real-life processes but not others on Test Task A and Test Task B. It would be important to further investigate why, under test conditions, the middle-scoring participants employed some of the processes but not others when composing from sources in future.

6.3 Summary

We will now summarise the major findings of Study 2, which set out to establish the cognitive parameters appropriate for reading-into-writing tasks to assess academic writing skills. Regarding the cognitive processes elicited by the real-life tasks, the results from the EFA revealed the underlying structure of reading-into-writing processes. Eleven distinct processes were identified: 1) planning and constructing task representation, 2) reconstructing writing plans, 3) careful reading, 4) search reading, 5) connecting and generating ideas, 6) organising intertextual relationships between ideas, 7) organising ideas in a textual structure, 8) low-level monitoring and revising during text production, 9) low-level monitoring and revising after text production, 10) high-level monitoring and revising during text production, and 11) high-level monitoring and revising after text production. In our view, exploratory factor analysis proved invaluable in providing empirical information about the clustering of the individual processes within each reading-into-writing phase elicited by the real-life tasks.

In addition, the results comparing students at different levels of performance showed that the high-scoring students (top 25%) reported employing most of the 11 processes significantly more than the low-scoring participants (bottom 25%). In other words, the use of these processes, at least to some extent, contributed to writers' performances, even though the nature of the relationship between processes and performance needs to be investigated in future studies. In the context of language assessment, it is important to define parameters which can account for differences in students' level of proficiency. Based on the results reported in this chapter, we feel there is a good case for considering these 11 processes as the target cognitive parameters of academic reading-into-writing skills. Nevertheless, one should note that the questionnaire data only indicates what students reported that they did, so we must be cautious when interpreting the results.

Taking the caveat of questionnaire data into account, the results of Study 2 added some insights into the nature of the reading-into-writing processes. For example, for the conceptualisation phase, six items of macro-planning and creating a task representation loaded on the same underlying factor. This implies that there is a close interplay between a writer's understanding of the task and their macro-planning processes in the real-life academic writing contexts. This further supports Shaw and Weir's (2007) view of the importance of presenting adequate contextual clues in the task prompt so that the candidates know the purpose of the writing and can plan what, how and to whom they are writing.

On the other hand, two items of *reconstructing the initial writing plans* loaded on a factor separate from the processes of macro-planning and task representation. This shows that in the context of reading-into-writing, writers adjust or recreate their writing plans and task representation as they interact with the reading sources and write on the basis of the reading. The finding supports Kellogg's (2001) hypothesis that advanced writers tend to be able to hold in mind their writing plans, and review the plan in response to the interaction with reading materials and to the text being generated. Gernsbacher (1990) argues that these processes are demanding because to be able to review the plans, the writers must hold their initial understanding of the task and writing plans active in working memory, and allocate regular attention to them while reading new materials and generating texts.

Another important observation from the findings is that the items of *connecting and generating ideas* loaded on the most dominant factor in the phase of meaning construction. This indicates the significant role of these processes when writers compose from sources in real-life academic writing contexts. In addition, careful reading, which has been the focus of many standardised reading tests as noted in Weir, Vidaković et al's survey (2013), is only one fraction of the reading-into-writing construct. According to the factor loadings, there is a clear distinction between the processes of careful reading and search reading. The descriptive statistics presented show that students actually employed search reading more than careful reading on both real-life academic writing tasks. This has an important implication that, to be able to compose from sources successfully in academic contexts, students need more than just careful comprehension reading skills. They need to be able to, for example, search for relevant information, connect important ideas within and across sources, and interpret relationships between these ideas.

The ability to organise ideas has been recognised as part of the reading-into-writing construct (e.g. Flower et al 1990, Plakans 2009a, Segev-Miller 2007, Spivey 1984, Spivey and King 1989). The results further show that, in real-life academic contexts, there are two different types of organising skill – one relates to the ability to organise intertextual relationships between ideas while the other relates to the ability to organise ideas into a textual structure.

In addition, for the monitoring and revising phase, the results show that the construct of revising during writing is different from revising after writing. This indicates the importance of encouraging students to monitor and revise their text not only during writing, but also to review and revise their text afterwards. In the writing literature, there is some evidence suggesting that students tend to focus on lower-level revisions concerning accuracy during writing but focus on higher-level revisions concerning ideas after writing. But there is limited research looking into revisions on reading-into-writing tasks. We know very little of how the variable of reading materials affects students' revision processes. It would be important to explore this in future studies.

As compared to reading comprehension and the ability to write an impromptu essay, some of these 11 processes identified in Study 2 appear to be unique to the reading-into-writing construct. This further supports the value of using the integrated task type to teach and assess EAP writing skills.

An important question to answer when defining the reading-into-writing construct is whether these 11 cognitive parameters identified can effectively distinguish differences between students at different levels. The results from Mann-Whitney U tests show that the high-scoring students reported employing eight processes (including *planning and constructing task representation, careful reading, search reading, connecting and generating ideas, organising intertextual relationships between ideas, organising ideas in a textual structure, low-level monitoring and revising during writing* and *high-level monitoring and revising during writing*) out of the 11 more than the low-scoring group. Six of the differences observed between the groups were significant.

Lastly, Study 2 investigated how well the two reading-into-writing tests elicited the target processes. We examined the extent to which students at different levels (high-, middle- and low-scoring groups) employed these 11 processes between the real-life and test conditions. The results yielded positive evidence for the cognitive validity of the two reading-into-writing task types. Both Test Task A (essay task with multiple verbal inputs) and Test Task B (essay task with multiple verbal and non-verbal inputs) were able to elicit from high-scoring and low-scoring students most of the cognitive processes in a similar manner to the way they employed the processes on the real-life tasks. The middle-achieving group, on the other hand, showed greater discrepancy in the way they employed some processes between the conditions.

To complete our exploration of the reading-into-writing construct, Chapter 7 reports results on the relationships between the participants' reading-into-writing test scores and their performance on real-life academic writing tasks. Based on the findings, we will discuss how confident we can be when drawing inferences of students' abilities in academic writing on the basis of their reading-into-writing test scores. What do their reading-into-writing test scores tell us about their abilities to write in real-life academic contexts?

7 Examining the relations between test scores and real-life performance

> This chapter builds on the empirical evidence in relation to the contextual and cognitive aspects of the construct of reading-into-writing reported in Chapters 5 and 6 by establishing the criterion-related validity of reading-into-writing test tasks to assess academic writing abilities.
>
> The aim is to orient the reader to the empirical evidence which demonstrates the predictive power of the reading-into-writing test scores in academic contexts.
>
> The chapter covers the following areas:
> - students' performance
> - the correlations between overall test scores and real-life academic performance
> - the correlations between analytical scores and real-life academic performance
> - the patterns of correlations.

Chapter 5 and Chapter 6 reported the results of the salient contextual features of the sampled real-life writing tasks and the key processes which students employed to complete these tasks. The two chapters also reported findings in relation to the two key *a priori* validity components of the socio-cognitive test validation framework (Weir 2005a): context validity and cognitive validity of the two reading-into-writing test formats (Test Task A – with multiple verbal inputs; Test Task B – with multiple verbal and non-verbal inputs). This chapter focuses on an *a posteriori* component: criterion-related validity, which concerns 'the extent to which test scores correlate with a suitable external criterion of performance with established properties' (Weir 2005a:35). We will first report the participants' proficiency level in English as measured by IELTS, and their performance on the two reading-into-writing tests and four real-life tasks. After that, we report the relations between their reading-into-writing test scores and real-life academic performance.

7.1 Students' performance

Proficiency level in English measured by IELTS

As reported in Chapter 4, the mean scores of the 291 participants' IELTS Reading and Writing were 5.88 and 5.54 respectively. As both reading-into-writing test tasks (Test Tasks A and B) and the selected real-life writing tasks involve considerable reading, the average of the participants' IELTS Reading and Writing bands and the distribution are presented here for reference (see Tables 7.1 and 7.2).

Table 7.1 Participants' IELTS bands

	Minimum	Maximum	Mean	Std Dev
IELTS Reading	5.00	7.50	5.88	0.60
IELTS Writing	4.50	7.00	5.54	0.49
Average IELTS Reading and Writing	5.00	7.00	5.81	0.43

Table 7.2 Frequency of the participants' average IELTS Reading and Writing bands

Average IELTS Reading and Writing band	Frequency	Per cent
7.0	5	2.3
6.5	23	10.5
6.0	91	41.6
5.5	83	37.9
5.0	17	7.8
Total	219	100

All IELTS scores were effective at the time of the investigation in line with the University of Bedfordshire's admission policy, i.e. within two years for effectiveness. Students who score IELTS 6.0 can be offered places on 3-year Bachelor's degrees; students who score IELTS 5.0 can be offered places on 4-year extended Bachelor's programmes, which include compulsory extra English classes in the first year. In this study, 54.4% of the participants had an IELTS average Reading and Writing band of 6.0 or above whereas 45.6% had an IELTS overall band of 5.0 or 5.5. According to information in relation to the indicative IELTS bands at CEFR levels provided by the test provider (IELTS 2017), 12.8% of the participants were at C1 level and 87.2% were at B2 level.

Although most participants in this study did not reach the target level of Test Task A, i.e. C1, the sampled proficiency range is still considered to be appropriate for the purpose of the investigation. This is because the sampled range reflects a typical IELTS score distribution of overseas undergraduate students admitted to study at UK universities. The results and implications drawn from this study therefore provide 1) a more realistic picture of the criterion-related validity of Test Task A, when the test is used as an admission test for UK universities; and 2) necessary criterion-related evidence of Test Task B as the university's diagnostic test of academic writing needs.

Performance on Test Task A

LTTC, the test provider, marked 160 performances on Test Task A, following their standard operationalised procedures. All scripts were double marked and 5% were marked by a third rater. Each script was scored using four analytical marking categories: 1) relevance and adequacy, 2) coherence and organisation, 3) lexical use, and 4) grammatical use. *Relevance and adequacy* concerns whether the text is relevant to the writing task, and whether all parts of the writing task are fully addressed. *Coherence and organisation* concerns whether the text shows coherence and cohesion, and whether the organisational structure of the text at different levels is clear. *Lexical use* and *grammatical use* concern the range and appropriateness of the lexical use and of grammatical use of the text respectively. Each category can be scored from 1 to 5 with 3 being the threshold (for more details, see Language Training and Testing Center 2014). An overall Band 3 on all of the four analytical categories is required to pass Test Task A. In real-life operationalised contexts, LTTC reports only the overall band (1 to 5) to candidates.

In this study, 17 participants (10.6%) passed Test Task A (i.e. obtained a minimum total analytical score of 12 with a minimum score of 3 on all analytical categories). The low passing rate on Test Task A was expected because only about 12 % of the participants were at C1 level based on their IELTS band. Ten of the 17 participants who passed Test Task A had an average reading and writing band of 6.5 or above. In order to generate more insightful information about the participants' performances on Test Task A, this chapter focuses the discussion on the participants' individual analytical scores and total analytical scores instead of the overall band.

Descriptive statistics of the 160 participants' scores on individual analytical categories and their total analytical scores on Test Task A are presented in Table 7.3. The participants' mean total analytical score on Test Task A was 8.72 with a standard deviation of 2.10. The means of the four analytical scores were seemingly close, ranging from 2.01 to 2.34. The mean score on *coherence and organisation* was highest whereas the mean score on *grammatical use* was lowest.

Examining the relations between test scores and real-life performance

Table 7.3 Descriptive statistics on Test Task A scores

	Max. possible score	Min.	Max.	Mean	Std Dev
Test Task A total scores	20	4.0	13.5	8.72	2.10
Relevance and adequacy	5	1.0	4.0	2.27	0.65
Coherence and organisation	5	1.0	3.5	2.34	0.60
Lexical use	5	1.0	3.0	2.15	0.58
Grammatical use	5	1.0	3.0	2.01	0.57

In order to understand more comprehensively the participants' performances on Test Task A, Table 7.4 presents the frequency of the four analytical scores on Test Task A. Test Task A is a criterion-referenced test which is aimed specifically at the C1 level. It reports how well candidates are doing relative to a pre-determined performance level on a specified set of goals. The figures show that more participants achieved Band 3, i.e. the pass band, on the categories *relevance and adequacy* (30%) and *coherence and organisation* (31.2%) than *lexical use* (19.4%) and *grammatical use* (15%).

Table 7.4 Frequency table of analytical scores on Test Task A

		Relevance and adequacy		Coherence and organisation		Lexical use		Grammatical use	
		Freq	Percentage	Freq	Percentage	Freq	Percentage	Freq	Percentage
Fail	1.0	17	10.6	13	8.1	15	9.4	19	11.9
	1.5	10	6.3	6	3.8	15	9.4	20	12.5
	2.0	52	32.5	51	31.9	67	41.9	85	53.1
	2.5	33	20.6	40	25.0	32	20.0	12	7.5
Pass	3.0	47	29.4	49	30.6	31	19.4	24	15.0
	3.5	0	0	1	0.6	0	0	0	0
	4.0	1	0.6	0	0	0	0	0	0
	5.0	0	0	0	0	0	0	0	0
	Total	160	100.0	160	100.0	160	100.0	160	100.0

Performance on Test Task B

The test provider, Centre for Research in English Language Learning and Assessment (CRELLA), marked 140 performances on Test Task B (essay task with multiple verbal and non-verbal inputs), and 30% of the scripts were double marked. Each script was scored by three analytical marking categories, i.e., content, organisation and language. The *content* category refers to the extent to which the writer has responded appropriately to the task and the specific instructions given about the relationship between the input reading material and the written output. It covers the inclusion of all essential key points, as well as communicative effect on the reader. The *organisation* category refers to the way in which the written production has been structured and organised in terms of the overall format, the grouping and sequencing of ideas in paragraphs, and the coherence of the argumentation. It covers the notion of cohesion and coherence at levels of sentences and paragraphs. The *language* category refers to the clarity of linguistic expression in English, including the selection and control of grammar and vocabulary items. It also includes stylistic choices relating to academic register.

Each category can be scored from 1 to 3. Score 1 indicates a significantly weak performance, score 2 indicates a below-adequate performance and score 3 indicates an adequate performance. Texts that were too short, completely off topic, illegible or plagiarised were scored 0. Test Task B was still at a trial stage when the study was conducted. Test scores were proposed to report both at the *overall* (i.e. the total analytical scores) and *analytical* levels. The trial grade boundaries were as follows:

A score of 8/9 = Grade A (no intervention required)
A score of 6/7 = Grade B (low-level intervention needed)
A score of 5 or < = Grade C (high-level intervention needed)

Descriptive statistics on the 140 performances on Test Task B are presented in Table 7.5. The participants' mean total analytical score on Test Task B was 4.99 out of 9 with a standard deviation of 1.76. The mean score on *organisation* was higher than the mean scores on *content* and *language*. Table 7.6 presents the frequency of the three analytical scores. Test Task B is a university diagnostic test of test takers' academic writing ability. 8.6%, 12.9% and 10.7% of participants scored Band 3 (which indicates an adequate or above-adequate performance) on the categories of *content*, *organisation* and *language*, respectively. Most participants were scored at Band 2 (which indicates a below-adequate performance) on *content* and *organisation* but most participants were scored Band 1 (which indicates a significantly weak performance) on *language*. Similar

Table 7.5 Descriptive statistics on Test Task B scores

	Max possible score	Min	Max	Mean	Std Dev
Test Task B total scores	9	0	9	4.99	1.76
Content (coverage of key points)	3	0	3	1.64	0.66
Organisation (cohesion and coherence)	3	0	3	1.78	0.68
Language (choice and control of lexis and grammar)	3	0	3	1.60	0.70

Table 7.6 Frequency table of analytical scores on Test Task B

	Content (coverage of key points)		Organisation (cohesion and coherence)		Language (choice and control of lexis and grammar)		Implication of score
	Freq	Percentage	Freq	Percentage	Freq	Percentage	
0	2	1.4	2	1.4	2	1.4	Too short, completely off topic, illegible or plagiarised
1.0	59	42.1	45	32.1	67	47.9	A significantly weak performance
2.0	67	47.9	75	53.6	56	40.0	A below-adequate performance
3.0	12	8.6	18	12.9	15	10.7	An adequate or above-adequate performance
Total	140	100.0	140	100.0	140	100.0	

to the results indicated by Test Task A, the participants seemed to perform less successfully on the *language* category than other analytical categories.

There are reasons to be somewhat cautious in interpreting the participants' performances on the two reading-into-writing tests. The participants may have been less familiar with reading-into-writing test tasks which involve multiple reading materials, even though they had been briefed about the format of Test Task A (with multiple verbal inputs) and Test Task B (with multiple verbal and non-verbal inputs) one or two weeks before they did the test. In addition, the participants might not have perceived Test Tasks A and B as high stakes for them because their scores on Test Tasks A and B would not affect their university grades. Although Test Task B was a university diagnostic test, the participants completed the task solely for research purposes and they did not receive any corresponding support based on their Test Task B scores. The functions of Test Task A (which is part of a level-specific proficiency test at C1 level) and Test Task B (which is part of an academic writing diagnostic test) are different. Therefore, it is not appropriate to make direct comparison of the test results between two test tasks.

Nevertheless, some similarities in the participants' performances on the two reading-into-writing test tasks were observed. In terms of the analytical scores, the results showed that the participants in this study were scored highest for the organisation category, followed by the content category, and lowest on the linguistic category on both reading-into-writing test tasks. It appears that both reading-into-writing test tasks provided a similar picture of the participants' strengths and weaknesses in terms of analytical categories. The major difference found between Test Task A and Test Task B scores was the range of scores. On Test Task A, almost no performance was scored Band 4 or Band 5 from a scale of 5 on all the four marking categories. On Test Task B, the full range of scores was achieved. This is most likely because Test Task A was set at C1 level whereas Test Task B was set at B2 level.

Performance on the real-life tasks

Each real-life performance (i.e. the essay task, the report task, the in-class test and the end-of-term case-study examination) can be awarded a score from 0 to 16, representing five bands (see Table 7.7).

Table 7.7 Real-life scores and the corresponding grades

Score	Band	Pass/Fail
16–14	A+/A/A-	Pass
13–11	B+/B/B-	
10–8	C+/C/C-	
7–5	D+/D/D-	
4–0	E	Fail

The four tasks were marked by different module teams, following the departmental marking procedures. Lecturers who marked the real-life performances were not informed of the students' IELTS scores or their performances on the two reading-into-writing test tasks.

The essay task was scored based on four categories: 1) examination of the data and description of the nature of the dataset; 2) discussion and justification of the techniques chosen; 3) reasons for rejecting the inappropriate techniques; and 4) discussion of other relevant issues. The report task was scored based on: 1) problem definition and structure of the text; 2) information identification (the number of sources, relevance to the topic, reliability of the sources); 3) critical reasoning; and 4) persuasion and influencing (see Appendix 1). The marking scheme of the in-class test and the end-of-term examination was not available to the researcher. The sub-scores of the tasks were also not available to the researcher. The real-life data reported in this chapter was the final standardised marks submitted to the university.

Table 7.8 presents the descriptive statistics of the scores for each selected real-life task. Participants in this study, as a whole group, performed best on the report task ($M = 9.72$, $SD = 2.60$) while scoring lowest on the exam ($M = 6.03$, $SD = 2.56$). The standard deviations of the four performances were moderate.

For the purpose of correlational analysis, the participants' mean scores of the four selected tasks i.e. the essay, report, question-and-answer test and case study examination tasks, were calculated. The participants' mean real-life score was 8.59 out of 16 ($SD = 2.24$).

Figure 7.1 shows the frequency of participants at each corresponding grade based on their mean real-life scores. Only one participant (0.5%) in this study got an average Grade A. 21% of the participants got an average Grade B and about 30% got Grade C. Most participants (45.2%) got an average Grade D and 3.7% got an average Grade E (Fail).

Examining the relations between test scores and real-life performance

Table 7.8 Descriptive statistics of real-life performances

Task	N[1]	Max possible score	Minimum	Maximum	Mean	Std Dev
Essay	161[2]	16	2	15	9.27	2.99
Report	136[3]	16	2	14	9.72	2.60
Test	145	16	2	15	8.84	2.98
Exam	143	16	2	14	6.03	2.56

Figure 7.1 Mean real-life grade

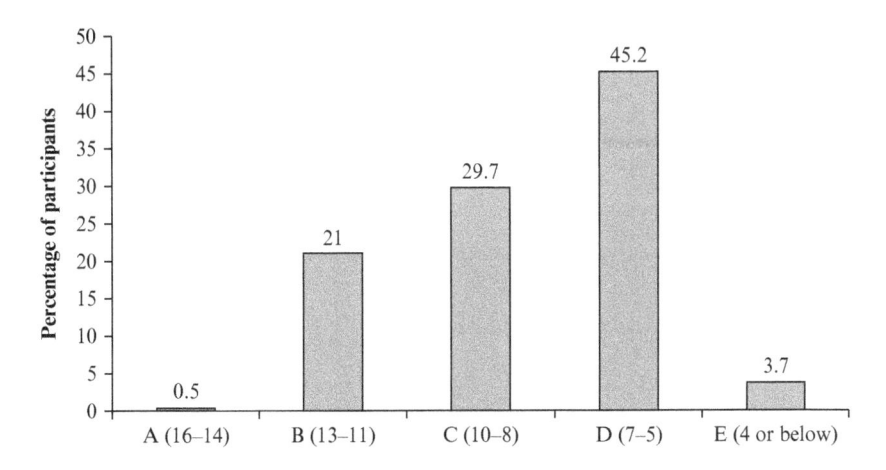

- A (16–14): 0.5
- B (13–11): 21
- C (10–8): 29.7
- D (7–5): 45.2
- E (4 or below): 3.7

(Percentage of participants)

7.2 Relationship between test scores and real-life academic performance

As test scores are used to infer test takers' ability in performing different writing tasks in the target context, we will first examine the extent to which the test scores (total scores and analytical scores) relate to the average scores of the four real-life writing tasks (see Tables 7.9 and 7.10). After that, to give an indication of the overall predictive power of the reading-into-writing test scores in academic contexts, we will examine the correlations between the test scores and the average scores of the four real-life writing tasks (see Table 7.11). Finally, to understand the relative strengths and weaknesses of the predictive power of the reading-into-writing test scores on a given scale, we will examine the graphic representation of the correlations between the test scores and the mean real-life scores (see Figures 7.2 and 7.3).

---

1 For the 219 participants in this study, 56 enrolled on one of the modules, 21 enrolled on two of the modules, 80 enrolled on three of the modules and 62 enrolled on all the modules.
2 73 out of the 161 participated in the investigation of cognitive processes.
3 70 out of the 136 participated in the investigation of cognitive processes.

Correlation between test scores and individual real-life scores

For the 160 participants who completed Test Task A, 96 completed the report task, 111 completed the essay task, 109 completed the in-class test, and 99 completed the end-of-term case study examination as part of their degree programme. As indicated in Table 7.9, the correlations between Test Task A and individual real-life scores ranged from 0.13 to 0.34. Test Task A scores correlated moderately with report scores at $r(94)=0.34$, $p<0.01$, but weakly with in-class test scores at $r(107)=0.21$, $p=0.03$ and essay scores at $r(109)=0.19$, $p=0.05$. Test Task A scores did not correlate significantly with the end-of-term examination scores.

Table 7.9 Correlation between Test Task A scores and individual real-life scores

		Essay (n=111)	Report (n=96)	Test (n=109)	Exam (n=99)
Test Task A	Pearson Correlation[4]	0.187*	0.343**	0.212*	0.126
	Sig. (2-tailed)	0.050	0.001	0.027	0.215

* Correlation is significant at the 0.05 level (2-tailed)
** Correlation is significant at the 0.01 level (2-tailed)

For the 140 participants who completed Test Task B, 95 completed the report task, 93 completed the essay task, 75 completed the question-and-answer test, and 69 completed the end-of-term case study examination as part of their degree programme. The correlations between Test Task B and individual real-life writing tasks ranged from 0.08 to 0.44 (see Table 7.10). Test Task B scores correlated moderately with question-and-answer test scores at $r(73)=0.44$, $p<0.01$ and with essay scores at $r(91)=0.39$, $p<0.01$, and weakly with report scores at $r(93)=0.28$, $p<0.01$. Test Task B scores correlated weakly with case study examination at $r(67)=0.08$, $p=0.48$ but, similar to Test Task A, the correlation between Test Task B scores and case study examination scores was non-significant.

Most test tasks are not designed to predict the test taker's writing ability on a single task type, but a representative range of task types that they are likely to encounter in the target context. The weak to moderate correlations between test scores and individual real-life scores are not surprising. Comparing between two test scores, Test Task B scores have better correlations with the real-life *essay* and *in-class test* scores, whereas Test Task A scores have better correlations with the real-life *report* and *end-of-term* scores.

Based on the results of contextual analysis (see Chapter 5), Test Task A

---

[4] Non-parametric correlation tests were also performed. The significant results were not affected by the use of parametric tests.

Table 7.10 Correlation between Test Task B scores and individual real-life scores

		Essay (n=93)	Report (n=95)	Test (n=75)	Exam (n=69)
Test Task B	Pearson Correlation	0.386**	0.283**	0.438**	0.082
	Sig. (2-tailed)	0.000	0.005	0.000	0.484

** Correlation is significant at the 0.01 level (2-tailed)

seems to be more comparable to the real-life essay task in terms of task features whereas Test Task B seems to be more comparable to the real-life report task. Therefore, the results, namely that Test Task A correlated with the real-life report task better, whereas Test Task B correlated with the real-life essay task better, are to some extent unexpected. It appears that task difficulty level might have had a bigger impact on the degree of correlation than task features. The real-life report task was regarded as more challenging than the real-life essay task by the judges, for example, in relation to cognitive demands, number of language functions to perform, and explicitness of textual organisation of the input texts. This may be one of the reasons why Test Task A (which is at C1 level) correlated with the real-life report task better whereas Test Task B (which is at a lower B2 level) correlated with the real-life essay task better.

Another interesting finding is that both Test Task A and Test Task B scores did not correlate significantly with the end-of-term examination scores. The first reason could be due to time effects. The participants completed the test tasks at the beginning of the term while the real-life tasks (i.e. the report task, the essay task and the in-class test) were assigned to the participants during the term, whereas the case-study examination was assigned at the end of the term. The correlations between test scores and the real-life scores might have dropped due to the time gap between the two events, which means that many other factors might have interfered with the correlations. For example, the participants' proficiency might have improved and their knowledge of academic writing might have improved. According to one of the lecturers, one major purpose of the examination was for the participants to demonstrate the subject knowledge they had acquired on the module. Therefore, the variable of subject knowledge might also have contributed to the examination scores more than the participants' writing ability.

The results so far show that Test Task A and Test Task B scores correlated with individual real-life tasks at different levels. It is therefore recommended in future to collect evidence from more than one task type, especially in high-stakes writing tests. As argued in the literature, such practice would help to generate a more comprehensive evaluation of test takers' academic writing ability (Shaw and Weir 2007, Weigle 2002).

Correlations between test scores and mean real-life scores

Having examined the correlations between the reading-into-writing test scores and the individual real-life tasks, we now turn to examine the extent to which the reading-into-writing test scores relate to the average scores of the four real-life writing tasks (see Table 7.11).

Table 7.11 Correlation between test scores and mean real-life scores

Test Task A (n=160)		Mean real-life score	Test Task B (n=140)		Mean real-life score
Total scores	Pearson Correlation	0.306**	Total scores	Pearson Correlation	0.379**
	Sig. (2-tailed)	0.000		Sig. (2-tailed)	0.000
Relevance and adequacy	Pearson Correlation	0.160*	Content	Pearson Correlation	0.300**
	Sig. (2-tailed)	0.043		Sig. (2-tailed)	0.000
Coherence and organisation	Pearson Correlation	0.226**	Organisation	Pearson Correlation	0.365**
	Sig. (2-tailed)	0.004		Sig. (2-tailed)	0.000
Lexical use	Pearson Correlation	0.306**	Language	Pearson Correlation	0.307**
	Sig. (2-tailed)	0.000		Sig. (2-tailed)	0.000
Grammatical use	Pearson Correlation	0.391**			
	Sig. (2-tailed)	0.000			

* *Correlation is significant at the 0.05 level (2-tailed)*
** *Correlation is significant at the 0.01 level (2-tailed)*

As shown in Table 7.11, Test Task A total scores correlated significantly with the mean real-life scores at a level of $r(158)=0.31$, $p>0.01$, explaining 9.36% variance of the real-life performances. Test Task B total scores correlated significantly with their mean real-life scores at a level of $r(138)=0.38$, $p>0.01$, explaining 14.36% variance of the real-life performances. It is encouraging to see that not only the total reading-into-writing task scores correlated well with students' real-life academic performance; most individual analytical scores of Test Task A and Test Task B correlated with the mean real-life scores at a level of 0.3 or above, except the categories of content (relevance and adequacy) and organisation (coherence and organisation) on Test Task A. To understand why some individual analytical scores correlated with real-life performance more than the others, we compared the descriptors of both marking schemes. It seemed that the descriptors of Test Task B were more task specific than those of Test Task A. The marking scheme of Test Task A was developed to assess Test Task A and another task (essay task with single non-verbal inputs) of the same test. In contrast, the marking scheme of Test Task B was developed specifically for Test Task B. The results seem to suggest that a more task-specific marking scheme, especially for the categories of contents and organisation, might contribute to better correlations between test scores and the target performance in real life. However, further evidence is needed to confirm this.

The figures in Table 7.11 are better than most previously reported figures in the literature. For example, Davies and Criper (1988) reported a correlation of 0.3 between ELTS scores and academic outcome. They concluded that language proficiency can explain about 10% of the variance of academic outcome, which is frequently quoted as a benchmark level of predictive power of test scores. Feast (2002) reported 0.39 between IELTS scores and academic outcome. Yen and Kuzma (2009) reported that IELTS scores correlated significantly with the first semester academic outcomes at 0.46 and the second semester's outcomes at 0.25. It is important to notice that these previous studies studied the relationships between overall IELTS scores (i.e. including all papers of IELTS) and academic outcomes whereas, in Study 3, we investigated the predictive power of Test Task A and Test Task B on their own. Most previous studies investigated the predictive power of the overall test scores rather than individual paper scores because the former was found to have a better predictive power than individual task scores. Of the individual paper scores, writing test scores were often found to have no or low correlations with academic success. For example, Cotton and Conrow (1998) and Humphreys et al (2010) found no significant correlation between the participants' IELTS writing scores (which include an independent writing task with input texts and an integrated writing task with non-verbal inputs) and their academic achievement. Kerstjens and Nery (2000) reported a significant correlation of 0.25 between their participants' IELTS writing test and academic scores. The results of Study 3 showed that both the reading-into-writing test tasks (Test Task A – essay task with multiple verbal inputs and Test Task B – essay task with multiple verbal and non-verbal inputs) each reported a better correlation with the academic outcomes than most figures in the literature, including those which used the overall test paper scores (e.g. Davies and Criper 1988, Feast 2002, Yen and Kuzma 2009) as well as individual writing scores (e.g. Cotton and Conrow 1998, Humphreys et al 2010, Kerstjens and Nery 2000).

Having established the numeric correlations between the two reading-into-writing test scores and students' academic performance in the TLU domain, we will now examine the graphic patterns of such correlations.

Defining Integrated Reading-into-Writing Constructs

7.3 Patterns of correlations between test scores and mean real-life scores

To understand what the reading-into-writing test scores can represent in relation to students' real-life academic performance, here we examine the patterns of the correlations between the test scores and the average real-life academic writing scores. The graphic representation of the correlations between the test scores and the mean real-life scores is presented in Figure 7.2 (Test Task A) and Figure 7.3 (Test Task B). The size and density of the plots indicate the strength of the correlation between the test scores and the real-life scores. The bigger and more concentrated the plots are, the stronger the correlation between the test scores and real-life scores is. The scatterplots are divided into five sections (Grade E to Grade A) by dotted lines. The relationships between the test scores and real-life scores are discussed with reference to the corresponding grade of the real-life scores.

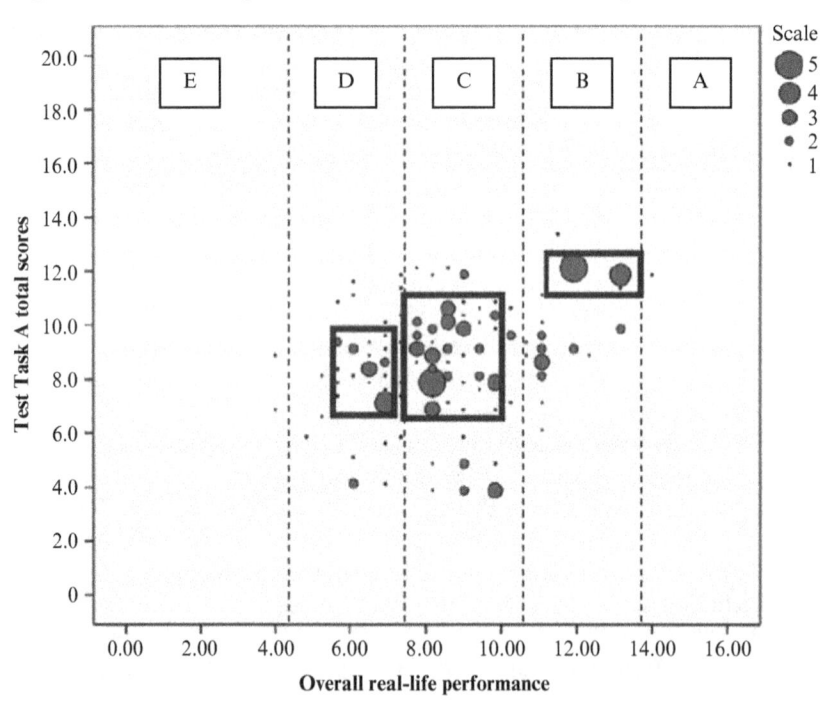

Figure 7.2 Relationships between Test Task A and real-life performance

As reported in Table 7.11, the participants' Test Task A scores (n=160) correlated with their mean real-life scores at $r(158)=0.31$, $p>0.01$. The correlation appears to be strongest and clearest between Test Task A score 12 and real-life Grade B. The plots at the real-life Grade B cluster most densely at the score of 12 on Test Task A. In other words, most participants who obtained a total score of 12 on Test Task A achieved an overall Grade B on the selected real-life tasks.

The plots at the real-life Grade C spread densely along a wide range of Test Task A scores whereas the plots at the real-life Grade D cluster densely between Test Task A scores 7 and 9. It appears that for those participants who obtained an overall real-life Grade C, other factors might have had a bigger impact on their academic achievement than their writing ability. Davies and Criper (1988) argued that individual non-linguistic characteristics might have a stronger impact on one's academic success than language proficiency.

The results also showed that for the participants who scored between 7 and 9 on Test Task A, they were most likely to achieve an overall Grade D and Grade C on the real-life tasks. It is interesting for future study to explore why, with a similar academic writing ability, some of these participants (Grade C or even Grade B) achieved better in the target context than the others (Grade D).

As mentioned, the passing requirement of Test Task A, which is a level-specific test at C1 level, requires a minimum of Band 3 on all four categories. Test Task A is part of GEPT Advanced, a test which has been recognised by many universities as a means to indicate if applicants have reached the minimum English language requirement. Results on Test Task A using a pass/fail dichotomy might not be entirely appropriate for university entry purposes if students want to study overseas. For example, in the UK, the latest UK Border Agency (UKBA) regulations require students who wish to apply to study at the level of Bachelor's degree under Tier 4 (General) of a points-based system to have a minimum of Level B2 of the CEFR (UK Border Agency 2013). There are similar English proficiency requirements for student visa applications in different English-speaking countries. Although GEPT Advanced has a High-Intermediate test at B2 level, the test does not seem to target the academic domain. It would seem more appropriate to adjust the score reporting method on GEPT Advanced, which was developed in the academic domain, to indicate the test takers who have reached B2 of the CEFR, which is the minimum threshold of English requirement for higher education in the UK. The results of this study showed that academic performance, especially at the levels of Grades D and B, could be predicted by different score ranges on Test Task A.

Having reported the findings regarding Test Task A, we will discuss the patterns of correlations between Test Task B scores and real-life scores (see Figure 7.3). As shown in Table 7.11, the participants' Test Task B scores (n=140) correlated with their mean real-life scores at $r(138)=0.38$, $p>0.01$. As the range of the total analytical scores on Test Task B is comparatively limited, i.e. from 0 to 9, the patterns of plots are expected to be less clear than those obtained on Test Task A.

According to Figure 7.3, the correlation pattern between Test Task B

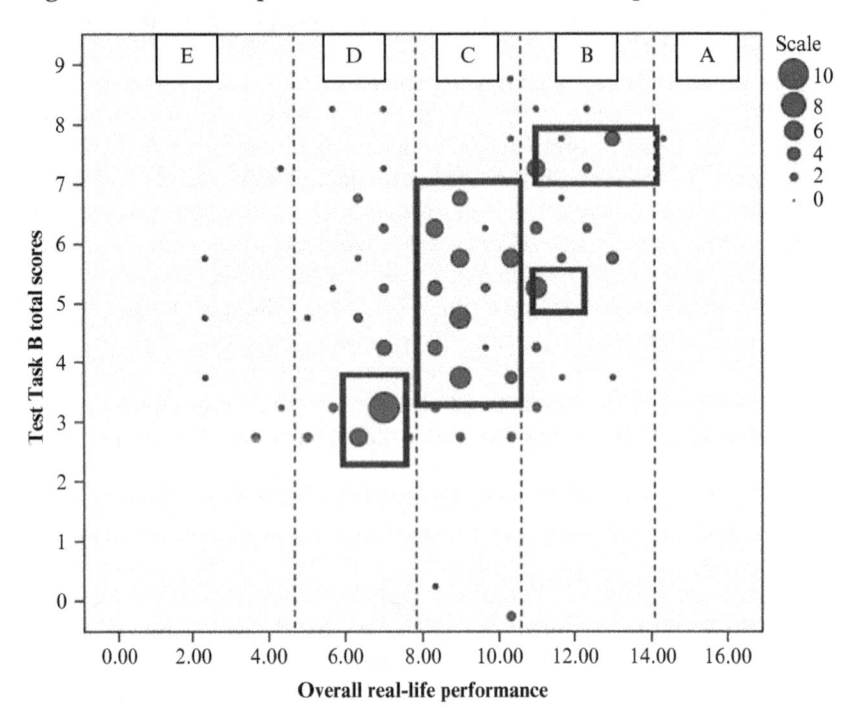

Defining Integrated Reading-into-Writing Constructs

Figure 7.3 Relationships between Test Task B and real-life performance

scores and real-life Grade D is the clearest. The plots at the real-life Grade D cluster most densely at the score of 3 on Test Task B. In other words, most participants who got a total score of 2.5 to 3.5 on Test Task B achieved an overall Grade D on the selected real-life tasks.

Like the pattern obtained on Test Task A, the plots at the real-life Grade C bunch densely along a wide range of Test Task B scores. Presumably other factors, such as subject knowledge and motivation, might have impacted the participants' academic achievement more than their academic writing ability. As mentioned previously, it is unfortunately beyond the scope of this study to investigate what other non-linguistic factors might have impacted on their performances on the selected real-life tasks.

Lastly, the plots at the real-life Grade B bunch most densely at the Test Task B score 5, and between 7 and 8. In other words, participants who scored 7 or 8 tended to achieve an overall Grade B on the real-life writing tasks. In addition, some participants who scored 5 on Test Task B obtained a better overall grade (Grade B) than the others (Grade C). It would be interesting in future studies to explore the reasons.

Test Task B was designed to indicate the test takers' need for academic writing support. As mentioned previously, Grade A (a score of 8 and 9) indicates no need for academic writing support, Grade B (a score of 6 and 7) indicates a low-level need for academic writing intervention, whereas Grade C (a score of 5 or below) indicates a high-level need for academic writing intervention. Considering the variable of academic writing proficiency solely, the results of this study seem to suggest that the cut-off scores of Test Task B which indicate different levels of academic writing support required might not be the most effective. Further evidence is needed to confirm the results and to investigate the most appropriate cut-off scores for the need of different levels of academic writing support.

7.4 Summary

In terms of criterion-related validity, the results of Study 3 indicated that the two reading-into-writing tests had a moderate predictive power for test takers' real-life academic writing performance. Test Task A and Test Task B correlated significantly to the participants' mean real-life academic scores at $r(158)=0.31$, $p>0.01$ and $r(138)=0.38$, $p>0.01$ respectively (see Table 7.11). In addition, five of the seven analytical scores had a significant correlation to the participants' mean real-life academic scores at the level of $r=0.3$ or above.

Nevertheless, the reading-into-writing test scores seem to be able to 'predict' performance in the target context better at the high and low levels than at the medium level (see Figures 7.2 and 7.3). In other words, participants who achieved comparatively well (Grade B) on real-life tasks tended to have scored comparatively high on the reading-into-writing tests. Participants who achieved comparatively poorly (Grade D) on real-life tasks tended to score comparatively poorly on the reading-into-writing tests. However, for participants who achieved at the medium level (Grade C), their scores on the reading-into-writing test tasks ranged widely. It appears that students' reading-into-writing abilities might have a limited impact on the medium-level academic achievement in the context of this study. Therefore, any high-stakes decisions, e.g. visa application and university admission, for these medium-level test takers need to be made with extra caution, and supported by other forms of evidence.

Chapter 7 has argued that the reading-into-writing task type has not only valid context validity and cognitive validity, as demonstrated in Chapters 5 and 6 respectively, but also has a better predictive power in relation to students' academic performance in the target language domain than most overall test paper scores and independent writing-only scores investigated in the literature. The results of Study 1 and Study 2 showed that the two reading-into-writing test tasks replicated a range of salient features of real-life academic writing tasks in terms of overall task setting and input text features, and elicited most of the 11 target cognitive processes from test takers. Weir (2005a) argued that the more valid the context and cognitive parameters a test task operationalises, the more accurate an estimate of the test takers' performance in the real-life target conditions the test can provide. This means that to achieve stronger correlations between test scores and students' performance in the TLU domain in real life, test developers must carefully consider the contextual and cognitive parameters they operationalise in their test tasks.

Studies 1, 2 and 3, for the first time in language testing literature, have provided empirical evidence in relation to the three major test validity components (i.e. context, cognitive and criterion-related) for defining the construct of reading-into-writing at the CEFR Level B2 or above in academic contexts. In Chapter 8, we will summarise the main findings and draw conclusions from the three empirical studies reported in this volume. Drawing upon the findings described in Chapters 5 to 7, in particular, we will seek to provide some practical guidance, together with a set of contextual and cognitive parameters, for test developers on a methodology for designing reading-into-writing tasks to assess academic writing abilities at the CEFR Level B2 or above. The final part of the chapter will highlight some possible directions for improving the representation of high-level reading-into-writing skills in the CEFR and for future research in relation to the construct of reading-into-writing.

Section 3
Connections in English Profile

8 Conclusions and recommendations

> This concluding chapter builds on the theoretical and empirical evidence of the construct of reading-into-writing in academic contexts established in the previous chapters.
>
> The aim is to orient the reader to a summary of the major findings in relation to the context, cognitive and criterion-related validity of reading-into-writing test tasks, and to some practical guidelines and recommendations for future test designs in relation to the overall task features and text selection.
>
> The chapter covers the following areas:
> - major findings of this volume
> - a framework for reading-into-writing
> - recommendations for the CEFR illustrative descriptors, test design and future research.

The motivation for the research reported in this volume was a desire to explore and define the construct of reading-into-writing at the CEFR Level B2 or above in academic contexts. This was caused by a concern that neither the traditional reading comprehension formats nor the impromptu writing task type fully represent the integrated nature of academic literacy, as described in Section 1.1. There remains a tendency in many standardised reading tests to focus on comprehension skills at sentence and paragraph levels, rarely targeting the processes of interpreting and integrating information at textual and intertextual levels. The same tendency is observed in many standardised writing tests to focus on ability in generating a grammatically correct and coherent text from one's background knowledge, rarely tapping into the writing skills of transforming information from multiple sources (see Section 1.1). It is hoped that this volume will provide the theoretical and empirical evidence necessary for establishing the construct validity of the integrated reading-into-writing task type which seeks to test students' ability in composing academic writing from sources.

Chapters 2 and 3 reviewed the theoretical base in relation to academic writing from sources, and past and current practice in reading and writing tests. The integrated reading-into-writing task type was first used in standardised language tests a century ago because it represents what people do in real life. The format then went out of favour a few times during the past century as the industry prioritised other aspects of test construct and practicality. As we have improved our understanding of academic literacy and construct validity, the integrated format has once again been used widely to represent more closely the ability of writing from sources. The empirical research reported in Chapters 5, 6 and 7 explores three major aspects of the construct validity of the integrated reading-into-writing task type in relation to task features, students' mental processes of writing from sources, and the relationship between test and real-life performance in three studies.

The findings of Study 1, Study 2 and Study 3 reported in Chapters 5 to 7 show evidence that the integrated reading-into-writing task type can validly and effectively measure students' ability in academic writing from sources. Test Task A (essay task with multiple verbal inputs) and Test Task B (essay task with multiple verbal and non-verbal inputs) resembled the criterial task features of the real-life writing tasks, elicited the key processes of writing from sources, and achieved good levels of correlations with the students' real-life academic written performance, indicating both the reading-into-writing tasks to be a valid format to assess academic writing ability.

It is clear, however, that the design of a well-functioning reading-into-writing task is not straightforward as it needs to take account not only of factors influencing reading and writing but also the interplay between the two. It was intended that one outcome of the empirical research reported in this volume would be to provide some practical guidance for test designers on how to construct a well-functioning reading-into-writing task to assess students' ability in academic writing from sources at the CEFR levels of B2 and C1. Thus, this chapter will seek to draw together some guidelines and recommendations for test developers in relation to the overall task features and text selection. The final part of this concluding chapter will consider some possible directions for future research in relation to using reading-into-writing tasks to assess writing from source at the levels of B2 and C1.

8.1 Summary of major findings

Contextual parameters for reading-into-writing tasks to assess academic writing

To consolidate the empirical evidence reported in this volume, we now summarise the major findings of Study 1, Study 2 and Study 3 in relation to the three aspects (context, cognitive and criterion-related) of the construct of reading-into-writing. As described in Section 4.1, an initial small-scale task survey indicated that essays and reports are commonly assigned to students in the context of this study, i.e. academic writing at the levels of B2 and C1 at

Conclusions and recommendations

a British university. Therefore, a *report* task and an *essay* task were sampled to represent the predominant real-life academic writing tasks in this study. Two formats of reading-into-writing test (Test Task A and Test Task B) were sampled from a list of standardised language tests (see Table 3.1). The overall task features of the sampled reading-into-writing real-life and test tasks were evaluated by 10 expert panel judges (for the detailed procedures, see Section 4.2).

As set out in Section 5.1, we now highlight the main findings of Study 1 in relation to the overall task features. Regarding the *genre*, there was a clear agreement from the judges that Real-life Task A was an essay task and Real-life Task B was a report task. However, the genre of the test tasks was to some extent artificial as both test tasks required students to produce an essay. The judges made an observation that each test task incorporated some features of other genres, and felt that the real-life tasks did not present a very clear *purpose of writing*. Both Test Task A and Test Task B received higher ratings for clarity of task purpose than the real-life tasks. Nevertheless, it is important to consider the fact that students in real-life academic contexts are given plenty of opportunities to clarify any unclear information whereas test takers do not usually have the same opportunities under test conditions.

While the *academic* and *professional topic domains* were dominant in the sampled real-life tasks, Test Task A was considered to be in the *academic* and *social domains* while Test Task B fell into the *professional* and *social domains*. Regarding the *scope of interaction between input and output* imposed on the writer, the real-life tasks were knowledge transforming tasks which required high-level processes. Both reading-into-writing tasks required the test takers to transform the ideas by selecting, organising and summarising relevant ideas from the input sources as well as evaluating different points of view. According to the judges, the test tasks did not require test takers to interpret, evaluate, and apply ideas in context to the extent that the real-life tasks did. However, they considered the level of cognitive demands of the test tasks to be appropriate under the test conditions.

Both real-life tasks required students to perform a range of *language functions*. Core language functions, those that were agreed by two or more pairs of the judges, required by the two real-life tasks included *describing, defining, reasoning, citing sources, evaluating, synthesising* and *expressing personal views*. In addition, the report task required the functions of *illustrating visuals, predicting* and *recommending,* whereas the essay task required the functions of *persuading* and *summarising*. A majority of these language functions identified as necessary for the completion of the real-life academic writing tasks were also required by the two reading-into-writing test tasks. As agreed by two or more pairs of the judges, Test Task A required test takers to perform *expressing personal views, summarising, citing sources, evaluating, recommending, reasoning, synthesising* and *describing*. Test Task B required test takers to perform, mostly necessarily, *reasoning, summarising, expressing personal viewpoints, evaluating, recommending, synthesising* and *illustrating visuals*.

As set out in Section 5.1, the real-life tasks were rated towards the positive end of a 5-point scale (1=unclear, 5=clear) *clarity of audience* and *clarity of marking criteria*. Both Test Task A and Test Task B received higher ratings for clarity of audience than the real-life tasks. The judges considered that the real-life academic writing tasks provided very detailed criteria (the report task scoring 4.5 and the essay task scoring 4.6 out of 5.0). The rating of the clarity of marking criteria for Test Task A (3.8) was slightly lower than the real-life tasks' ratings, whereas Test Task B scored 4.6. Shaw and Weir (2007:71) argued strongly for the importance of providing clear and unambiguous information on the intended audience and marking criteria in any valid writing test. The results of Study 1 showed that the two reading-into-writing test tasks functioned well with regard to clarity of task purpose.

Having summarised the overall task features, we will now highlight the main findings about the complexity of the input materials of the reading-into-writing tasks, as reported in Section 5.2. In line with previous studies which showed that most academic writing tasks involve integration of external reading materials (Bridgeman and Carlson 1983, Carson 2001, Grabe 2003, Horowitz 1986a, 1986b, Johns 1993, Weir 1983), the two sampled real-life tasks (essay and report) required students to write based upon *multiple texts* and *non-verbal materials*, though integration of non-verbal materials seems to be more essential for the completion of the report task than the essay task. In addition, the real-life input texts contained a variety of *input genres*, such as news/magazine articles, journal articles and book chapters, and different non-verbal materials, such as graphs, tables, pictures and diagrams. One of the most heavily criticised aspects of the use of independent writing-only tasks to assess academic writing ability is that such tasks lack authenticity as they do not engage test takers in making use of any reading materials; and therefore, all corresponding cognitive processes of integrating external resources into written production would not be assessed (Carson 2001, Hamp-Lyons and Kroll 1997, Johns 1993, Johns and Mayes 1990, Plakans 2008, 2010, Weigle 2002). The results of Study 1 showed that Test Task A replicated the real-life academic performance conditions by requiring the test takers to write based upon two essays, whereas Test Task B required the test takers to write based upon one report and one news article, each passage containing a diagram. In addition to genre, the difficulty level of a reading-into-writing task would also be affected by the *discourse mode* of the input texts (Parodi 2007). The results showed that the real-life input texts contained a combination of *expository* and *argumentative/evaluative* texts, whereas the reading-into-writing test tasks limited their input texts to be either *expository* or *argumentative*. Test Task A required test takers to summarise argumentative texts while Test Task B required test takers to summarise expository texts. As argued by Brewer

(1980), the cognitive demands of integrating expository and argumentative texts are different. Integration of expository texts would normally require the processes of constructing induction, classification and comparison, whereas integrating argumentative texts would normally require a reader to establish the author's position, reasons, supporting evidence and counterarguments. As students are required to integrate *expository* and *argumentative* texts in real-life academic contexts, academic writing tests should sample both discourse modes in their tasks. In addition, based on the ratings of a 5-point scale on the *concreteness of ideas* (1=abstract, 5=concrete) and the *explicitness of textual organisation* (1=inexplicit, 5=explicit), ideas in the reading-into-writing test input texts were regarded as noticeably more concrete and more explicitly organised than the content of the real-life input texts.

We will now summarise the findings of the complexity of input texts analysed by automated textual analysis tools.

Linguistic complexity of input texts

As described in Section 4.2, this study built on the automated textual analysis procedures employed in recent studies (e.g. Green et al 2010, Green et al 2012, Weir 2012, Wu 2014) in the language testing literature to analyse the *lexical complexity*, *syntactic complexity* and *degree of cohesion* of the real-life input texts and the reading-into-writing test tasks. The results, as set out in Section 5.2, revealed very specific information about the level of lexical complexity, syntactic complexity and degree of cohesion of the real-life input texts in terms of a set of carefully selected automated textual analysis indices (also see Table 5.2).

These indices on the real-life input texts were compared descriptively with those obtained in Green et al's (2010) study on the textual features of undergraduate reading texts to better understand the level of the real-life input texts. Generally speaking, the difficulty level of the input texts, which the participants in this study integrated in their writing assignments, was close to those undergraduate coursebook texts in Green et al's study (2010). However, the results suggested three areas of discrepancy in the linguistic features between the real-life input texts and undergraduate coursebook texts (for the detailed statistics see Table 5.3):

- the real-life input texts contained more frequent words (the first 1,000 and the first 2,000) and fewer low-frequency words than the undergraduate texts
- the real-life input texts contained slightly more *words before the main verbs of the main clauses* than the undergraduate texts, and a slightly lower density of connectives (*logical operator incidence score*) than the undergraduate texts

- adjacent sentences in the real-life input texts seemed to be less conceptually similar than those in the undergraduate coursebook texts.

Based on descriptive statistics, the findings suggested some distinctive features of the texts which were used for general study purposes and those for writing purposes in real-life academic contexts. Real-life input texts for academic writing sampled in this study were slightly more challenging in syntactic features but less challenging in word frequency than the undergraduate coursebook texts analysed in Green et al's (2010) study. While further evidence is needed to confirm the results, the findings might provide insights for test developers when they develop input texts in reading-into-writing tests and those in reading comprehension tests.

We now summarise the results of the complexity levels of the real-life and test task input texts. The difficulty level of sampled Test Task A input texts was comparable to the level of the real-life input texts, in terms of lexical complexity (as indicated by the proportion of first 1,000 frequency words, proportion of first 2,000 frequency words, proportion of academic words, frequency level of content words, average syllables per word and type-token ratio (TTR) of all content words), syntactic complexity (as indicated by the average sentence length, mean number of words before the main verb in verb phrases and proportion of logical operators), and degree of text cohesion (as indicated by the percentage of adjacent sentences with one or more repeated arguments, word stems, content words, proportion of adjacent anaphor references, and adjacent semantic similarity). A few indices suggested that Test Task A input texts were more challenging than the real-life input texts in terms of lexical complexity due to a higher proportion of low-frequency words, but less challenging than the real-life input texts in terms of syntactic complexity due to a higher similarity of sentence structures and a lower average number of modifiers per noun phrase in the texts. Recommendations are further discussed in Section 8.4.

Due to the small number of testlets available for Test Task B, only descriptive statistical analysis was performed on the textual indices between Test Task B and real-life input texts. Results suggested that the Test Task B input texts appeared to be more challenging than the real-life input texts in terms of most lexical features and syntactic features, but were more cohesive than the real-life input texts. In terms of the lexical complexity, even though Test Task B input texts contained a slightly higher proportion of high-frequency words than the real-life input texts, Test Task B input texts had a higher proportion of academic words and low-frequency words and a higher proportion of unique content words (TTR). In terms of syntactic complexity, it seemed to be more demanding to process the noun phrases and to sort out the logical connections between ideas in the Test Task B input texts than the real-life input texts. Nevertheless, the results of the text cohesion indices indicated that it would be easier to process the main themes in Test Task B input texts than in the real-life input texts.

Many researchers argued that, as far as academic writing is concerned, the integrated reading-into-writing test type is perhaps the most valid task type to simulate real-life writing conditions (Hamp-Lyons and Kroll 1996, Plakans 2008, Weigle 2004, Weir, Vidaković et al 2013). The findings of Study 1 showed that the two reading-into-writing test tasks had good context validity as they largely resembled the real-life academic writing tasks in terms of the overall task setting and input text features.

Cognitive processes essential for reading-into-writing

Having summarised the results of Study 1, we will highlight the key findings of Study 2. The second strand of the research investigated the cognitive processes employed by 219 participants on two real-life academic writing tasks and two reading-into-writing test tasks through a carefully developed and validated WPQ. A total of 443 questionnaires were collected regarding real-life and test conditions in the study – 70 questionnaires on the real-life essay task, 73 on the real-life report task, 160 on the reading-into-writing Test Task A (essay task with multiple verbal inputs), and 140 on the reading-into-writing Test Task B (essay task with multiple verbal and non-verbal inputs). Results collected from the two real-life academic writing tasks provided empirical evidence of the target cognitive processes to be measured in an academic writing test in terms of explicit cognitive parameters. Results collected from the two reading-into-writing test tasks revealed the extent to which the integrated task type activated these cognitive processes in the same manner as they were activated by the real-life academic writing tasks. Overall, both reading-into-writing test tasks demonstrated good cognitive validity. The results are summarised below.

Based upon the literature review, as set out in Section 2.3, writers normally go through several cognitive phases when they write from sources, though the phases can be overlapping or looping back. The study considers the following five phases to be most relevant to the discussion of academic writing: *conceptualisation*, *meaning construction, organising, translation,* and *monitoring and revising* (Field 2004, Kellogg 1994, Shaw and Weir 2007). Considering the constraints of the questionnaire, this study focused broadly on the phases which are more metacognitive (i.e. easier to be self-reported) and did not investigate the processes of translation and micro-planning. Although there is a rich body of research on the cognitive processes involved in each of these cognitive phases (e.g. Flower et al 1990, Hayes 1996, Hayes and Flower 1983, Kellogg 1994, 1996, Khalifa and Weir 2009, Shaw and Weir 2007, Spivey, 1990, 1991, 1997, Spivey and King 1989), we still lack a comprehensive model which accounts for the processes involved in writing from sources, especially in the L2 contexts (Hirvela 2004). Building upon these studies, this study investigated the underlying structure of the cognitive processes activated within each cognitive phase by two real-life academic writing tasks by EFA.

The results showed that the hypothesised academic writing phases arising from the literature review were largely supported by the statistical analysis of the questionnaire data collected in this study. Each academic writing phase activated under the real-life academic conditions involved two or more distinct yet correlated underlying cognitive processes. The conceptualisation phase involved the processes of planning and constructing task representation, and reconstructing writing plans. The meaning construction phase involved three underlying processes: careful reading, search reading, and connecting and generating ideas. The organising phase involved the processes of organising intertextual relationships between ideas and organising ideas in a textual structure. Finally there was a clear distinction between the monitoring and revising processes during and after text production at both low and high levels. This study considers that these 11 cognitive processes involved in the four cognitive phases would be appropriate as the target cognitive processes for a valid academic writing test.

Having identified the target cognitive parameters, the study investigated whether these parameters could help to distinguish the higher-scoring and lower-scoring writers. Shaw and Weir (2007) argued that when identifying the cognitive parameters to be examined in a test, it is important to demonstrate 'how writers at different levels would employ these cognitive processes with 'educationally significant differences' (2007:142). The results showed that the high-scoring students reported employing eight of the 11 cognitive processes (i.e. *planning and constructing task representation, careful reading, search reading, connecting and generating ideas, organising intertextual relationships between ideas, organising ideas in a textual structure, lower-level monitoring and revising during text production* and *higher-level monitoring and revising during text production*) more than the low-scoring group. Six of the differences were statistically significant. The findings that the high-scoring participants employed most of these processes more than the low-scoring participants on the real-life tasks add further support to the case for considering these 11 cognitive processes as the target cognitive process parameters for a valid academic writing test.

The study then investigated whether these cognitive parameters could also distinguish processes employed by high-scoring writers from those by low-scoring writers on the two sample reading-into-writing test tasks. The results showed that, on Test Task A, the high-scoring participants reported employing six of the processes (which included *reconstructing writing plans, search reading, organising ideas in a textual structure, lower-level monitoring and revising during text production, lower-level monitoring and revising after text production* and *higher-level monitoring and revising after text production*)

Conclusions and recommendations

more than the low-scoring group, though all differences obtained were non-significant (p>0.05). It should be noted that, as mentioned in Chapter 3, Test Task A was designed to indicate whether the test takers had reached a particular level, i.e. C1 in this context. Most (87.2%) of the participants in this study were at B2 level, as indicated by their IELTS scores. The profile of the participants might have limited the effectiveness of these 11 cognitive parameters distinguishing the processes reported by high-scoring and low-scoring writers on Test Task A. Regarding Test Task B, the high-scoring participants reported employing nine of the cognitive processes more than the low-scoring group. The differences of seven processes (which included *planning and constructing task representation, search reading, organising intertextual relationships between ideas,* and the four *monitoring and revising* processes) between the two groups were significant (p<0.05).

Any writing test tasks, whether independent or integrated, which are cognitively valid should elicit from test takers the cognitive processes which they would normally employ in non-test conditions. In addition, Shaw and Weir (2007:142) emphasised that valid cognitive parameters identified should also be able to demonstrate how writers at different levels would employ them differently. The final step was therefore to examine the extent to which the 11 cognitive processes sufficiently resembled the cognitive processes which the writers used in non-test conditions.

The analysis took level of performance into consideration and showed that both reading-into-writing test tasks were able to elicit from high-scoring and low-scoring participants most of the cognitive processes to a similar extent as they did when composing from sources in real life.

However, the middle group showed greater discrepancy in how they employed these processes between the test and real-life conditions. They tended to employ some processes more in the real-life conditions than the test conditions. They employed the processes of *conceptualisation* and all *monitoring and revising* processes significantly less on Test Task A than on real-life tasks.

They employed the processes of *connecting and generating ideas, low-level monitoring and revising after text production* and *higher-level monitoring and revising after text production* significantly less on Test Task B than on real-life tasks. When compared to the high-scoring group, the middle-achieving group might not be able to employ all processes with full automaticity as they were at the transitional stage of developing their academic writing ability. Due to limited cognitive capacity, they may need more time to complete the processes. It would be essential in future research to investigate why, under test conditions, the middle group employed some of the real-life processes but not others on these two types of reading-into-writing tasks. Recommendations for further research will be discussed later.

Understanding relations between test and real-life performance

Four points of reference (i.e. two writing tasks, one in-class test and one end-of-term case study examination) were selected for the last strand of investigation. Test Task A scores correlated significantly with the mean real-life scores at a moderate level of $r(158)=0.31$, $p>0.01$, explaining 9.36% variance of the real-life performances. Test Task B scores correlated significantly with their mean real-life scores at a moderate level of $r(138)=0.38$, $p>0.01$, explaining 14.36% variance of the real-life performances. The correlations between Test Task A scores and academic performance, and between Test Task B scores and academic performance reported in this study are apparently better than most previously reported figures in the literature.

The patterns of the correlations between the two reading-into-writing test scores and academic performance were very similar. The two reading-into-writing test scores seemed to be able to 'predict' performance in the target context better at high and low levels than at the medium level. In addition, the reading-into-writing test scores seemed to be able to predict academic outcome at the comparatively high and low levels, i.e. Grade B and Grade D in this study.

Nevertheless, the results showed that academic writing ability might have limited impact on medium-level academic performance. Therefore, any high-stakes decisions for these medium-level test takers need to be made with extra caution, and supported by other forms of evidence.

The results of the correlations between test scores and real-life scores not only reviewed a general pattern concerning the validity of the two reading-into-writing test tasks in predicting academic performance, but also indicated how score interpretation can be improved to fulfil the test purposes. The latest UKBA regulations require students who wish to apply to study at the level of Bachelor's degree in the UK under Tier 4 (General) of a points-based system to have a minimum of Level B2 of the CEFR (UK Border Agency 2013). Results on Test Task A (i.e. GEPT Advanced test) using a pass/fail dichotomy might no longer be entirely appropriate for university entry purposes. It would seem more appropriate to adjust the score reporting method on GEPT Advanced to indicate the test takers who have reached the minimum threshold of English requirement for higher education in the UK, i.e. B2 of the CEFR. The results of this study showed that academic performance, especially at the levels of Grades B and D, could be predicted by different score ranges on Test Task A.

On the other hand, Test Task B was designed to indicate the test takers' need for academic writing support. As mentioned previously, a score of 8 and 9 out of 9 indicates no need for academic writing support, a score of 6 and 7 indicates a low-level need for academic writing intervention, whereas a score of 5 or below indicates a high-level need for academic writing intervention. Nevertheless, the results of this study seemed to suggest that these cut-off scores of Test Task B

Conclusions and recommendations

which indicate the different levels of academic writing support required might not be the most effective. Based on the correlation pattern between Test Task B and real-life performance, most participants who scored 7 or 8 tended to achieve an overall Grade B on the real-life writing tasks. Therefore, a score of 7 or above seemed to indicate no need for academic writing support. In addition, most participants who got a total score of 2.5 to 3.5 on Test Task B achieved an overall Grade D on the selected real-life tasks. Therefore, a score of 4 or below seemed to indicate a high-level need for academic writing intervention. Evidence in future research is required to confirm these.

8.2 Towards a framework for reading-into-writing at B2/C1 levels

To the best of the author's knowledge, the research reported in this volume is the first study to validate two types of operationalised reading-into-writing test tasks by 1) comparing the contextual features of the test tasks with those of the real-life academic writing tasks, 2) comparing the cognitive processes which they elicit from test takers with the cognitive processes elicited by the real-life academic writing tasks, and 3) investigating the relationships between the test scores and academic outcomes.

The three strands of investigation (Study 1, Study 2 and Study 3) have added valuable empirical information of the construct of writing from sources at the B2 and C1 levels. Reading-into-writing tasks at the B2 and C1 levels possess a unique set of contextual and cognitive parameters which are not the same as those defined in the independent reading tests (e.g. Khalifa and Weir 2009) or independent writing tests (e.g. Shaw and Weir 2007). This means test developers, university admissions officers and other stakeholders need to consider the role of integrated reading-into-writing tasks as against independent reading tasks and independent writing tasks in assessing academic skills, if they would like to be more certain of their students' ability to cope with academic writing.

As set out in Section 3.3, the research reported in this volume was fuelled by a desire to expand Weir's (2005a) socio-cognitive test development and validation framework from its current applications in independent to integrated language skills. Weir's framework has been adopted by the English Profile, and thus is influencing large-scale projects worldwide, e.g. the Japanese adaptation of the CEFR for their national English language education system (Japanese Grants-in-Aid for Scientific Research); and the former Yugoslav Republic of Macedonia (FYROM) syllabus framework for Modern Foreign Languages (TEMPUS IV). As described in Section 1.1, the aims of the English Profile are to inform practical task design in pedagogy, materials development and curriculum planning worldwide, as well as supporting effective teaching and learning at different educational levels. Therefore, by attempting to build a framework for reading-into-writing based upon Weir's work, the research reported in this volume also contributes to the English Profile, which lacks a description of reading-into-writing skills. Based on a synthesis of the literature of reading-into-writing, as reviewed in Chapters 2 and 3, as well as the empirical evidence reported in Chapters 5 to 7, we propose a framework for reading-into-writing to define the construct of reading-into-writing in terms of explicit contextual and cognitive parameters and a reference of the predictive power to real-life academic performance (see Table 8.1).

The explicit contextual and cognitive parameters and the level of predictive power of reading-into-writing presented in Table 8.1 were developed based on both theoretical foundations and empirical evidence. The framework for reading-into-writing contributes to 1) clarifying the nature of academic reading-into-writing skills, particularly the criterial task features and cognitive processes distinguishing academic skills at CEFR Level B2 or above (this would potentially have an important impact on major international test providers, helping them to achieve test quality to secure recognition and accreditation); and to 2) enhancing the international higher education experience through clearer specification of academic English writing skills and through improving assessment products and practice. It is hoped that the framework, which has good theoretical and practical value, will lead to more accurate assessment of students' academic writing abilities at the CEFR Levels B2 and C1. This is vitally important to students and their receiving institutions because the development of more valid assessment tasks will lead to improved selection/gatekeeping procedures for entry to academic and commercial institutions, and also to better-targeted remedial language instruction where needed.

Next we will provide specific recommendations regarding how this framework for reading-into-writing contributes to expanding the CEFR illustrative descriptors and better test designs, followed by recommendations for future research in the area.

8.3 Recommendations for expanding the CEFR illustrative descriptors

As described in Section 1.1, the CEFR plays a significant role in the field of language testing as it has become a norm for high-stakes language tests to be aligned to the CEFR (Harsch and Hartig 2015). While standard setting of aligning tests to the CEFR is usually performed in an *a posteriori* fashion, the CEFR is also increasingly used during test development and item writing as a point of reference of different communicative skills and linguistic competencies. However, the limitations of using the CEFR scales in developing language tests have been discussed in the literature (e.g. Fulcher 2004, Weir 2005b). Among them, we highlight two points observed by Weir (2005b:282):

Conclusions and recommendations

- the scales are premised on an incomplete and unevenly applied range of contextual variables/performance conditions
- little account is taken of the nature of cognitive processing at different levels of ability.

Table 8.1 A framework for integrated reading-into-writing at the levels of B2 and C1

Contextual parameters
Overall task setting
Time and length
Purpose
Topic domain
• Academic
• Professional
Genre (e.g. essay, report, summary)
Scope of interaction between input and output
• Organising ideas from different sources
• Transforming ideas from different sources
Language functions to perform
• e.g., describing, defining, reasoning, illustrating visuals, citing sources, evaluating, predicting, recommending, synthesising, expressing personal views, summarising, reasoning
Clarity of intended reader
Knowledge of criteria
• Contents (integration and transformation of ideas)
• Structure
• Language (use of sources)
Input text features
Input format (e.g. single, multiple, text-based, graph-based inputs)
Genre (e.g. articles, reports, case studies, abstracts, proposals)
Non-verbal input (e.g. diagrams, tables, charts)
Discourse mode
• Argumentative
• Expository
Concreteness of ideas
Explicitness of textual organisation
Lexical complexity
• High-frequency words (K1)
• High-frequency words (K1 + K2)
• Academic words
• Low-frequency words (Offlist)
• Log frequency content words
• Average syllables per word
• Type-token ratio (TTR) (content words)
Syntactic complexity
• Average words per sentence
• Logical operator incidence score
• Mean number of modifiers per noun phrase
• Mean number words before the main clause in sentences
• Sentence syntax similarity

173

Defining Integrated Reading-into-Writing Constructs

Table 8.1 (continued)

Contextual parameters

Degree of cohesion
- Adjacent overlap argument
- Adjacent overlap stem
- Adjacent overlap content word
- Proportion of adjacent anaphor references
- Adjacent semantic similarity (LSA)

Cognitive parameters

Cognitive phases	Cognitive processes
Conceptualisation	• Macro-planning and constructing task representations
	• Reconstruction of writing plans
Meaning construction	• Careful reading
	• Search reading
	• Connecting and generating ideas
Translation and micro-planning[1]	• Translating
	• Micro-planning
Organising	• Organising intertextual relationships between ideas
	• Organising ideas in a textual structure
Monitoring and revising	• Lower-level monitoring and revising during text production
	• Lower-level monitoring and revising after text production
	• Higher-level monitoring and revising during text production
	• Higher-level monitoring and revising after text production

Predictive validity of reading-into-writing test tasks
Correlations between Test Task A (essay with multiple verbal inputs) scores and academic performance: $r=0.31$ ($p<0.01$)
Correlations between Test Task B (essay with multiple non-verbal inputs) scores and academic performance: $r=0.38$ ($p<0.01$)

Another limitation of the CEFR is that its speaking scales are more developed than those of the other three skills and there is limited coverage of integrated reading-into-writing skills. As described in Chapter 2, regarding written production, the current CEFR illustrative scales only covered *overall written production*, *creative writing*, and *reports and essays*. There is a need to enhance the CEFR scales in relation to how language users write from sources. A companion volume to the CEFR is being prepared to extend the notion of mediation, which would be relevant to the integrated constructs.

When doing so, we have taken account of Weir's (2005b) views of the CEFR's lack of attention to the cognitive processes involved in different language skills and its insufficient description of the contexts in which these activities take place. Based on the findings of Study 2 reported in Chapter 6 as well as the cognitive parameters in the framework for reading-into-writing in Table 8.1, we put forward a list of descriptors which might be useful to

---

1 The processes of translation and micro-planning were not investigated in this study (for reasons, see Chapter 5).

describe the reading-into-writing processes language users at B2 or above use when they write from sources in academic contexts, as follows:

Planning and constructing task representation
- I can understand the task demands and context well.
- I can plan what I need to write to make my text relevant and adequate to the task.
- I can plan according to the purpose of writing.
- I can plan about how my text would suit the expectations of the intended reader.
- I can evaluate my understanding of the task during my writing.

Reconstructing writing plans
- I can adjust my writing plans, if necessary, based on what I read from the source texts.
- I can adjust my writing plans, if necessary, while writing.

Search reading
- I can search quickly for part(s) of the texts which might help complete the task.
- I can take notes on or underline the important ideas in the source texts.
- I can focus on part(s) of the texts which are relevant to the task.

Careful reading
- I can read through the sources to understand the main ideas.
- I can read the sources carefully for a sustained interpretation of the materials.

Connecting and generating ideas
- I can develop a better understanding of the topic from the reading sources.
- I can connect the important ideas in the source texts to what I know already.
- I can develop new interpretations or ideas while writing.
- I can make further connections across the source texts while writing.

Organising textual/intertextual relationships between ideas
- I can organise the main ideas in each source based on how they relate to each other.

Defining Integrated Reading-into-Writing Constructs

- I can prioritise the ideas from different sources in relation to their importance to the task.
- I can organise the main ideas across the source texts based on how they relate to each other.

Organising ideas in a textual structure

- I can structure main ideas of my text before writing.
- I can organise my ideas as I write.
- I can remove ideas which are irrelevant, redundant or repetitive from the text.
- I can recombine or reorder some ideas so that they fit the structure of my writing.

Monitoring and revising during and after writing

- I can check that the quotations are properly made.
- I can check that I have put the ideas of the source texts into my own words.
- I can check the accuracy and range of the sentence structures.
- I can check the appropriateness and range of vocabulary.
- I can check that my text is coherent.
- I can check that my text is relevant.
- I can check that my text is well organised.
- I can check that I have included my own viewpoint on the topic after writing.
- I can check that I included all appropriate main ideas from the source texts.
- I can check the possible effect of my writing on the intended reader.

These proposed descriptors are by no means a complete inclusion of all reading-into-writing processes involved in writing from sources in academic contexts. Nevertheless, they could be useful as a starting point to fill the gaps of the current CEFR in describing learner proficiency in integrated reading-into-writing skills at CEFR Level B2 and above. We have reasonable confidence of the validity of these descriptors because:

- They were derived from a synthesis of previous literature (for details see Chapter 2).
- They were validated by empirical evidence collected in a real-life academic context and their underlying structure was indicated by Exploratory Factor Analyses (for details see Section 6.1).
- According to the results of statistical analyses, these descriptors, at least to some extent, distinguish writers at different levels of performance

Conclusions and recommendations

(i.e. high-, middle- and low-scoring groups) in both real-life and test conditions. The results showed that the high-scoring students employed most of these cognitive processes more frequently than the low-scoring students (for details see Chapter 6).

Therefore, we believe that these descriptors, to some degree, characterise the reading-into-writing processes of language users at the CEFR Level B2 or above in academic contexts. Nevertheless, research might be needed to align these descriptors to the current CEFR written production descriptors. Other research is needed to determine which of these descriptors best signify the progression from B2 to C1. In addition, to complete the illustrative scale of integrated reading-into-writing/writing from sources, more research is needed to investigate the learners' reading-into-writing processes at the other CEFR levels, not all of which have yet been sufficiently addressed. Recommendations for future research in the area will be provided in Section 8.3.

8.4 Recommendations for future task design

A clear explication of the cognitive and contextual demands of academic writing skills is critical for developing tasks to teach and assess such skills. Urquhart and Weir (1998:172) argued that appropriate texts need to be selected for readers to perform the target reading activities developed for them. Their notion is also applicable for our discussion of reading-into-writing here. Language testers and EAP teachers need to be familiar with the features of the reading-into-writing tasks which the students will encounter in their academic studies.

We have identified a set of contextual parameters which are useful to describe the features of reading-into-writing tasks in academic contexts (for details see Chapter 5 and the framework for reading-into-writing in Table 8.1). Based on the discrepancies between real-life academic writing tasks and reading-into-writing test tasks observed in Study 1, we provide practical advice to help item writers, teachers or other English Profile users to select and modify reading materials, and develop valid reading-into-writing tasks that reflect target language at the appropriate levels.

1. Consider appropriate time and length

In real-life conditions, students usually have greater flexibility in how much time they spend on planning, reading, rereading, writing and revising. However, under test conditions, test takers would need to manage their time allocation carefully in order to complete the task. For example, the findings in this volume indicate that some students spent too much time on reading and are over-engaged in careful reading processes. We feel that it would be useful

Defining Integrated Reading-into-Writing Constructs

for test developers to provide some guidelines on time management in reading-into-writing test tasks for students and their teachers. The length of each input text and the expected output would need to be determined with care and consideration of the target processes. For example, assuming all other variables being equal, a reading-into-writing task which requires students to summarise facts and details might have longer input texts than one which requires a summary of different arguments.

2. Incorporate a wider range of other common academic writing genres

'Essay' is arguably the most popular genre used in reading-into-writing/writing tests. While essay is one of the most common academic writing genres, there are two issues raised. First, as observed by the judges in Study 1, the essay genre used in most tests is almost an artificial form of 'language test essay'. Second, other common academic writing genres, such as report, critical review and summary, are mostly underrepresented.

3. Avoid the use of topics in the social domain

While topics in academic and professional domains should be most appropriate for EAP reading-into-writing, the judges felt that both test tasks contained rather general contents, which were usually connected to the social domain, in their input texts. As argued in Chapter 5, it is not always straightforward to determine the topic domain of a reading-into-writing task. Nevertheless, while EAP writing tests should not include topics which involve contents at a high level of specific knowledge, item writers should avoid sourcing materials from the social domain.

4. Incorporate a wider range of language functions, e.g. defining, illustrating visuals, recommending

As observed in Study 1, while the two reading-into-writing test tasks required students to perform some core language functions, both required fewer functions than the real-life tasks did. It is important to cover these language functions, which is part of the academic writing construct, even though not all functions need to be tested in every single testlet.

5. Incorporate a wider range of input genres and discourse modes

Another challenge of developing valid reading-into-writing tasks is the selection of reading inputs which have sufficient idea units within quite a tight word limit and are at the appropriate level for comprehension. Item writers need to be aware of the possible effects of their manipulating input texts on task complexity.

Real-life academic writing tasks always require students to integrate contents from a range of input genres with varied discourse modes. However, due to the need for standardisation, the range of the input genres and types of texts of test tasks are usually limited. For example, all input texts on Test Task A (from 10 testlets) were regarded as belonging to a simplified version of the argumentative essay genre whereas Test Task B (from one testlet) contained texts belonging to simplified versions of the expository report and news/magazine article genre. It is important for test developers to monitor if a sufficient range of the input genres and text types is represented across the testlets.

6. Be aware of the impact on lexical complexity when manipulating the idea units

The findings showed that the lexical complexity of both reading-into-writing test task input texts was more demanding than the real-life input texts. This is likely to be the result of input text manipulation of incorporating sufficient 'idea units' into the input texts with a usually tight word limit. Test Task A input texts had a greater density of *low-frequency words*, mostly proper nouns, than the real-life input texts, whereas Test Task B input texts had a higher proportion of academic words and low-frequency words and a higher TTR of all content words than the real-life input texts. While standardising the text length of the input texts, test developers have to monitor if lexical complexity of the input texts was increased unnecessarily due to the process of text manipulation.

7. Be cautious with the use of cohesive devices

The results of Study 1 suggested that it was less demanding to build the textual representation of the test task input texts than that of the real-life input texts because the test task input texts were more explicitly organised and more cohesive than the real-life input texts. It is reasonable that test task input texts have a higher degree of cohesion than the real-life input texts, so that test takers would be able to process the texts under more demanding conditions, e.g. greater time restrictions. However, a tendency of overusing cohesive devices in the test task input texts was observed. Item writers should avoid relying too much on the use of cohesive devices to improve coherence of the input texts.

Following the specific and practical advice on future task design, we provide some more generic recommendations for researching integrated reading-into-writing in the future.

8.5 Recommendations for future research

The research reported in this volume has extended Weir's socio-cognitive framework from independent language skills to integrated reading-into-writing at the levels of B2 and C1. It is hoped that this represents a solid step towards building a more complete construct definition of reading-into-writing at other CEFR levels also. Before giving some recommendations for further research in the future, we consider the limitations of the current study. The generalisability of the results reported in this volume on 1) the target parameters of the real-life academic writing tasks, and 2) the validation evidence of the two types of reading-into-writing test tasks, is limited for reasons described in the next sections.

Limitations of the current research

Sampling

A total of 219 participants took part in the three validation studies. As indicated by the participants' IELTS Reading and Writing bands, 12.8% of the participants were at C1 level whereas the majority of the participants (87.2%) were at B2 level. While the proficiency level of the participants was considered appropriate for the context of this study, future studies are advised to include more participants at C1. In addition, students' background was homogenous in the sense that they all came from the Business School in the UK academic context. A comparatively homogenous profile of background knowledge was suitable for the cognitive investigation in this study. Nevertheless, future studies are advised to investigate the cognitive processes and test results of students from a variety of disciplinary backgrounds and/or from different national contexts.

We sampled two real-life academic writing tasks and two reading-into-writing test tasks in our investigation. Although the tasks were sampled based on a range of carefully chosen criteria to ensure that they are representative of the wider pool, the sample size remains small.

For the investigation of the input text features, the 10 most-cited input texts were selected for each real-life academic writing task for analysis. Twenty input texts from 10 testlets of Test Task A were analysed. However, at the time of the study, limited test papers of Test Task B were available for analysis. Only two input texts from Test Task B were analysed. Therefore, the results regarding the contextual features of Test Task B should be interpreted as no more than indicative.

Two reading-into-writing task types (i.e. *essay with multiple verbal inputs* and *essay with multiple verbal and non-verbal inputs*) were investigated. Future studies are advised to investigate other reading-into-writing task types, giving priority to those which have not received much attention in the literature, for

Conclusions and recommendations

instance, tasks which require test takers to process multiple reading texts for both the reading comprehension section and writing section.

Lastly, as explained in Chapter 4, the test scores and real-life academic writing scores reported in this study were achieved by standardised scoring procedures administrated by the test providers and the university. Therefore, the results of the predictive validity reported in Chapter 7 need to be interpreted in light of the appropriateness of the scoring procedures used.

Research instruments

In Study 1, we employed the methods of expert judgement and automatic textual analysis to investigate task features but they have their own limitations (for discussion, see for example Green et al 2012, Weir 2012, Wu 2014). Therefore, it is not advisable to use either one of them alone. The procedures for expert judgement of the contextual features of the reading-into-writing tasks were refined based on the experience of the two pilots. Firstly, it is necessary to clarify which part of the tasks the analytic categories in the proforma should be applied to, e.g. the prompt, the input texts, and/or the output. Besides, it appeared that some categories, e.g. cognitive demands, topic domains, concreteness of ideas, required subjective judgement. In order to minimise irregularity, we asked the judges to complete the judgement individually and then discuss their results in pairs. Results arising from the pair discussions instead of individual judgements were reported.

In Study 1, we analysed a set of input texts for each task. We found it more effective to analyse the overall task setting and the features of input texts in two separate expert judgement meetings. As it is well documented that judges might refer to the same criteria with a varying degree (e.g. Engelhard 2009, Longford 1996, Van Nijlen and Janssen 2008), we feel that the analysis of the linguistic complexity of the input texts, especially for lexical and syntactic complexity, should be supplemented by automated textual analysis tools. As demonstrated in Study 1, tools such as CohMetrix and VocabProfile could usefully supplement the expert judgement in comparing features of the test task input texts with those of real-life input texts in a systematic and quantitative manner. Nevertheless, as explained in detail in Chapter 4, some indices were difficult to interpret, repetitive of each other, or not useful or effective in determining the complexity of a text. A careful selection of the indices was essential. Besides, these automatic tools are upgraded regularly. For example, we used CohMetrix version 2.0 in our investigation. The tool was then upgraded to new versions in which substantial changes were made. These changes unfortunately make it difficult to compare the results of this study and previous studies with those of future studies. In addition, CohMetrix has also been criticised for being very opaque because the formulas of some of the devices are not very transparent, and hence reduce the interpretability of the results.

We investigated students' writing processes through the WPQ in Study 2, though think-aloud protocol has been regarded as the most persuasive way of demonstrating the processes employed (for example see Hayes and Flower 1983, Plakans 2010, Spivey 1997). Think-aloud was, however, considered inappropriate and impractical in the context of our investigation due to the large number of participants. Measures were taken to ensure the validity and usefulness of the questionnaire designed. Following the recommendations of Purpura (1998) on the use of cognitive process questionnaires, the questionnaire was developed based upon human information processing theory. In addition, the psychometric characteristics of the questionnaire and the underlying construct validity of the questionnaire were verified by a series of statistical analyses. The questionnaire was constructed paying particular attention to all the processes which seemed to be most relevant to our discussion of the cognitive validity of academic writing from sources. The questionnaire, however well developed, can only seek evidence of the participants' perceptions of what they did. One should, therefore, be cautious of this limitation when interpreting the findings. Future studies should attempt to triangulate the questionnaire data by another instrument, such as post-test interview or keystroke logging.

Besides, as we aimed to investigate the cognitive processes elicited by operationalised reading-into-writing test tasks and real-life academic writing tasks, the mode of writing was not investigated as a variable of the writing process. Both test tasks were paper-based (PB) whereas the real-life test tasks were expected to be mainly computer-based (CB) (even though some participants might have completed the real-life tasks on paper and then typed out the script). Although a large body of research has concluded that student performances across the CB and PB modes can be considered comparable (e.g. Puhan, Boughton and Kim 2007, Taylor, Jamieson, Eignor and Kirsch 1998, Weir et al 2007), we should not assume that the processes involved in the modes are exactly the same. Future studies should investigate how the mode of writing influences the employment of the cognitive processes. For example, PB writing might require more rigid organisational planning, which stronger test takers engage in but the weaker ones often do not. It would also require the rapid creation of graphic handwritten forms. By contrast, CB writing would allow for massive recursive editing and would rely upon a very different process of execution (Severinson Eklundh and Kollberg 2003, Weir et al 2007). Grammatical errors such as spelling can be corrected retrospectively, and therefore immediate accuracy would be far less of an issue.

Directions for future research

To conclude, the research reported in this volume offers an in-depth construct investigation into the theory and practice of using reading-into-writing to

Conclusions and recommendations

assess the ability of academic writing from sources. The findings, to a large extent, supported the context, cognitive and criterion-referenced validity of two reading-into-writing task types (*essay with multiple verbal inputs* and *essay with multiple verbal and non-verbal inputs*). The work has extended Weir's (2005a) socio-cognitive framework to integrated assessment by providing explicit contextual and cognitive parameters to define the construct of reading-into-writing. We hope that the outcomes of this research put us in a better position for describing the salient features of integrated reading-into-writing tasks, identifying the key cognitive processes involved in writing from sources in academic contexts, and understanding the relationships between reading-into-writing test scores and real-life performance. However, this work is by no means finished. As noted by Cumming (2013), the construct of reading-into-writing is complex and multidimensional and it can be utilised at different assessment contexts and for different purposes. We view the work presented in this volume as a starting point to a systematic approach to researching integrated reading-into-writing assessment.

We mentioned some suggestions for follow-up research when we discussed the findings in Chapters 5, 6 and 7. Here we reflect on the key findings presented in this volume and recommend some directions for researching integrated reading-into-writing in the future. The findings identified 11 key processes writers would normally use when they compose from sources in academic writing contexts. Some of the processes can hardly be elicited by most traditional reading comprehension items and impromptu writing tasks. We need to investigate more closely how these reading-into-writing processes influence students' written performance. The outcomes would have important implications for rating scale development.

Based on the findings, a set of Can Do statements which might be useful to describe learners' reading-into-writing abilities at the levels of B2 or above has emerged. On the one hand, more evidence is needed to determine which of these processes would best differentiate between B2 and C1. On the other, further research is needed to investigate learners' reading-into-writing processes at the other CEFR levels. Another particularly important area of the reading-into-writing construct is to understand how learners at different CEFR levels make use of source texts in their writing. Without such evidence, it is difficult to determine the criterial characteristics of integrated reading-into-writing performance at each CEFR level.

Last but not least, there is a need to better understand the impact of different contextual parameters and features of input texts on task level and students' performances. For example, how do we interpret students' reading-into-writing abilities from a performance of *summarising main ideas of an article*, *presenting an argument in response to contrasting viewpoints*, or *reporting an issue from different sources*?

Although the scale of research efforts needed to gain a comprehensive understanding of the construct of reading-into-writing seems pronounced, we believe there is high value in using integrated tasks in teaching and assessing literacy skills at different levels for different purposes.

On a final note, this volume has provided an overview of the literature of reading-into-writing and reported the results of three empirical studies to define the construct of reading-into-writing in academic contexts at the CEFR level of B2 or above. Through establishing a framework for reading-into-writing in this volume, we have clarified the nature of academic reading-into-writing skills in relation to the criterial task features and cognitive processes which distinguish academic skills at the CEFR levels of B2 and C1. It is hoped that the explicit specification of academic reading-into-writing skills provided in this volume will lead to the development of better teaching and assessment tasks for academic writing. We also hope to inspire researchers to contribute to this exciting, but much under-researched, area of integrated language skills.

References and further reading

Ackerman, J M (1990) Reading, writing and knowing: The role of disciplinary knowledge in comprehension and composing, *Research in the Teaching of English* 25 (2), 133–178.
Alderson, J C (2000) *Assessing Reading*, Cambridge: Cambridge University Press.
Alderson, J C (2005) *Diagnosing Foreign Language Proficiency: The Interface Between Learning and Assessment*, London: Continuum.
Alderson, J C, Clapham, C and Wall, D (1995) *Language Test Construction and Evaluation*, Cambridge: Cambridge University Press.
Alderson, J C, Figueras, N, Kuijper, H, Nold, G and Takala, S (2006) Analysing tests of reading and listening in relation to the Common European Framework of Reference: The experience of the Dutch CEFR construct project, *Language Assessment Quarterly* 31 (1), 3–30.
Armbruster, B B, Anderson, T H and Ostertag, J (1987) Does text structure/summarization instruction facilitate learning from expository text? *Reading Research Quarterly* 22 (3), 331–346.
Asencion, Y (2004) *Validation of reading-to-write assessment tasks performed by second language learners*, unpublished PhD dissertation, Northern Arizona University.
Asencion-Delaney, Y (2008) Investigating the reading-to-write construct, *Journal of English for Academic Purposes* 7, 140–150.
Association of Language Testers in Europe (2011) *The CEFR Grid for Writing Tasks 3.1*, available online: /rm.coe.int/16806979e0
Bachman, L F (1990) *Fundamental Considerations in Language Testing*, Oxford: Oxford University Press.
Bachman, L F and Palmer, A S (1996) *Language Testing in Practice*, Oxford: Oxford University Press.
Bachman, L F, Davidson, F, Ryan, K and Choi, I-C (1995) *An Investigation into the Comparability of Two Tests of English as a Foreign Language*, Studies in Language Testing volume 1, Cambridge: UCLES/Cambridge University Press.
Beck, I L, McKeown, M G, Sinatra, M G and Loxterman, J A (1991) Revising social studies text from a text processing perspective: Evidence of improved comprehensibility, *Reading Research Quarterly* 27, 251–276.
Belcher, D and Hirvela, A (2001) *Linking Literacies: Perspectives on L2 Reading-writing Connections*, Ann Arbor: University of Michigan Press.
Bereiter, C and Scardamalia, M (1987) *The Psychology of Written Composition*, Hillsdale: Lawrence Erlbaum Associates.
Biber, D, Conrad, S and Cortes, V (2004) If you look at . . .: Lexical bundles in university teaching and textbooks, *Applied Linguistics* 25, 371–405.
Brewer, W F (1980) Literary theory, rhetoric, and stylistics: Implications for psychology, in Spiro, R J, Bruce, B C and Brewer, W F (Eds) *Theoretical Models and Processes of Reading Comprehension*, Hillsdale: Lawrence Erlbaum Associates, 221–239.
Bridgeman, B and Carlson, S (1983) *Survey of Academic Writing Tasks Required*

of Graduate and Undergraduate Foreign Students, Princeton: Educational Testing Service.
Bridges, G (2010) Demonstrating cognitive validity of IELTS Academic Writing Task 1, *Research Notes* 42, 24–33.
British National Corpus (2007) *British National Corpus*, available online: www.natcorp.ox.ac.uk
Britt, M A and Sommer, J (2004) Facilitating textual integration with macro-structure focusing tasks, *Reading Psychology* 25 (4), 313–339.
Brown, G and Yule, G (1983) *Discourse Analysis*, Cambridge: Cambridge University Press.
Brown, J D, Hilgers, T and Marsella, J (1991) Essay prompts and topics: Minimizing the effect of mean differences, *Written Communication* 8, 533–556.
Bulté, B and Housen, A (2012) Defining and operationalising L2 complexity, in Housen, A, Kuiken, F and Vedder, I (Eds) *Dimensions of L2 Performance and Proficiency*, Amsterdam: John Benjamins Publishing Company, 21–46.
Burtis, P J, Bereiter, C, Scardamalia, M and Tetroe, J (1983) The development of planning in writing, in Kroll, B M and Wells, G (Eds) *Explorations in the Development of Writing*, New York: Wiley, 153–174.
Cambridge University Press (2015) *English Profile: Introducing the CEFR for English*, available online: www.englishprofile.org/images/pdf/theenglishprofilebooklet.pdf
Campbell, C (1990) Writing with others' words: Using background reading text in academic compositions, in Kroll, B (Ed) *Second Language Writing: Research Insights for the Classroom*, Cambridge: Cambridge University Press, 211–230.
Canale, M (1983) From communicative competence to communicative language pedagogy, in Richards, J C and Schmidt, R W (Eds) *Language and Communication*, London: Longman, 2–27.
Carson, J (2001) A task analysis of reading and writing in academic contexts, in Hirvela, A (Ed) *Linking Literacies: Perspectives on L2 Reading-writing Connections*, Ann Arbor: University of Michigan Press, 48–83.
Carson, J and Leki, I (Eds) (1993) *Reading in the Composition Classroom: Second Language Perspectives*, Boston: Heinle and Heinle.
Casey, L B, Miller, N D, Stockton, M B and Justice, W V (2016) Assessing Writing in Elementary Schools: Moving away from a Focus on mechanics, *Language Assessment Quarterly* 13 (1), 42–55.
Chan, S H C (2011) *Demonstrating cognitive validity and face validity of PTE Academic Writing items, Summarize Written Text and Write Essay*, Pearson Research Summaries and Notes, available online: s3.amazonaws.com/files.formstack.com/uploads/1801396/26959953/182961858/26959953_demonstratingcognitiveandfacevalidityofpteacademicwritingitems_2011.pdf
Chan, S H C (2017) Using keystroke logging to understand writers' processes on a reading-into-writing test, *Language Testing in Asia* 7 (1), 1–10.
Chan, S H C, Inoue, C and Taylor, L (2015) Developing rubrics to assess the skill of reading-into-writing: a case study, *Assessing Writing* 26, 20–37.
Chan, S H C, Wu, R Y F and Weir, C J (2014) Examining the context and cognitive validity of the GEPT Advanced Writing Task 1: A comparison with real-life academic writing tasks, *LTTC-GEPT Research Report* 3, 1–89.
Charge, N and Taylor, L (1997) Recent developments in IELTS, *ELT Journal* 51 (4), 374–380.
Cherkes-Julkowski, M, Sharp, S and Stolzenberg, J (1997) *Rethinking Attention Deficit Disorders*, Cambridge: Brookline Books.
Clapham, C (1996) *The Development of IELTS: A Study of the Effect of*

References and further reading

Background on Reading Comprehension, Studies in Language Testing volume 4, Cambridge: UCLES/Cambridge University Press.

Cobb, T (2003) *VocabProfile*, available online: www.lextutor.ca/vp/eng/

Cohen, A (1984) On taking language tests: What the students report, *Language Testing* 1, 70–81.

Cooper, A and Bikowski, D (2007) Writing at the graduate level: What tasks do professors actually require? *Journal of English for Academic Purposes* 6, 206–221.

Cotton, F and Conrow, F (1998) An investigation of the predictive validity of IELTS amongst a group of international students studying at the University of Tasmania, *IELTS Research Reports* 1 (4), 72–115.

Council of Europe (2001) *Common European Framework of Reference for Languages: Learning, Teaching, Assessment*, Cambridge: Cambridge University Press.

Council of Europe (2009) *Relating Language Examinations to the Common European Framework of Reference for Languages: Learning, Teaching, Assessment (CEFR): A Manual*, Strasbourg: Council of Europe.

Council of Europe (2018) *Common European Framework of Reference for Languages: Learning, Teaching, Assessment. Companion Volume with New Descriptors*, Strasbourg: Council of Europe.

Coxhead, A (2000) A new academic wordlist, *TESOL Quarterly* 34 (2), 213–238.

Crossley, S A and McNamara, D S (2010) Cohesion, coherence, and expert evaluations of writing proficiency, in Ohlsson, S and Catrambone, R (Eds) *Proceedings of the 32nd Annual Conference of the Cognitive Science Society*, Austin: Cognitive Science Society, 984–989.

Crossley, S A and McNamara, D S (2012) Predicting second language writing proficiency: The role of cohesion, readability, and lexical difficulty, *Journal of Research in Reading* 35 (2), 115–135.

Crossley, S A, Clevinger, A and Kim, Y (2014) The role of lexical properties and cohesive devices in text integration and their effect on human ratings of speaking proficiency, *Language Assessment Quarterly* 11 (3), 250–270.

Crossley, S A, Greenfield, J and McNamara, D (2008) Assessing text readability using cognitively based indices, *TESOL Quarterly* 42 (3), 475–493.

Crossley, S A, Louwerse, M M, McCarthy, P M and McNamara, D S (2007) A linguistic analysis of simplified and authentic texts, *Modern Language Journal* 91 (2), 15–30.

Cumming, A (1997) The testing of second language writing, in Clapham, C (Ed) *The Encyclopedia of Language and Education Volume 7: Language Assessment*, Dordrecht: Kluwer, 51–63.

Cumming, A (2013) Assessing integrated writing tasks for academic purposes: Promises and perils, *Language Assessment Quarterly* 10 (1), 1–8.

Cumming, A, Grant, L, Mulcahy-Ernt, P and Powers, D E (2004) A teacher-verification study of speaking and writing prototype tasks for a new TOEFL, *Language Testing* 21 (2), 107–145.

Cumming, A, Kantor, R, Baba, K, Erdosy, U, Eouanzoui, K and James, M (2005) Differences in written discourse in independent and integrated prototype tasks for next generation TOEFL, *Assessing Writing* 10, 5–43.

Davies, A (2008) *Assessing Academic English: Testing English Proficiency, 1950–1989 – The IELTS Solution*, Studies in Language Testing volume 23, Cambridge: UCLES/Cambridge University Press.

Davies, A and Criper, C (1988) *ELTS Validation Project Report: English Language Testing Service Research Report 1*, London: British Council/UCLES.

Douglas, D (2000) *Assessing Language for Specific Purposes: Theory and Practice*, Cambridge: Cambridge University Press.

Engelhard, G (2009) Evaluating the judgments of standard-setting panelists using Rasch measurement theory, in Smith, E and Stone, G (Eds) *Criterion-referenced Testing: Practice Analysis to Score Reporting Using Rasch Measurement Models*, Maple Grove: JAM Press, 312–346.

Enright, M, Grabe, W, Koda, K, Mosenthal, P, Mulcahy-Ernt, P and Schedl, M (2000) *TOEFL 2000 Reading Framework: A Working Paper*, TOEFL Monograph MS-17, Princeton: Educational Testing Service.

Esmaeili, H (2002) Reading-to-write reading and writing tasks and ESL students' reading and writing performance in an English language test, *The Canadian Modern Language Review* 58, 599–622.

Eysenck, M W and Keane, M (2005) *Cognitive Psychology* (Fifth edition), Hove: Psychology Press.

Fabrigar, L R, Wegener, D T, MacCallum, R C and Strahan, E J (1999) Evaluating the use of exploratory factor analysis in psychological research, *Psychological Methods* 4 (3) 272–299.

Feak, C and Dobson, B (1996) Building on the impromptu: A source-based writing assessment, *College ESL* 6 (1), 73–84.

Feast, V (2002) The impact of IELTS scores on performance at university, *International Education Journal* 3 (4), 70–89.

Field, J (2004) *Psycholinguistics: The Key Concepts*, London: Routledge.

Field, J (2008) *Listening in the Language Classroom*, Cambridge: Cambridge University Press.

Field, J (2011) Cognitive validity, in Taylor, L (Ed) *Examining Speaking: Research and Practice in Assessing Second Language Speaking,* Studies in Language Testing volume 30, Cambridge: UCLES/Cambridge University Press, 65–111.

Field, J (2013) Cognitive validity, in Geranpayeh, A and Taylor, L (Eds) *Examining Listening: Research and Practice in Assessing Second Language Listening*, Studies in Language Testing volume 35, Cambridge: UCLES/Cambridge University Press, 77–151.

Fitzgerald, J (1987) Research on revision in writing, *Review of Educational Research* 57, 481–506.

Fitzgerald, J and Shanahan, T (2000) Reading and writing relations and their development, *Educational Psychologist* 35 (1), 39–50.

Flower, L S (1990) Reading-to-write: Understanding the task, in Flower, L, Stein, V, Ackerman, J, Kantz, M J, McCormick, K and Peck, W C (Eds) *Reading to Write. Exploring a Cognitive and Social Process*, New York: Oxford University Press, 35–73.

Flower, L S, Hayes, J R, Carey, L, Schriver, K and Stratman, J (1986) Detection, diagnosis and the strategies of revision, *College Composition and Communication* 37 (1), 16–55.

Flower, L S, Stein, V, Ackerman, J, Kantz, M J, McCormick, K and Peck, W C (1990) *Reading-to-write: Exploring a Cognitive and Social Process*, New York: Oxford University Press.

Fulcher, G (2004) Deluded by artifices? The Common European Framework and harmonization, *Language Assessment Quarterly* 1 (4), 253–266.

Fulcher, G (2010) *Practical Language Testing*, London: Hodder Education.

Galbraith, D and Torrance, M (1999) Conceptual processes in writing: From problem solving to text production, in Torrance, M and Galbraith, D (Eds) *Knowing What to Write: Conceptual Processes in Text Production*, Amsterdam: Amsterdam University Press, 1–12.

Gebril, A and Plakans, L (2014) Assembling validity evidence for assessing academic writing: Rater reactions to integrated tasks, *Assessing Writing* 21, 56–73.

Geranpayeh, A and Taylor, L (Eds) (2013) *Examining Listening: Research and Practice in Assessing Second Language Listening,* Studies in Language Testing volume 35, Cambridge: UCLES/Cambridge University Press.

Gernsbacher, M A (1990) *Language Comprehension as Structure Building*, Hillsdale: Lawrence Erlbaum Associates.

Goldman, S R and Rakestraw, J A (2000) Structural aspects of constructing meaning from text, in Kamil, M L, Mosenthal, P B, Pearson, P D and Barr, R (Eds) *Handbook of Reading Research Volume III*, Hillsdale: Lawrence Erlbaum Associates, 311–335.

Gomulicki, B R (1956) Recall as an abstractive process, *Acta Psychologica* 12, 77–94.

Grabe, W (2001) Reading-writing relations: Theoretical perspectives and instructional practices, in Belcher, D and Hirvela, A (Eds) *Linking Literacies: Perspectives on L2 Reading-writing Connections*, Ann Arbor: University of Michigan Press, 15–47.

Grabe, W (2003) Reading and writing relations: Second language perspectives on research and practice, in Kroll, B (Ed) *Exploring the Dynamics of Second Language Writing*, Cambridge: Cambridge University Press, 243–259.

Grabe, W (2009) *Reading in a Second Language: Moving from Theory to Practice*, New York: Cambridge University Press.

Grabe, W and Kaplan, F L (1996) *Theory and Practice of Writing: An Applied Linguistic Perspective*, London: Longman.

Graesser, A C, McNamara, D S and Kulikowich, J M (2011) Coh-Metrix: Providing multilevel analyses of text characteristics, *Educational Researcher* 40 (5), 223–234.

Graesser, A C, Cai, Z, Louwerse, M and Daniel, F (2006) Question Understanding Aid (QUAID): A web facility that helps survey methodologists improve the comprehensibility of questions, *Public Opinion Quarterly* 70, 3–22.

Graesser, A C, McNamara, D, Louwerse, M M and Cai, Z (2004) Coh-Metrix: Analysis of text on cohesion and language, *Behavior Research Methods, Instruments, & Computers* 36 (2), 193–202.

Graham, S (2006) Writing, in Alexander, P A and Winne, P H (Eds) *Handbook of Educational Psychology*, Hillsdale: Lawrence Erlbaum Associates, 457–477.

Graham, S and Harris, K R (1996) Self-regulation and strategy instruction for students who find writing and learning challenging, in Levy, C M and Ransdell, S (Eds) *The Science of Writing: Theories, Methods, Individual Differences and Applications*, Hillsdale: Lawrence Erlbaum Associates, 347–360.

Graham, S and Harris, K (2000) The role of self-regulation and transcription skills in writing and writing development, *Educational Psychologist* 35, 3–12.

Green A (1998) *Verbal Protocol Analysis in Language Testing Research*, Studies in Language Testing volume 5, Cambridge: UCLES/Cambridge University Press.

Green, A (2007) *IELTS Washback in Context: Preparation for Academic Writing in Higher Education,* Studies in Language Testing volume 25, Cambridge: UCLES/Cambridge University Press.

Green, A (2012) *Language Functions Revisited: Theoretical and Empirical Bases for Language Construct Definition Across the Ability Range*, English Profile Studies volume 2, Cambridge: UCLES/Cambridge University Press.

Green, A (2014) *Exploring Language Assessment and Testing: Language in Action*, New York: Routledge.

Green, A, Ünaldi, A and Weir, C J (2010) Empiricism versus connoisseurship: Establishing the appropriacy of texts in tests of academic reading, *Language Testing* 27 (2), 191–211.

Green, A, Weir, C J, Chan, S H C, Field, J, Taylor, L, Bax, S and Nakatsuhara, F (2012) *Textual features of CAE reading texts: CAE texts compared with reading*

texts from FCE, CPE and IELTS and with essential undergraduate textbooks, unpublished research report.
Hale, G, Taylor, C, Bridgeman, B, Carson, J, Kroll, B and Kantor, R (1996) *A Study of Writing Tasks Assigned in Academic Degree Programs*, TOEFL Research Reports RR-95-44, Princeton: Educational Testing Service.
Hamp-Lyons, L and Kroll, B (1996) Issues in ESL writing assessment, *College ESL* 6 (1), 52–72.
Hamp-Lyons, L and Kroll, B (1997) *TOEFL 2000 – Writing: Composition, Community, and Assessment*, TOEFL Monograph 5, Princeton: Educational Testing Service.
Harrison, J and Barker, F (Eds) (2015) *English Profile in Practice*, English Profile Studies volume 5, Cambridge: UCLES/Cambridge University Press.
Harsch, C and Hartig, J (2015) What are we aligning tests to when we report test alignment to the CEFR? *Language Assessment Quarterly* 12 (4), 333–362.
Harsch, C and Rupp, A A (2011) Designing and scaling level-specific writing tasks in alignment with the CEFR: A test-centered approach, *Language Assessment Quarterly* 8 (1), 1–33.
Hartmann, D K (1995) Eight readers reading: The intertextual links of proficient readers reading multiple passages, *Reading Research Quarterly* 30, 520–561.
Hawkins, J A and Filipović, L (2012) *Criterial Features in L2 English: Specifying the Reference Levels of the Common European Framework*, English Profile Studies volume 1, Cambridge: UCLES/Cambridge University Press.
Hayes, J R (1996) A new framework for understanding cognition and affect in writing, in Levy, C M and Ransdell, S (Eds) *The Science of Writing: Theories, Methods, Individual Differences, and Applications*, Hillsdale: Lawrence Erlbaum Associates, 1–28.
Hayes, J R and Flower, L (1980) Identifying the organisation of writing processes, in Gregg, L W and Steinberg, E R (Eds) *Cognitive Processes in Writing*, Hillsdale: Lawrence Erlbaum Associates, 3–30.
Hayes, J R and Flower, L (1983) Uncovering cognitive processes in writing: An introduction to protocol analysis, in Mosenthal, P, Tamor, L and Walmsley, S (Eds) *Research on Writing: Principles and Methods*, New York: Longman, 207–220.
Hirvela, A (2004) *Connecting Reading and Writing in Second Language Writing Instruction*, Ann Arbor: University of Michigan Press.
Horowitz, D M (1986a) Essay examination prompts and the teaching of academic teaching, *English for Specific Purposes* 5, 107–120.
Horowitz, D M (1986b) What professors actually require: Academic tasks for the ESL classroom, *TESOL Quarterly* 20, 445–460.
Horowitz, D M (1991) ESL writing assessments: Contradictions and resolutions, in Hamp-Lyons, L (Ed) *Assessing Second Language Writing in Academic Contexts*, Norwood: Ablex, 71–86.
Hughes, A (2003) *Testing for Language Teachers* (Second edition), Cambridge: Cambridge University Press.
Humphreys, P, Haugh, M, Fenton-Smith, B, Lobo, A, Michael, R and Walkinshaw, I (2012) Tracking international students' English proficiency, *IELTS Research Report Online Series* 1, 1–41.
Hyland, K (2002) *Teaching and Researching Writing, Applied Linguistics in Action Series*, London: Longman.
IELTS (2017) *Common European Framework for IELTS*, available online: www.ielts.org/ielts-for-organisations/common-european-framework
Johansson, V (2008) Lexical diversity and lexical density in speech and writing: A developmental perspective, *Working Papers* 53, 61–79.

Johns, A M (1981) Necessary English: A faculty survey, *TESOL Quarterly* 15, 51–57.
Johns, A M (1993) Reading and writing tasks in English for academic purposes classes: Products, processes and resources, in Carson, J G and Leki, I (Eds) *Reading in the Composition Classroom: Second Language Perspectives*, Boston: Heinle and Heinle, 274–289.
Johns, A M and Mayes, P (1990) An analysis of summary protocols of university ESL students, *Applied Linguistics* 11 (3), 253–271.
Johnson, M D (2017) Cognitive task complexity and L2 written syntactic complexity, accuracy, lexical complexity, and fluency: A research synthesis and meta-analysis, *Journal of Second Language Writing* 37, 13–38.
Kaakinen, J K and Hyönä, J (2005) Perspective effects on expository text comprehension: Evidence from think-aloud protocols, eyetracking, and recall, *Discourse Processes* 40, 239–257.
Kaakinen, J K, Olkoniemi, H, Kinnari, T and Hyönä, J (2014) Processing of written irony: An eye movement study, *Discourse Processes* 51, 287–311.
Kane, M (2012) Validating score interpretations and uses, *Language Testing* 29 (1), 3–17.
Kellogg, R T (1987) Effects of topic knowledge on the allocation of processing time and cognitive effort to writing, *Memory and Cognition* 15, 256–266.
Kellogg, R T (1994) *The Psychology of Writing*, New York: Oxford University Press.
Kellogg, R T (1996) A model working memory in writing, in Levy, C M and Ransdell, S (Eds) *The Science of Writing: Theories, Methods, Individual Differences and Applications*, Hillsdale: Lawrence Erlbaum Associates, Publishers, 57–71.
Kellogg, R T (1999) Components of working memory in writing, in Torrance, M and Jeffery, G (Eds) *The Cognitive Demands of Writing: Processing Capacity and Working Memory Effects in Text Production*, Amsterdam: Amsterdam University Press, 43–61.
Kellogg, R T (2001) Competition for working memory among writing processes, *American Journal of Psychology* 114 (2), 175–192.
Kennedy, C and Thorp, D (2007) A corpus-based investigation of linguistic responses to an IELTS Academic Writing task, in Taylor, L (Ed) *IELTS Collected Papers: Research in Speaking and Writing Assessment*, Studies in Language Testing volume 19, Cambridge: UCLES/Cambridge University Press, 316–377.
Kerstjens, M and Nery, C (2000) Predictive validity in the IELTS test: A study of the relationship between IELTS scores and students' subsequent academic performance, *IELTS Research Reports* 3, 85–108.
Khalifa, H and Weir, C J (2009) *Examining Reading: Research and Practice in Assessing Second Language Reading*, Studies in Language Testing 29, Cambridge: UCLES/Cambridge University Press.
Kintsch, W (1974) *The Representation of Meaning in Memory*, Hillsdale: Lawrence Erlbaum Associates.
Kintsch, W and Van Dijk, T A (1978) Toward a model of text comprehension and production, *Psychological Review* 85, 363–394.
Knoch, U, Macqueen, S and O'Hagan, S (2014) An investigation of the effect of task type on the discourse produced by students at various score levels in the TOEFL iBT Writing Test, *ETS Research Report Series* 23, 14–43.
Koizumi, R (2012) Relationships between text length and lexical diversity measures: Can we use short texts of less than 100 tokens? *Vocabulary Learning and Instruction* 1(1), 60–69.

Lado, R (1961) *Language Testing: The Construction and Use of Foreign Language Tests*, London: Longman.
Language Training and Testing Center (2012) *About GEPT*, available online: www.lttc.ntu.edu.tw/E_LTTC/E_GEPT.htm
Language Training and Testing Center (2014) *GEPT Advanced Marking Criteria*, available online: www.lttc.ntu.edu.tw/GEPT1/Advanced/06.test_score.htm
Ledoux, K, Traxler, M J and Saab, T Y (2007), Syntactic priming in comprehension: Evidence from event-related potentials, *Psychological Science* 18, 135–143.
Lee, W, Kantor, R and Mollaun, P (2002) *Score reliability as an essential prerequisite for validating new writing and speaking tasks for TOEFL*, paper presented at the Annual TESOL Convention, Salt Lake City, April 2002.
Leki, I (1993) Reciprocal themes in ESL reading and writing, in Carson, J G and Leki, I (Eds) *Reading in the Composition Classroom. Second Language Perspectives*, Boston: Heinle and Heinle, 221–233.
Leki, I and Carson, J G (1994) Students' perceptions of EAP writing instruction and writing needs across the disciplines, *TESOL Quarterly* 28, 81–101.
Leki, I and Carson, J G (1997) Completely different worlds: EAP and the writing experiences of ESL students in university courses, *TESOL Quarterly* 31, 39–69.
Lenski, S D and Johns, J L (1997) Patterns of reading-to-write, *Reading Research and Instruction* 37, 15–38.
Levelt, W J M (1989) *Speaking: From Intention on Articulation*, Cambridge/London: ACL-MIT Press.
Lewkowicz, J (1997) The integrated testing of a second language, in Clapham, C (Ed) *Encyclopedia of Language and Education Volume 7: Language Testing and Assessment*, Dordrecht: Kluwer Academic Publishers, 121–130.
Lim, G S (2013) Components of an elaborated approach to test validation, *Research Notes* 51, 11–14.
Lindgren, E and Sullivan, K P H (2006) Analysing online revision, in Sullivan, K P H and Lindgren, E (Eds) *Studies in Writing, Computer Keystroke-logging and Writing: Methods and Applications*, Amsterdam: Elsevier, 157–188.
Longford, N (1996) Reconciling experts' differences in setting cut scores for pass-fail decisions, *Journal of Educational and Behavioral Statistics* 21 (3), 203–213.
Lowenthal, D (1980) Mixing levels of revision, *Visible Language* 14, 383–387.
Lumley, T (2005) *Assessing Second Language Writing: The Rater's Perspective*, Frankfurt: Peter Lang.
Macarthur, C A, Graham, S and Harris, K R (2004) Insights from instructional research on revision with struggling writers, in Allal, L, Chanquoy, L and Largy, P (Eds) *Revision: Cognitive and Instructional Processes*, Amsterdam: Kluwer Academic Press, 125–137.
Mathison, M A and Spivey, N N (1993) *Writing from Academic Sources: Authorship in Writing the Critique*, Berkeley: National Center for the Study of Writing and Literacy.
McCarthy, Y K and Leinhardt, G (1998) Writing from primary documents: A way of knowing in history, *Written Communication* 15, 25–68.
McNamara, D S, Louwerse, M M, Cai, Z and Graesser, A (2005) *Coh-Metrix version 1.4*, available online: www.researchgate.net/publication/200772661_Coh-Metrix_version_14
Messick, S (1989) Validity, in Linn, R L (Ed) *Educational Measurement* (Third edition), London: Macmillan, 13–103.
Mislevy, R J (1992) Foundations of a new test theory, in Frederiksen, R J, Mislevy, R J and Bejar, I I (Eds) *Test Theory of a New Generation of Tests*, Hillsdale: Lawrence Erlbaum Associates, 19–39.

Moore, T and Morton, J (1999) Authenticity in the IELTS academic module writing test: A comparative study of task 2 items and university assignments, in Tulloh, R (Ed) *IELTS Research Report 1999 Volume 2*, Canberra: IELTS Australia, 64–106.

Moore, T and Morton, J (2005) Dimensions of difference: A comparison of university writing and IELTS writing, *Journal of English for Academic Purposes* 4, 43–66.

Murray, D M (1978) Internal revision: A process of discovery, in Cooper, C R and Odell, L (Eds) *Research on Composing*, Urbana: National Council of Teachers of English, 113–139.

Norris, J M and Ortega, L (2009) Towards an organic approach to investigating CAF in instructed SLA: The case of complexity, *Applied Linguistics* 30, 555–578.

Odell, L (1980) Business writing: Observations and implications for teaching composition, *Theory into Practice* 19, 225–232.

Oller, J W (1979) *Language Tests at School*, London: Longman.

Parodi, G (2007) Reading–writing connections: Discourse-oriented research, *Reading and Writing* 20 (3), 225–250.

Pearson (2010) *PTE Academic Tutorial*, available online: pearsonpte.com/wp-content/uploads/2014/10/Tutorial.pdf

Perfetti, C A (1997) Sentences, individual differences and multiple texts: Three issues in text comprehension, *Discourse Processes* 23, 337–355.

Perfetti, C A, Britt, M A and Georgi, M C (1995) *Text-based Learning and Reasoning: Studies in History*, Hillsdale: Lawrence Erlbaum Associates.

Perfetti, C A, Rouet, J F and Britt, M A (1999) Toward a theory of document representation, in van Oostendorp, H and Goldman, S R (Eds) *The Construction of Mental Representations During Reading*, Hillsdale: Lawrence Erlbaum Associates, 99–122.

Perl, S (1979) The composing processes of unskilled college writers, *Research in the Teaching of English* 13 (4), 317–336.

Pickering, M J and Branigan, H P (1998) The representation of verbs: evidence from syntactic priming in language production, *Journal of Memory and Language* 39, 633–651.

Plakans, L (2008) Comparing composing processes in writing-only and reading-to-write test tasks, *Assessing Writing* 13, 111–129.

Plakans, L (2009a) The role of reading strategies in integrated L2 writing tasks, *Journal of English for Academic Purposes* 8, 252–266.

Plakans, L (2009b) Discourse synthesis in integrated second language writing assessment, *Language Testing* 26 (4), 561–587.

Plakans, L (2010) Independent vs integrated writing tasks: A comparison of task representation, *TESOL Quarterly* 44 (1), 185–194.

Plakans, L and Gebril, A (2012) A close investigation into source use in integrated second language writing tasks, *Assessing Writing* 17 (1), 18–34.

Plakans, L and Gebril, A (2013) Using multiple texts in an integrated writing assessment: Source text use as a predictor of score, *Journal of Second Language Writing* 22 (3), 217–230.

Pollitt, A and Taylor, L (2006) Cognitive psychology and reading assessment, in Sainsbury, M, Harrison, C and Watts, A (Eds) *Assessing Reading: From Theories to Classrooms*, Cambridge: National Foundation for Educational Assessment, 38–49.

Puhan, G, Boughton, K A and Kim, S (2007) Examining differences in examinee performance in paper and pencil and computerized testing, *Journal of Technology, Learning and Assessment* 6 (3), 1–22.

Purpura, J E (1997) An analysis of the relationships between test takers' cognitive and metacognitive strategy use and second language test performance, *Language Learning* 47 (2), 289–325.

Purpura, J E (1998) The development and construct validation of an instrument designed to investigate selected cognitive background characteristics of test takers, in Kunnan, A J (Ed) *Validation in Language Assessment*, Hillsdale: Lawrence Erlbaum Associates, 111–140.

Purves, A C, Soter, A, Takala, S and Vahapassi, A (1984) Towards a domain-referenced system for classifying assignments, *Research in the Teaching of English* 18 (4), 385–416.

Rayner, K and Pollatsek, A (1989) *The Psychology of Reading*, Englewood Cliffs: Prentice-Hall.

Read, J (1990) Providing relevant content in an EAP writing test, *English for Specific Purposes* 9 (2), 109–121.

Roscoe, J T (1969) *Fundamental Research Statistics for the Behavioral Sciences*, New York: Holt, Rinehart and Winston.

Ruiz-Funes, M (2001) Task representation in foreign language reading-to-write, *Foreign Language Annals* 34 (1), 226–234.

Sasaki, M (2000) Effects of cultural schemata on students' test-taking processes for cloze tests: A multiple data source approach, *Language Testing* 17, 85–114.

Scardamalia, M and Bereiter, C (1987) Knowledge telling and knowledge transforming in written composition, in Rosenberg, S (Ed) *Advances in Applied Psycholinguistics Volume 2: Reading, Writing and Language Learning*, Cambridge: Cambridge University Press, 142–175.

Scardamalia, M and Bereiter, C (1996) Adaptation and understanding: A case for new cultures of schooling, in Vosniadou, S, DeCorte, E, Glaser, R and Mandl, H (Eds) *International Perspectives on the Design of Technology-supported Learning Environments*, Hillsdale: Lawrence Erlbaum Associates, 149–163.

Scardamalia, M and Paris, P (1985) The function of explicit discourse knowledge in the development of text representations and composing strategies, *Cognition and Instruction* 2, 1–39.

Segev-Miller, R (2007) Cognitive processes in discourse synthesis: The case of intertextual processing strategies, in Rijlaarsdam, G, Torrance, M, Van Waes, L and Galbraith, D (Eds) *Writing and Cognition: Research and Applications*, Amsterdam: Elsevier, 231–250.

Seifert, C M, Robertson, S P and Black, J B (1985) Types of inferences generated during reading, *Journal of Memory and Language* 24, 405–422.

Severinson Eklundh, K and Kollberg, P (2003) Emerging discourse structure: Computer-assisted episode analysis as a window to global revision in university students' writing, *Journal of Pragmatics* 35 (6), 869–891.

Shaw, S and Weir, C J (2007) *Examining Writing: Research and Practice in Assessing Second Language Writing*, Studies in Language Testing volume 26, Cambridge: UCLES/Cambridge University Press.

Shi, L (2004) Textual borrowing in second language writing, *Written Communication* 21 (2), 171–200.

Smagorinsky, P (1994) Think-aloud protocol analysis: Beyond the black box, in Smagorinsky, P (Ed) *Speaking about Writing*, Thousand Oaks: Sage, 3–19.

Spivey, N N (1984) *Discourse Synthesis: Constructing Texts in Reading and Writing*, Outstanding Dissertation Monograph Series, Newark: International Reading Association.

Spivey, N N (1990) Transforming texts: Constructive processes in reading and writing, *Written Communication* 7 (2), 256–287.

Spivey, N N (1991) The shaping of meaning: options in writing the comparison, *Research in the Teaching of English* 25, 390–418.
Spivey, N N (1997) *The Constructivist Metaphor: Reading, Writing and the Making of Meaning*, San Diego: Academic Press.
Spivey, N N (2001) Discourse synthesis: Process and product, in McInnis, R G (Ed) *Discourse Synthesis: Studies in Historical and Contemporary Social Epistemology*, Westport: Praeger, 379–396.
Spivey, N N and King, J R (1989) Readers as writers composing from sources, *Reading Research Quarterly* 24 (1), 7–26.
Stevenson, M, Schoonen, R and de Glopper, K (2006) Revising in two languages: A multi-dimensional comparison of online writing revisions in L1 and FL, *Journal of Second Language Writing* 15 (3), 201–233.
Stratman, J and Hamp-Lyons, L (1994) Reactivity in concurrent think-aloud protocols: Issues for research, in Smagorinsky, P (Ed) *Speaking about Writing*, Thousand Oaks: Sage, 89–112.
Taylor, L (Ed) (2011) *Examining Speaking: Research and Practice in Assessing Second Language Speaking*, Studies in Language Testing volume 30, Cambridge: UCLES/Cambridge University Press.
Taylor, L (2013) *Testing Reading through Summary: Investigating Summary Completion Tasks for Assessing Reading Comprehension Ability*, Studies in Language Testing volume 39, Cambridge: UCLES/Cambridge University Press.
Taylor, C, Jamieson, J, Eignor, D and Kirsch, I (1998) *The Relationship Between Computer Familiarity and Performance on Computer-based TOEFL Test Tasks*, ETS Research Report 61, available online: www.ets.org/Media/Research/pdf/RR-98-08.pdf
Tierney, R J and Shanahan, T (1991) Research on the reading-writing relationship: Interactions, transactions, and outcomes, in Barr, R, Kamil, M L, Mosenthal, P and Pearson, P D (Eds) *Handbook of Reading Research Volume II*, Mahwah: Longman, 246–280.
Trinity College London (2012) *Integrated Skills in English. Theoretical Background and Research*, London: Trinity College London internal test development documents.
Trinity College London (2013) *Exam Information: Integrated Skills in English (ISE)*, London: Trinity College London.
UK Border Agency (2013) *Knowledge of English*, available online: www.gov.uk/tier-4-general-visa/knowledge-of-english
UK Council for International Student Affairs (2012) *Annual report 2011–2012*, London: UK Council for International Student Affairs.
University of Bedfordshire (2013) *Business School About Us*, available online: www.beds.ac.uk/howtoapply/departments/businessschool/about-us
University of Reading (2013) *About the Test of English for Educational Purposes (TEEP)*, available online: www.reading.ac.uk/ISLI/english-language-courses/english-language-tests/islc-teep-about-teep.aspx
Urquhart, A H and Weir, C J (1998) *Reading in a Second Language: Process, Product and Practice*, Harlow: Longman.
Van Dijk, T A and Kintsch, W (1983) *Strategies of Discourse Comprehension*, New York: Academic Press.
Van Nijlen, D and Janssen, R (2008) Modeling judgments in the Angoff and contrasting groups method of standard setting, *Journal of Educational Measurement* 45 (1), 45–63.
Weigle, S C (1999) Investigating rater/prompt interactions in writing assessment: Quantitative and qualitative approaches, *Assessing Writing* 6 (2), 145–178.

Weigle, S C (2002) *Assessing Writing*, Cambridge: Cambridge University Press.
Weigle, S C (2004) Integrating reading and writing in a competency test for non-native speakers of English, *Assessing Writing* 9 (9), 27–55.
Weir, C J (1983) *Identifying the language problems of the overseas students in tertiary education in the United Kingdom*, unpublished PhD dissertation, University of London.
Weir, C J (1988) Construct validity, in Hughes, A, Porter, D and Weir, C J (Eds) *ELT Validation Project: Proceeding of a Conference Held to Consider the ELTS Validation Project Report*, English Language Testing Service Research Report 1 (ii), Cambridge: British Council/UCLES, 15–25.
Weir, C J (1990) *Communicative Language Testing*, Englewood Cliffs: Prentice Hall.
Weir, C J (2005a) *Language Testing and Validation: An Evidence-based Approach*, Basingstoke: Palgrave Macmillan.
Weir, C J (2005b) Limitations of the Common European Framework for developing comparable examinations and tests, *Language Testing* 22 (3), 281–300.
Weir, C J (2012) *TEAP Writing Project: A review of the washback concept in language education with particular implications for Japan and the EIKEN Foundation of Japan organisation,* unpublished research report.
Weir, C J, Chan, S H C and Nakatsuhara, F (2013) *Examining the Criterion-related Validity of the GEPT Advanced Reading and Writing Tests: Comparing GEPT with IELTS and Real-life Academic Performance*, LTTC-GEPT Research Reports RG-01, Taiwan: Language Training and Testing Center.
Weir, C J, O'Sullivan, B, Jin, Y and Bax, S (2007) Does the computer make a difference? The reaction of candidates to a computer-based versus a traditional hand-written form of the IELTS Writing component: effects and impact, in McGovern, P and Walsh, S (Eds) *IELTS Research Reports Volume 7*, IELTS Australia and British Council, 311–347.
Weir, C J, Hawkey, R, Green, A, Ünaldi, A and Devi, S (2008) The relationship between the academic reading construct as measured by IELTS and the reading experiences of students in their first year of study at a British university, *IELTS Research Report* 9, 97–156.
Weir, C J, Vidaković, I and Galaczi, E (2013) *Measured Constructs: A History of Cambridge English Language Examinations 1913–2012*, Studies in Language Testing volume 37, Cambridge: UCLES/Cambridge University Press.
Wiley, J and Voss, J F (1999) Constructing arguments from multiple sources: Tasks that promote understanding and not just memory for text, *Journal of Educational Psychology* 91 (2), 301–311.
Wu, R Y F (2014) *Validating Second Language Reading Examinations: Establishing the Validity of the GEPT Through Alignment with the Common European Framework of Reference*, Studies in Language Testing volume 41, Cambridge: UCLES/Cambridge University Press.
Yen, D and Kuzma, J (2009) Higher IELTS score, higher academic performance? The validity of IELTS in predicting the academic performance of Chinese students, *Worcester Journal of Learning and Teaching* 3, 1–7.
Yu, G (2008) Reading to summarize in English and Chinese: A tale of two languages? *Language Testing* 25 (4), 521–551.
Yu, G (2013) From integrative to integrated language assessment: Are we there yet? *Language Assessment Quarterly* 10 (1), 110–114.
Yu, G and Lin, S (2014) *A Comparability Study on the Cognitive Processes of Taking Graph-based GEPT Advanced and IELTS Academic Writing Tasks*, LTTC-GEPT Research Reports, Taiwan: LTTC-GEPT.

Appendix 1

Real-life tasks

Real-life Task A – Essay task

You must choose ONE of the four questions listed below as the basis of the 5,000-word essay. Each question is linked to a 'stimulus' article which you will find listed below and then in full on subsequent pages.

You have the opportunity to hear *a briefing* from your tutors on all four questions on _____ – times and rooms will be posted on___. There will be a second meeting in which you may seek clarification on any aspect of the questions. At this meeting you will be encouraged to form 'study groups' with other students who have chosen the same question for the purposes of the initial research phase of the essay development.

Theme	Stimulus article	Question
1. Leadership, Leadership Competences	1. How Leadership Has Changed	1. What evidence is there *in the last five* years to substantiate the concept of 'Cross-Enterprise Leadership'?
2. Innovation, New Product/Service Launches	2. MT Expert – Innovation: Why Doing is Better than Thinking	2. Notwithstanding the enthusiasm of the authors of the 'Innovation' article, aren't there limits to the 'launch in beta' approach for products and services in general?
3. Strategic Planning, The Business Environment	3. The Strategic Plan	3. The Strategic Plan: is it relevant anymore?
4. Gender Diversity, Women in the Workplace	4. When Diversity Differentiated for Success	4. Gender diversity seems to be alive and well at IBM Daksh, but shouldn't women be recruited and promoted solely on the basis of merit?

Marking scheme of Real-life Task A (Teacher Version)

The aim of this unit is to give students the opportunity to demonstrate their knowledge and skills in the following areas:

- **problem definition and structure**
- **information identification, retrieval and analysis**
- **critical reasoning/justification**
- **persuasion and influencing.**

Students submit a 5,000-word individual essay around their group topic derived from their own critical analysis but based on the findings and discussions of their group. The essay is presented in the format of a researched journal article with full referencing and sourcing of the evidence base on which it is derived. Each group of eight students is given a different topic related to their area of study. Primary data gathering does not form part of the task. Markers should note that to avoid 'chunking' a limit of 10% of verbatim quotation, even if in quotation marks, was set in the classes.

Problem definition and structure

The questions provided are open ended and different approaches to answering them are discussed in the groups but ultimately it is the responsibility of each individual to decide how to structure the response.

A   An excellent answer will demonstrate a comprehensive consideration of the issues and configure the response to enable different arguments to be presented in a logical order.

B   A good answer will structure the problem in a logical way demonstrating a breadth.

C   An average answer will show consideration of some of the issues reasonably.

D   A poor response will take a very narrow view and consider a limited range of issues.

E   A referral answer will not consider the issues posed in the question in a coherent or detailed way.

F   A failing answer will not demonstrate an understanding of the issues posed in the question.

Appendix 1

Information identification, retrieval and analysis

This is measured by the amount of data the student has found, its relevance to the topic and the student's judgement in terms of its reliability – how old is it, who produced it, is it based on personal opinion or well-conducted research? etc.

It is not appropriate to suggest a minimum number of references as some areas are better documented than others but a good piece of work is unlikely to have fewer than eight references including work from academic journals. Poor or failing pieces of work may rely on one textbook and/or some 'Google' articles.

An appropriate, accurate and consistent style of referencing should also be taken into account under this heading.

Critical reasoning/justification

This section is concerned with the way the student actually uses the information they have collected in producing the essay.

- Is the student able to evaluate critically the data they have collected?
- Are the points well made?
- Are they based on the evidence presented?
- Is evidence used well to support the opinion being expressed?
- Is the information presented in a logical way?
- Can the student synthesise an argument?

A A well-constructed piece of work which clearly demonstrates the student's ability to synthesise complex arguments. It has a logical flow and all the points made follow from and are supported by the evidence.

B A well-constructed piece of work. Literature critically evaluated not merely a précis. Good use of secondary data sources.

C A range of appropriate points made but more as a list than as a unified piece of work. Secondary sources usually provided to support the points made.

D A limited number of points made. Poor use of any external data to support the points. Poor structure.

E Some evidence of an attempt to provide an answer to the question but insufficient detail to pass.

F A random collection of statements based on the student's own point of view with no attempt to use evidence to support the arguments.

Persuasion and influencing

We should not penalise students whose first language is not English so this heading is not about the ability to write completely grammatical English although facility in the language is an undeniable advantage.

It is about the way in which the whole piece of work is constructed and is the sum of the parts mentioned above. It is unlikely that a badly constructed, poorly referenced and argued piece of work will persuade and influence.

A   The work will be well argued and the conclusions will follow naturally from the evidence presented. No doubt will be left in the reader's mind as to their validity. A conclusion that contradicts perceived wisdom and is well justified will be particularly welcomed.
B   The work will be soundly argued and the conclusions will be largely convincing but some doubt could remain in the reader's mind as to their validity.
C   The work will be reasonably argued but the conclusions will not be entirely convincing from the evidence presented. The reader will have some doubt as to their validity.
D   Poorly argued with rather unconvincing conclusions. The reader may well doubt that the conclusions are valid.
E   Poorly argued and with conclusions that just do not follow from the evidence presented.
F   Little or no argument and very poor conclusion.

Real-life Task B – Report task

Write a report (maximum 2,000 words) explaining, with appropriate referenced theory, the methodology that you intend to use in order to produce a four-step ahead forecast for your dataset. The report should cover the following areas:

1. An examination of the data and description of the nature of the dataset with which you have been supplied (40%).
2. Discussion and justification of the three techniques you have decided to use (30%).
3. Your reasons for rejecting other techniques that you consider inappropriate (20%).
4. Some discussion of other forecasting issues that should be considered when attempting to produce medium- to long-term forecasts (10%).

The following is a guide as to how your work will be marked:

	F/F-	E	D (Range)	C (Range)	B (Range)	A (Range)
Examination of Data (40%)						
Examination of the data and description of the nature of the dataset.	Work is of little or no merit whatsoever.	Poor charts. Little evidence of examination of the data.	Some errors in the charting of the data. Poor examination of the patterns in the data supported by little evidence.	Some errors in the charting of the data. Some examination of the patterns in the data supported by little evidence.	Accurate charting of the data. Thorough examination of the patterns in the data supported by some evidence.	Accurate charting of the data. Thorough examination of the patterns in the data supported by comprehensive evidence.
Selection of Techniques (30%)	F/F-	E	D (Range)	C (Range)	B (Range)	A (Range)
Discussion and justification of the three techniques you have decided to use.	Work is of little or no merit whatsoever.	Selection of inappropriate techniques with no real justification.	Selection of inappropriate techniques but some attempt at justification.	A satisfactory discussion and limited identification of problems you foresee and/or limitations, of the techniques when applied to **YOUR** data.	A comprehensive and **CRITICAL** discussion, including any problems you foresee and/or limitations, of the techniques when applied to **YOUR** data, although there may be some weaknesses and omissions.	A comprehensive and **CRITICAL** discussion, including any problems you foresee and/or limitations, of the techniques when applied to **YOUR** data.

	F/F-	E	D (Range)	C (Range)	B (Range)	A (Range)
Rejection of Techniques (20%) Your reasons for rejecting other techniques that you consider inappropriate.	Work is of little or no merit whatsoever.	Rejection of techniques with no real justification.	Rejection of inappropriate techniques and some attempt at justification.	A satisfactory discussion, giving clear reasons as to the unsuitability of the rejected techniques, when applied to YOUR data.	A comprehensive and **CRITICAL** discussion, giving detailed reasons as to the unsuitability of the rejected techniques, when applied to YOUR data, although there may be some weaknesses and omissions.	A comprehensive and **CRITICAL** discussion, giving detailed reasons as to the unsuitability of the rejected techniques, when applied to YOUR data.
Other Issues (10%) Discussion of other forecasting issues that should be considered when attempting to produce medium- to long-term forecasts.	Work is of little or no merit.	Shows little understanding of the issues. Poor referencing.	Some relevant points made, but no examples. Limited evidence of understanding of the main issues. Maybe some errors in referencing.	Some relevant points made with limited examples. Evidence of some understanding of the main issues. Maybe some errors in referencing.	Interesting points with examples provided. Evidence of some understanding of the main issues. Accurate referencing.	Interesting points with examples provided. Evidence of clear understanding of the main issues. Creativity evidenced in the discussion. Accurate referencing.

Appendix 2 Contextual parameter proforma

Overall task setting (productive demands)	
1. Purpose and intended reader	1 Unclear 2 3 4 5 Clear
2. Time and length	Time allowance: Number of words required:
3. Topic domain	Personal Social Academic Professional Not at all — Definitely Not at all — Definitely Not at all — Definitely Not at all — Definitely 1 2 3 4 5 1 2 3 4 5 1 2 3 4 5 1 2 3 4 5
4. Genre (response)	Please specify:
5. Interaction between input and response (please tick the most suitable option)	☐ Telling personal experience / viewpoints ☐ Summarising / organising given ideas ☐ Transforming given ideas into new representations
Overall task setting (productive demands)	
6. Language functions to perform (you may tick more than one)	☐ Classifying ☐ Citing sources ☐ Describing ☐ Defining ☐ Evaluating ☐ Persuading ☐ Predicting ☐ Recommending ☐ Reasoning ☐ Summarising ☐ Synthesising ☐ Expressing personal views ☐ Illustrating visuals ☐ Others (Please specify):

Defining Integrated Reading-into-Writing Constructs

7. Clarity of intended reader	1 Unclear	2	3	4	5 Clear
8. Knowledge of criteria	1 Unclear	2	3	4	5 Clear
Input text features					
9. Input format	☐ Single verbal ☐ Single non-verbal ☐ Multiple verbal ☐ Multiple non-verbal ☐ Multiple verbal and non-verbal				
10. Genre (input)	☐ Book chapter ☐ Journal article ☐ News / magazine article ☐ Proposal ☐ Report ☐ Review ☐ Others (Please specify):				
11. Non-verbal input	☐ Table ☐ Graph ☐ Diagram ☐ Picture ☐ Others (Please specify):				
Conceptual complexity					
12. Discourse mode	☐ Narrative ☐ Descriptive ☐ Expeditionary ☐ Argumentative ☐ Others (Please specify):				
13. Concreteness of ideas	1 Abstract	2	3	4	5 Concrete
14. Explicitness of textual organisation	1 Inexplicit	2	3	4	5 Explicit
Linguistic complexity					
15. Lexical complexity	See automated textual analysis				
16. Syntactic complexity	See automated textual analysis				
17. Degree of coherence	See automated textual analysis				

Appendix 3

A list of deleted automated textual indices and reasons for deletion

	Reasons	**CohMetrix (Cohm) indices deleted**
1	They overlapped with other indices – they showed very similar or no difference when compared to the results of other indices. For instance, 40 (Flesch-Kincaid grade level) and 39 (Flesch reading ease) are already covered by 38 (Average syllables per word and 37 (Average words per sentence). Celex measures are covered by word frequency measures.	• Cohm 24 Number of conditional expressional, incidence score • Cohm 25 Number of negations, incidence score • Cohm 34 Number of sentences • Cohm 39 Flesch reading ease • Cohm 40 Flesch-Kincaid grade level* • Cohm 55 Sentence syntax similarity adjacent • Cohm 57 All within paragraphs
2	They were difficult to interpret in as it is affected by other variables, e.g. genre. For instance, 23 (ratio of pronouns to noun phrase) is affected by text type.	• Cohm 12 Incidence of negative additive connections • Cohm 13 Incidence of negative temporal connections • Cohm 14 Incidence of negative causal connections • Cohm 23 Ratio of pronouns to noun phrase • Cohm 30 Personal pronoun incidence score
3	They were not applicable to the data in this study due to the sampling procedures of the real-life texts.	• Cohm 33 Number of paragraphs • Cohm 35 Number of words • Cohm 36 Average sentences per paragraph
4	They were not useful or effective in determining the complexity of a text because: the index produced a score which is difficult to interpret; insufficient explanation was provided in the CohMetrix menu; and/or results obtained contradict human judgement.	• Cohm 7 Incidence of causal verbs, links and particles • Cohm 8 Ratio of causal particles to causal verbs • Cohm 9 Incidence of positive additive connectives • Cohm 10 Incidence of positive temporal connectives • Cohm 11 Incidence of positive causal connectives • Cohm 15 Incidence of all connectives • Cohm 19 Argument overlap, all distances • Cohm 20 Stem overlap all distances unweighted • Cohm 21 Anaphor reference, all distances

Defining Integrated Reading-into-Writing Constructs

	<ul><li>Cohm 22 Noun phrase incidence score (per thousand words)</li><li>Cohm 28 LSA all sentences combination mean</li><li>Cohm 29 LSA paragraph to paragraph mean</li><li>Cohm 31 Mean hyponymy values of nouns</li><li>Cohm 32 Mean hyponymy value of verbs</li><li>Cohm 42 Higher level constituents per word</li><li>Cohm 45 Celex, raw, mean for content words</li><li>Cohm 47 Celex raw minimum in sentence for content words</li><li>Cohm 48 Celex, logarithm, minimum in sentence for content words (0–6)</li><li>Cohm 49 Concreteness, mean for content words</li><li>Cohm 51 Incidence of negative logical connectives</li><li>Cohm 52 Ratio of intentional particles to intentional content</li><li>Cohm 53 Incidence of intentional actions, events and particles</li><li>Cohm 54 Mean of tense and aspect repetition scores</li><li>Cohm 59 Mean of location and motion ratio scores</li><li>Cohm 60 Concreteness</li></ul>

* Most previous studies reported a scale of 0–16 but CohMetrix provides the scale of 0–12.

Appendix 4

Expert judgement feedback evaluation questionnaire

Based on the experience applying the contextual parameter proforma, how confident do you feel when you choose your response? Please tick 1, 2, 3 or 4 to indicate how confident you were. If your answer is 2 or 1, please specify the reason.

4 = very confident 3 = confident 2 = not confident 1 = not confident at all

	4	3	2	1	Reasons
Part 1 – Overall task setting					
• Purpose					
• Topic domain					
• Genre					
• Cognitive demands					
• Language functions					
• Intended reader					
• Knowledge of criteria					
Part 2 – Input text features					
• Input format					
• Verbal input genre					
• Non-verbal input					
• Discourse mode					
• Concreteness of ideas					
• Explicitness of textual organisation					

Appendix 5

Reliability analysis on the questionnaire (54 items)

Original item no.	Questionnaire items	Mean	Standard deviation	Item-total correlation	Reliability	Changes made
Conceptualisation phase						
1	I read the task prompt (i.e. instructions) carefully.	3.34	0.684	<0.3	0.737	Item 1 was meant to measure a process of task representation, i.e. building an initial understanding of the writing task. However, it did not yield an item-total correlation higher than 0.30, which means that the participants did not employ this process similarly to how they employed other task representation processes. As the wording of the item contained 'read' and 'carefully', the item might measure a careful reading process. The item was regrouped to meaning construction. It reported an item-total correlation to other reading items at 0.48.
2	I thought of what I might need to write to make my essay relevant and adequate to the task.	3.17	0.930	0.536		
3	I thought of how my essay would suit the expectations of the intended reader.	2.90	0.861	0.458		
5	I thought about the purpose of the task.	2.98	0.938	0.602		
4	I understood the instructions for this writing task very well.	3.10	0.831	0.457		
12	I read the task prompt again while reading the source texts.	3.02	1.000	0.434		
25	I read the task prompt again while I was writing.	2.84	1.032	0.395		

6	I read through the whole of each source text carefully.	2.95	0.801	0.403	Two new items added based on qualitative data.
				0.806	Item 1 was added.
7	I read the whole of each source text more than once.	2.80	0.944	0.335	
8	I used my knowledge of how texts like these are organised to find parts to focus on.	3.20	0.846	<0.3	Item 8 was meant to measure a process of generating and connecting – relating a writer's *a priori* genre knowledge to the source texts. However, it did not yield an item-total correlation higher than 0.30 as other generating and connecting items did. As the wording of the item contained 'organised', the item was regrouped to organising ideas. It reported an item-total correlation to organising at 0.56.
9	I searched quickly for part(s) of the texts which might answer the question.	3.20	0.842	0.549	
10	I read some relevant part(s) of the texts carefully.	3.27	0.809	0.618	
11	I used my knowledge of the topic to help me to understand the texts.	Dropped due to inadequate sampling.			
13	I took notes on or underlined the important ideas in the source texts.	3.23	0.959	0.499	
14	I linked the important ideas in the source texts to what I know already.	2.92	0.879	0.576	
16	I developed a better understanding of the topic while I was reading the source texts.	2.92	0.870	0.462	
23	I developed new ideas while I was writing.	2.85	0.843	0.400	
24	I made connections across the source texts.	2.77	0.813	0.426	
26	I selectively reread the source texts.	2.66	0.868	0.396	

Organising phase

Organising

15	I organised the main ideas in each source based on how they relate to each other.	2.93	0.855	0.451	0.744	Item 8 was added. Another new item was added based on qualitative data.
17	I organised the main ideas across the source texts based on how they relate to each other.	3.10	0.899	0.552		
18	I recombined or reordered the ideas to fit the structure of my essay.	2.85	0.865	0.607		
19	I organised the ideas to be put in the writing before starting to write.	2.91	0.932	0.591		
20	I removed some ideas I planned to write.	2.87	0.903	0.448		
21	I tried to use the same organisational structure as in one of the source texts.	2.60	0.892	0.261		
22	I sometimes paused to organise my ideas while I was writing.	2.91	0.869	0.321		

Monitoring and revising phase

27	I monitored and edited the content development of my text.	Dropped due to qualitative feedback.			9.27	Nil
28	I checked that the content was relevant.	2.89	0.945	0.615		
29	I checked that I included all appropriate main ideas from all the source texts.	2.95	0.894	0.583		
30	I checked that I included my own viewpoint on the topic.	2.99	0.972	0.577		

31	I checked that the essay was well organised.	2.76	0.941	0.570
32	I checked that the essay was coherent.	2.84	0.897	0.587
33	I checked that the quotations were properly made.	2.80	0.899	0.484
34	I checked that I had put the ideas of the source texts into my own words.	3.01	0.944	0.596
35	I checked the possible effect of my writing on the intended reader.	2.59	0.949	0.386
36	I monitored and edited the linguistic aspect of my text.	Dropped due to qualitative feedback.		
37	I checked the accuracy of the sentence structures.	Items 37 and 38 were combined due to high correlation between two items.		
38	I checked if the range of sentence structures was adequate.			
39	I checked the appropriateness of vocabulary.	Items 39 and 40 were combined due to high correlation between two items.		
40	I checked the range of vocabulary.			
41	After revising the first draft, I monitored and edited the content development of my text.	Dropped due to qualitative feedback.		
42	After revising the first draft, I checked that the content was relevant.	2.56	1.194	0.746
43	After revising the first draft, I checked that I included all appropriate main ideas from all the source texts.	2.59	1.157	0.746

44	After revising the first draft, I checked that I included my own viewpoint on the topic.	2.67	1.161	0.804
45	After revising the first draft, I checked that the essay was well organised.	2.51	1.173	0.746
46	After revising the first draft, I checked that the essay was coherent.	2.61	1.496	0.565
47	After revising the first draft, I checked that the quotations were properly made.	2.54	1.112	0.734
48	After revising the first draft, I checked that I had put the ideas of the source texts into my own words.	2.65	1.168	0.304
49	After revising the first draft, I checked the possible effect of my writing on the intended reader.	2.39	1.120	0.700
50	After revising the first draft, I monitored and edited the linguistic aspect of my text.	Dropped due to qualitative feedback.		
51	After revising the first draft, I checked the accuracy of the sentence structures.	Items 51 and 52 were combined due to high correlation between two items.		
52	After revising the first draft, I checked if the range of sentence structures was adequate.			
53	After revising the first draft, I checked the appropriateness of vocabulary.	Items 53 and 54 were combined due to high correlation between two items.		
54	After revising the first draft, I checked the range of vocabulary.			

Appendix 6

Writing process questionnaire items

1	I read the whole task prompt (i.e. instructions) carefully.
2	I thought of what I might need to write to make my text relevant and adequate to the task.
3	I thought of how my text would suit the expectations of the intended reader.
4	I understood the instructions for this writing task very well.
5	I thought about the purpose of the task.
6	I read through the whole of each source text slowly and carefully.
7	I read the whole of each source text more than once.
8	I used my knowledge of how texts like these are organised to find parts to focus on.
9	I searched quickly for part(s) of the texts which might help complete the task.
10	I read part(s) of the texts which are relevant to the task carefully.
11	I considered the task requirements while I was reading the source texts.
12	I took notes on or underlined the important ideas in the source texts.
13	I prioritised important ideas in the source texts in my mind.
14	I linked the important ideas in the source texts to what I know already.
15	I organised the main ideas in each source based on how they relate to each other.
16	I organised the main ideas across the source texts based on how they relate to each other.
17	I developed a better understanding of the topic while I was reading the source texts.
18	I changed my writing plans while reading the source texts.
19	I organised the ideas to be put in the writing before starting to write.
20	I recombined or reordered the ideas to fit the structure of my writing.
21	I removed some ideas I planned to write.
22	I considered the structure of the source texts while organising my writing.
23	I sometimes paused to organise my ideas while writing.
24	I developed new ideas while writing.
25	I made further connections across the source texts while writing.
26	I considered the task requirements while writing.
27	I selectively read the source texts again while writing.
28	I changed my writing plans while writing.

29	I checked that the content was relevant while writing.
30	I checked that my text was well organised while writing.
31	I checked that my text was coherent while writing.
32	I checked that I included all appropriate main ideas from the source texts while writing.
33	I checked that I included my own viewpoint on the topic while writing.
34	I checked that the quotations were properly made while writing.
35	I checked that I had put the ideas of the source texts into my own words while writing.
36	I checked the possible effect of my writing on the intended reader while writing.
37	I checked the accuracy and range of the sentence structures while writing.
38	I checked the appropriateness and range of vocabulary while writing.
39	I checked that the content was relevant after writing.
40	I checked that my text was well organised after writing.
41	I checked that my text was coherent after writing.
42	I checked that I included all appropriate main ideas from the source texts after writing.
43	I checked that I included my own viewpoint on the topic after writing.
44	I checked that the quotations were properly made after writing.
45	I checked that I had put the ideas of the source texts into my own words after writing.
46	I checked the possible effect of my writing on the intended reader after writing.
47	I checked the accuracy and range of the sentence structures after writing.
48	I checked the appropriateness and range of vocabulary after writing.

Appendix 7

Analysis of eigenvalues and scree plots (real-life data)

The conceptualisation phase

Factor	Initial eigenvalues		
	Total	% of variance	Cumulative %
1	2.829	35.363	35.363
2	1.401	17.517	52.880
3	0.934	11.670	64.550
4	0.765	9.567	74.117
5	0.615	7.690	81.806
6	0.541	6.757	88.563
7	0.489	6.112	94.675
8	0.426	5.325	100.000

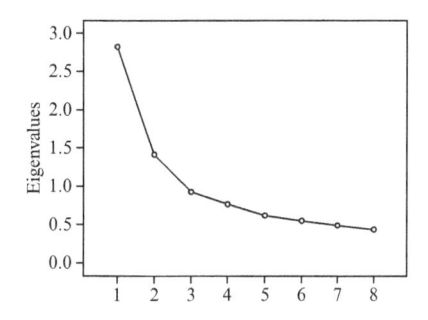

The meaning construction phase

Factor	Initial eigenvalues		
	Total	% of variance	Cumulative %
1	3.454	34.541	34.541
2	1.388	13.880	48.420
3	1.016	10.161	58.582
4	0.863	8.627	67.209
5	0.849	8.485	75.694
6	0.698	6.982	82.676
7	0.562	5.619	88.295
8	0.473	4.732	93.027
9	0.356	3.560	96.587
10	0.341	3.413	100.000

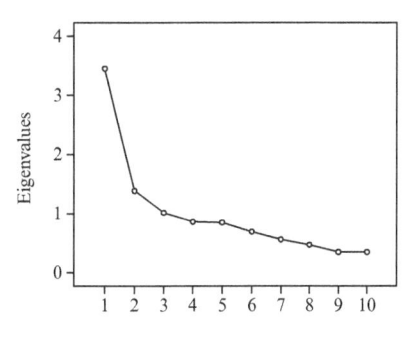

The organising phase

Factor	Initial eigenvalues		
	Total	% of variance	Cumulative %
1	3.488	38.753	38.753
2	1.360	15.110	53.863
3	1.190	13.228	67.091
4	0.736	8.178	75.268
5	0.609	6.771	82.040
6	0.500	5.557	87.596
7	0.461	5.124	92.721
8	0.395	4.393	97.113
9	0.260	2.887	100.000

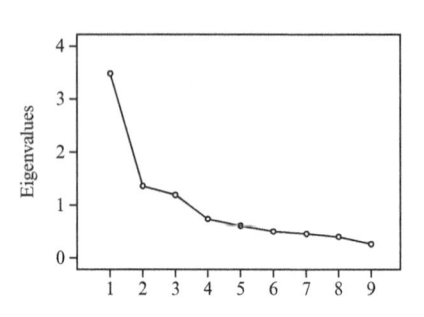

The monitoring and revising phase at lower level

Factor	Initial eigenvalues		
	Total	% of variance	Cumulative %
1	3.816	47.703	47.703
2	1.847	23.087	70.790
3	0.895	11.190	81.979
4	0.632	7.899	89.879
5	0.311	3.884	93.762
6	0.225	2.808	96.571
7	0.157	1.965	98.535
8	0.117	1.465	100.000

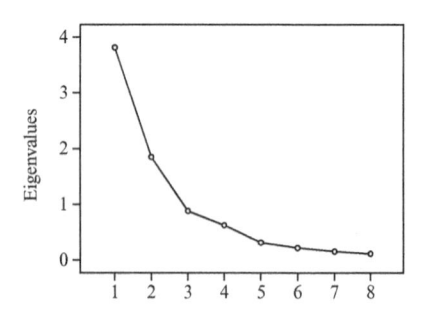

Appendix 7

The monitoring and revising phase at higher level

Factor	Initial eigenvalues		
	Total	% of variance	Cumulative %
1	5.150	42.920	42.920
2	2.922	24.351	67.271
3	0.864	7.198	74.469
4	0.681	5.673	80.141
5	0.603	5.023	85.164
6	0.536	4.464	89.628
7	0.370	3.081	92.709
8	0.272	2.271	94.980
9	0.213	1.777	96.757
10	0.175	1.454	98.211
11	0.140	1.170	99.381
12	0.074	0.619	100.000

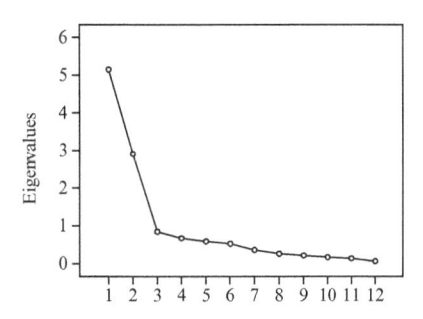

Author index

A
Ackerman, J M 3, 19, 34, 45, 111, 135, 140, 167
Alderson, J C 20, 23, 25, 46
Association of Language Testers in Europe 67
Anderson, T H 45
Armbruster, B B 45
Asencion, Y 4
Asencion-Delaney Y 3, 7, 43, 46

B
Baba, K 36, 42, 47–48, 52
Bachman, L F 17–18, 23, 46, 42, 57–58, 115
Bax, S 25, 38, 68, 69, 165, 181, 182
Beck, I L 25
Belcher, D 45
Bereiter, C 2, 21–22, 27, 35, 88, 91, 122, 129
Biber, D 98
Bikowski, D 16
Black, J B 36
Boughton, K A 182
Branigan, H P 100
Brewer, W F 21, 114, 164
Bridgeman, B 15, 16, 26, 42, 64, 164
Bridges, G 56
British National Corpus 68, 70
Britt, M A 25, 46
Brown, G 35, 99
Brown, J D 44
Bulté, B 98
Burtis, P J 35

C
Cai, Z 68, 98–99, 100
Campbell, C 45
Canale, M 27
Carey, L 122
Carlson, S 15–16, 42, 64, 164
Carson, J 4, 16–17, 26, 42–43, 45, 64, 164
Casey, L B 68
Chan, S H C 4, 25, 38, 49–50, 56, 59, 68, 69, 122, 165, 181
Charge, N 51
Cherkes-Julkowski, M 37

Choi, I C 23
Clapham, C 20, 46, 86, 111
Clevinger, A 101
Cobb, T 68
Cohen, A 27
Conrad, S 98
Conrow, F 153
Cooper, A 16
Cortes, V 98
Cotton, F 153
Council of Europe 1, 5–8, 20, 22, 68–69
Coxhead, A 24, 68, 70
Criper, C 153, 155
Crossley, S A 68, 98, 101
Cumming, A 22, 36, 42, 45–50, 52, 183
Cambridge University Press 5

D
Daniel, F 98
Davidson, F 23
Davies, A 51, 153, 155
De Glopper, K 122
Devi, S 74
Dobson, B 22, 86
Douglas, D 18–22, 44, 86, 111,

E
Eignor, D 182
Engelhard, G 181
Enright, M 23
Eouanzoui, K 36, 42, 47–48, 52
Erdosy, U 36, 42, 47–48, 52
Esmaeili, H 4, 45, 74
Eouanzoui, K 36, 42, 47–48, 52
Eysenck, M W 35

F
Fabrigar, L R 117
Feak, C 22, 86
Feast, V 153
Fenton-Smith, B 153
Field, J 10, 23, 25, 27–30, 32–35, 37–39, 68, 69, 74–76, 122, 127, 129, 165, 167, 181
Figueras, N 23
Fitzgerald, J 38–39

Author index

Flower, L 3–4, 19, 34, 39, 43, 45, 73–74, 111, 122, 135, 140, 167, 182
Fulcher, G 57, 172

G

Galaczi, E 2, 22, 25, 29, 42, 44, 45, 46, 48, 50, 51, 52, 61, 140, 167
Galbraith, D 22
Gebril, A 49–50
Georgi, M C 46
Geranpayeh, A 59
Gernsbacher M A 119, 140
Goldman, S R 25
Gomulicki, B R 36
Grabe, W 4, 17, 23, 24, 30–31, 34–35, 45–46, 164
Graesser, A C 68, 98–100
Graham, S
Grant, L 36, 45–46, 49–50, 52
Green, A B 1, 24 25, 45, 49, 57, 65, 68–69, 71, 74, 96, 98, 101–104, 165–166, 181,
Greenfield, J 98

H

Hale, G 16, 26
Hamp-Lyons, L 43, 64, 74, 164, 167
Harris, K R 39
Harsch, C 5, 172
Hartig, J 172
Haugh, M 153
Hawkey, R 74
Hayes, J R 30–31, 34, 39, 73–74, 122, 167, 182,
Hilgers, T 44
Hirvela, A 7, 27–28, 45, 168
Horowitz, D M 16, 41–42, 64, 164
Housen, A 98
Hughes, A 17, 19, 42, 44–45, 58
Humphreys, P 153
Hyland, K 35, 111
Hyönä, J 100–101

I

IELTS 51
Inoue, C 4, 49, 50, 56, 59

J

James, M 36, 42, 47–48, 52
Jamieson, J 182
Janssen, R 181
Jin, Y 38, 74, 182
Johansson, V 98
Johns, A M 16–17, 37, 42–43, 45, 64
Johns, J L 4, 17
Johnson, M D 96
Justice, W V 68

K

Kaakinen, J K 100–101
Kane, M 57
Kantor, R 16, 26, 36, 42, 47–48, 52
Kantz, M J 3, 19, 34, 45, 111, 135, 140, 167
Kaplan, F L 30–31, 34–35
Keane, M 35
Kellogg, R T 30, 32–33, 38–39, 75, 111, 122, 129, 167
Kennedy, C 100
Kerstjens, M 153
Khalifa, H 23, 28–29, 36, 43, 59, 74, 87, 129, 167, 171
Kim, S 182
Kim, Y 101
King, J R 3, 7, 20, 29–30, 36–37, 43, 73, 135, 140, 167
Kinnari, T 101
Kintsch, W 20, 27, 29, 36, 43,
Kirsch, I 182
Knoch, U 96
Koda, K 23
Koizumi, R 24
Kollberg, P 2, 39, 182
Kroll, B 16, 26, 43, 64, 164, 167
Kuijper, H 23
Kulikowich, J M 68
Kuzma, J 153

L

Lado, R 57
Ledoux, K 100
Lee, W 49
Leinhardt, G 46
Leki, I 4, 16, 42, 43, 45, 64
Lenski, S D 4, 17, 45
Levelt, W J M 32
Lewkowicz, J 48
Lim, G S 59
Lin, S 46
Lindgren, E 122
Lobo, A 153
Longford, N 181
Louwerse, M M 68, 98, 99, 100
Lowenthal, D 27
Loxterman, J A 25
Language Training and Testing Center 56, 66, 111, 144
Lumley, T 22

M

Macarthur, C 39
MacCallum, R C 117
Macqueen, S 96
Marsella, J 44
Mathison, M A 29
Mayes, P 37, 43, 164

219

McCarthy, P M 68
McCarthy, Y K 46
McCormick, K 3, 19, 34, 45, 135, 140, 167
McKeown, M G 25
McNamara, D S 68, 98, 99, 100
Messick, S 57, 58, 61
Michael, R 153
Miller, N D 68
Mollaun, P 49
Moore, T 26, 42
Morton, J 26, 42
Mosenthal, P 23
Mulcahy-Ernt, P 42, 45, 46, 49, 50, 52
Murray, D M 27

N
Nakatsuhara, F 24, 25, 68, 69, 165, 181
Nery, C 153
Nold, G 23
Norris, J M 98

O
O'Hagan, S 96
Odell, L 27
Olkoniemi, H 101
Oller, J W 44
Ortega, L 98
Ostertag, J 45
O'Sullivan, B 38, 74, 182

P
Palmer, A S 17, 18, 42, 57, 58, 115
Paris, P 34
Parodi, G 164
Pearson 52
Peck, W C 3, 19, 34, 45, 135, 140, 167
Perfetti, C A 25, 46
Pickering, M J 100
Plakans, L 4, 30, 34, 43, 46, 49, 50, 56, 73, 140, 164, 167, 182
Pollatsek, A 98, 99
Pollitt, A 42
Powers, D E 42
Puhan, G 182
Purpura, J E 27, 74, 182
Purves, A C 21, 22

R
Rakestraw, J A 25
Rayner, K 98, 99
Read, J 20 86
Robertson, S P 36
Roscoe, J T 72
Rouet, J F 25
Ruiz-Funes, M 34
Rupp, A A 5
Ryan, K 23

S
Saab, T Y 100
Scardamalia, M 2, 22, 27, 28, 31, 34, 35, 36, 37, 39, 43, 88, 91, 122, 129
Schedl, M
Schoonen, R 122
Schriver, K 122
Segev-Miller, R 64, 140
Seifert, C M 36
Severinson Eklundh, K 2, 39, 182
Shanahan, T 21, 45
Sharp, S 37
Shaw, S 17, 18, 19, 22, 26, 28, 31, 32, 34, 35, 37, 38, 39, 42, 59, 66, 74, 85, 91, 122, 140, 152, 164, 167, 168, 169, 171
Shi, L 47
Sinatra, M G 25
Smagorinsky, P 73–74
Sommer, J 25
Soter, A 21, 22
Spivey, N N 3, 7, 20, 25, 29–30, 36, 37, 43, 73, 74, 116, 129, 135, 140, 167, 182
Stein, V 3, 19, 45, 135, 140, 167
Stevenson, M 122
Stockton, M B 68
Stolzenberg, J 37
Strahan, E J 117
Stratman, J 73, 122
Sullivan, K P H 122

T
Takala, S 21, 22, 23
Taylor, C 16, 26, 182
Taylor, L B 4, 20, 24, 42, 49, 50, 51, 52, 56, 59, 182
Tetroe, J 35
Thorp. D 100
Tierney, R J 45
Torrance, M 22
Traxler, M J 100
Trinity College London 56

U
UK Border Agency 56, 155, 170
UK Council for International Student Affairs 64
Ünaldi, A 24, 65, 68, 69, 71, 74, 96, 101–104, 165, 166
University of Bedfordshire 64
University of Reading 51
Urquhart, A H 20, 36, 116, 177

V
Vahapassi, A 21, 22
Van Dijk, T A 20, 27, 29, 43
Van Nijlen, D 181

Vidaković, I 2, 22, 25, 29, 42, 44, 45, 46, 48, 50, 51, 52, 61, 140, 167

W
Walkinshaw, I 153
Wall, D 46
Wegener, D T 117
Weigle, S C 2, 3, 4, 17, 19, 20, 21, 22, 42–45, 50, 56, 67, 152, 164, 167
Weir, C J 2, 10, 16, 17, 18, 19, 20, 22, 23, 24, 25, 26, 28, 29, 30, 31, 32, 34, 35, 36, 37, 38, 39, 42, 43, 44, 45, 46, 48, 50, 51, 52, 57, 58, 59, 61, 64, 66, 68, 69, 71, 74, 85, 87, 91, 96, 103, 104, 116, 122, 129, 140, 142, 152, 157, 164, 165, 167, 168, 169, 171, 172, 174, 177, 180, 181, 182, 183
Wiley, J 46
Wu, R Y F 23–25, 47, 59, 67, 68, 69, 71, 165, 181

Y
Yen, D 153
Yu, G 4, 21, 41, 43, 46, 47, 56
Yule, G 35, 99

Subject index

A
Academic Word List (AWL) 24, 70
Analysis
  cognitive processing 27, 30, 39–40, 59, 72–79, 83, 173
  contextual parameter 39, 47, 63, 66–72, 85–92, 95, 162–165, 177, 183
  qualitative 76–77, 125
  quantitative 181
A priori cognitive validity 71, 142
Argumentative 3, 20–21, 34, 55, 93, 113–114, 164–165, 173, 179
Authenticity
  interactional 42–44
  situational 42–44
Automated textual analysis 10, 24, 25, 63, 67–72, 81, 83, 85, 96, 165, 181
AWL *see* Academic Word List (AWL)

B
British National Corpus (BNC) 68, 70, 97
BNC *see* British National Corpus (BNC)

C
C1 Advanced 48
C2 Proficiency 48–49
CAE *see* Certificate in Advanced English (CAE)
Cambridge English: Advanced 24, 49, 53–55, 68–69; see also C1 Advanced; Certificate in Advanced English (CAE)
Certificate in Advanced English (CAE) 49, 51
Cambridge English: Proficiency 53–55, 69; see also C2 Proficiency; Certificate of Proficiency in English (CPE)
CEFR *see* Common European Framework of Reference for Languages (CEFR)
Certificate in Advanced English (CAE) 49, 51
Certificate of Proficiency in English (CPE) 51
Cognitive demands 21, 26, 29–30, 47, 83, 96, 114, 151, 163, 165, 177, 181
Coherence 19, 25, 38, 39, 53, 55, 68, 75, 91, 97, 100–102, 107, 122, 129, 144–147, 152, 179

Cohesion 23, 25, 55, 69, 70, 83, 96, 100, 101, 104–109, 144, 146, 147, 165–167, 174, 179
Cohesive device 6, 25, 100, 179
Common European Framework of Reference for Languages (CEFR) 1–11, 20, 22, 26, 27, 33, 47, 50, 52–56, 60, 61, 66–68, 72, 82, 114, 137, 143, 155, 158, 161, 162, 170–177, 180, 183–184
Comparability 23, 78
Comprehension 8, 20, 29–30, 33, 36, 43–47, 100, 141, 161, 166, 178, 181, 183
Complexity
  grammatical/syntactic/structural 19, 48, 68–71, 83, 92–109, 165–166, 173, 181
  lexical 19, 48, 55, 68–71, 83, 92–109, 165–166, 173, 179, 181
  text 6, 20, 23–26, 34, 47, 54,
Conceptualisation 32–35, 39, 74, 77, 115–119, 125, 139, 167–169, 174
Concreteness 25, 83, 94, 96, 113, 165, 173, 181
Connecting 2, 30, 35–37, 75, 100, 119–120, 124–141, 168–169, 174–175
Construct
  Definition 5, 22, 26, 50, 180
  Validation 26, 57
Content problem space 37
Content words 70, 96–109, 166, 173, 179
Contextual features 10, 26, 35, 43, 47, 59, 60, 64, 66, 81, 84–114, 125, 142, 171, 180, 181
Correlation
  item-total 77
CPE *see* Certificate of Proficiency in English (CPE)
Cronbach's α 77

D
Decoding 27, 29, 33, 98, 129
Descriptive statistics 72, 79, 105–106, 140, 144–149, 166
Discourse
  mode 18, 83, 93, 96, 113, 114, 164, 165, 173, 178–179
  synthesis 3, 26, 30, 33, 39, 43, 74, 115, 119–120, 135

Subject index

Domain
    academic 20, 86–88, 110, 111
    social 20. 86–88, 110, 111
    professional 20, 86–88, 110, 111

E
EAP *see* English for academic purposes (EAP)
Educational Testing Service (ETS) 52
EFA *see* Exploratory factor analysis (EFA)
EMI *see* English as Medium of Instruction (EMI)
English as Medium of Instruction (EMI) 33
English for academic purposes (EAP) 4, 16, 33, 39, 44, 45, 64, 111, 141, 177, 178
English for specific purposes (ESP) 44, 111
ESP *see* English for specific purposes (ESP)
Essay
    impromptu 3, 22, 24, 26, 119, 141, 161, 183
ETS *see* Educational Testing Service (ETS)
Execution
Expert judgement 10, 24, 67–72, 81, 83, 84, 109, 112, 115, 124, 181
Exploratory factor analysis (EFA) 63, 79, 83, 117, 122, 127, 130, 139, 168

G
Generating 21, 28, 30, 38, 75, 119–141, 161, 168, 169, 174, 175
Genre 7, 17–20, 23, 30, 33, 35, 42, 65, 67, 75, 83, 85, 93, 96–98, 109–116, 129, 134, 163, 164, 173, 178–179
General English Proficiency Test (GEPT) 4, 24, 47, 48, 52, 53, 66, 68, 69, 155, 170
Georgia State Test of English Proficiency (GSTEP) 2, 55, 56
GEPT *see* General English Proficiency Test (GEPT)
GSTEP *see* Georgia State Test of English Proficiency (GSTEP)

H
High-frequency words 70, 97, 103–108, 166, 173
High-stakes tests 42, 52, 172

I
IELTS 3, 16, 23, 24, 42, 43, 51, 52, 55, 56, 68, 69, 72, 78, 79, 142, 143, 144, 148, 153, 169, 180
Independent samples t-tests 78–79
Inferencing 2, 29, 31, 36
Input
    non-verbal 3–4, 16, 20, 21, 51–57, 60, 80, 83, 84, 92–93, 96, 109, 112, 113, 115, 116, 130, 141, 142, 145, 147, 153, 162, 164, 167, 173, 174, 180, 183
    verbal 3–4, 20, 31–32, 52, 56, 57, 60, 83, 84, 92–93, 96, 110, 113, 115, 116, 130–131, 141, 142, 145, 147, 153, 162, 167, 174, 180, 183
Intended reader 19–20, 30, 35, 36, 67, 75, 83, 91, 96, 110, 112, 118, 124, 129, 130, 134, 173, 175, 176
Interaction 5, 6, 10, 18, 19, 21, 22, 30, 32, 42, 43, 87–89, 110, 111, 119, 121, 140, 163, 173
Interfactor correlations matrix 118–124
Internet-based Test of English as a Foreign Language (TOEFL iBT) 4, 48, 49, 52, 55

J
Judges 66–71, 85–96, 110, 112, 130, 151, 163, 164, 178, 181

K
Kaiser-Meyer-Olkin (KMO) 117
KMO *see* Kaiser-Meyer-Olkin (KMO)
Knowledge
    telling 2, 21, 22, 28, 35–37, 43, 88
    transforming 2, 21, 22, 27, 28, 35, 36, 39, 43, 64, 88, 111, 135, 163

L
Language Training and Testing Center (LTTC) 42, 52, 59, 66, 144
Language functions 1, 7, 19, 20, 22, 26, 38, 43, 67, 75, 83, 89–90, 96, 110, 112, 114, 151, 163–164, 173 178
Latent Semantic Analysis (LSA) 70, 97, 101, 104, 106, 108, 174
Length
    sentence 24, 99, 103, 108, 166
    text 18, 23–24, 179
Lexical
    access 29
    search 29, 33, 129
Level-specific proficiency tests 52–56, 131, 147, 155
Likert scale 72, 85
Listening-into-writing 48
LSA *see* Latent Semantic Analysis (LSA)
LTTC *see* Language Training and Testing Center (LTTC)

M
Mann-Whitney test 72, 79, 105, 106, 125, 126, 128, 132, 133, 141
Meaning construction 29, 35, 37, 39, 74, 77, 115, 119–121, 129, 140, 167, 168, 174
Memory
    long-term 17, 21–22, 30–35, 43
    working 31–33, 98, 101, 119, 122, 129, 140

Metacognitive 27–28, 30, 32, 167
Monitoring 23, 27–28, 32, 33, 38–39, 75–75, 77, 115, 116, 122–129, 132–141, 167–169, 174, 176

N
Non-parametric 79, 83, 105, 150

O
Organisation 6, 23, 25, 32, 34, 37, 38, 50, 53–55, 74–75, 91–92, 94–96, 111, 113, 114, 125, 144–147, 151–153, 165, 173, 182
Organising 21, 22, 27, 30, 33, 36–39, 75, 77, 88, 89, 111, 115, 116, 120–121, 125–141, 163, 167–169, 173–176
Output 18, 19, 21, 23, 53–58, 67, 86, 88–89, 95, 105, 109–111, 146, 163, 173, 178, 181

P
Parameter
  cognitive 11, 27, 33, 41, 57, 60, 64, 79, 83, 114, 115, 127, 131, 134–135, 139, 141, 157–158, 167–174, 183
  contextual 39, 47, 63, 66–67, 71, 72, 84, 85, 95, 162, 177, 183
Parsing 24, 29, 33, 99, 100, 129
Pearson Test of English (PTE) 52, 55
Pilot study 66–69, 74–77
Planning
  micro-planning 32, 167, 174
  macro-planning 27, 32, 35, 75, 115, 117, 119, 124, 139–140, 174
Principal Axis Factor Method 117
Processes
  high-level 1–2, 25, 45, 50, 64, 88, 111, 115, 116, 124, 126–128, 132–134, 136, 138, 139, 141, 158, 163
  low-level 27, 76, 98, 116, 126, 128, 132, 133, 134, 136, 138, 139, 141, 146, 157, 169, 170
  linear 20, 21–22, 28, 31–33, 69, 74–75
  recursive 28, 33, 182
PTE see Pearson Test of English (PTE)

R
Rater 49–50, 144
Rating scale 46, 48–50, 183
Reading
  careful 36, 43–45, 75, 115, 116, 119–120, 124–141, 168, 174, 175, 177
  expeditious 36, 43, 125
Readability
  CohMetrix 24, 25, 68–71, 99, 181
  Flesch-Kincaid Grade Level 24–25, 69
  Flesch Reading Ease 24–25, 69

Reliability
  Internal 77
Reviewing 30–31, 117
Rhetorical problem space 37

S
Sampling 63–66, 69, 76, 77, 117, 180–181
Scanning 31, 75
Search reading 75, 119, 120, 124–141, 168–169, 174, 175
Secure English Language Tests (SELTs) 56
SELTs see Secure English Language Tests (SELTs)
Significance level 78–79
Skill
  Receptive 19, 28–29, 74, 129
  Productive 19, 28, 32, 33, 74
Skimming 75
Socio-cognitive approach 58–60
Socio-cognitive validation framework 58, 142, 171, 180, 183
Specification 1, 17–18, 48, 64, 65, 69, 71, 95, 172, 184
Standardisation 2, 4, 11, 29, 40–44, 48–61, 66, 80, 93, 140, 148, 161–163, 181
Syntax 70, 97, 100–108,173
Summarisation
  Summarise 3, 6, 8, 9, 20, 23, 25, 26, 29, 32, 43, 45, 46, 52–56, 88–90, 97, 98, 110, 111, 116, 163–164, 173, 178, 183
  Summary 4, 7, 16, 18, 20, 21, 45, 47–48, 50-52, 55, 85, 173, 178
Synthesise 8, 16, 26, 28, 54, 90, 99–100, 110

T
Target language use (TLU) 2, 17, 90, 99, 114, 115, 153, 158
Task
  prompt 3, 18, 33, 74, 137, 140
  setting 18, 56, 67, 71, 81, 83, 84, 92, 109, 110, 124, 157, 167, 173, 181
  representation 34–35, 43, 75, 115–119, 124–141, 168, 169, 174, 175
TEAP see Test of English for Academic Purposes (TEAP)
TEEP see Test of English for Educational Purposes (TEEP)
Test of English as a Foreign Language (TOEFL) 3, 16, 23
Test of English for Academic Purposes (TEAP) 52, 68
Textual/inter-textual 2, 10, 23–25, 29, 34, 36, 43–46, 47, 50, 63, 65, 68–75, 81–83, 85, 94–113, 121, 125–141, 161, 165–169, 173–176, 179, 181
The Test of English for Educational Purposes (TEEP) 16, 51

Subject index

Think-aloud protocols 30, 34, 35, 49, 73, 75, 182
TLU *see* Target language use (TLU)
TOEFL *see* Test of English as a Foreign Language (TOEFL)
TOEFL iBT *see* Internet-based Test of English as a Foreign Language (TOEFL iBT)
Topic domain 67, 83, 86–88, 95, 96, 110, 163, 173, 178, 181
Translating 30, 31, 33, 38, 75, 174
TTR *see* Type-token ratio (TTR)
Type-token ratio (TTR) 24, 68, 70, 97, 98, 102, 103, 105, 106, 107, 108, 166, 173, 179

U

UK Visas & Immigration (UKVI) 56
Undergraduates 16, 34, 35, 42, 45, 65, 68, 69, 72 76, 101–104, 109, 110, 116–130, 144, 165, 166

V

Validation 10, 11, 26, 28, 39, 41, 42, 49, 57, 58, 64, 66, 71, 77, 81, 83, 142, 171, 180

Validity
  cognitive 10, 11, 18, 27, 32–33, 42–44, 56–60, 63, 64, 72–83, 116, 130, 137, 141, 142, 157, 161, 162, 169, 174, 182, 183
  consequential 58
  construct 26, 57–58, 61, 74, 161, 162, 182
  context 10–11, 17, 18, 42–43, 58–59, 63, 66–72, 81–84, 115–116, 142, 157, 167, 173
  criterion-related 10, 11, 58, 59, 63, 80–82, 142, 144, 157, 158, 161, 162
VocabProfile 24, 68–71, 181
Vocabulary 1, 20, 23, 24, 55, 68, 69, 75, 97, 111, 123, 146, 176

W

Washback
  positive 45–46, 50
  negative 46
Wilcoxon signed-ranks test 79, 106, 126, 127, 128, 132, 133
Words
  academic 69, 70, 97, 98, 102–109, 166, 173, 179
  low-frequency 70, 97, 102–109, 165, 166, 173, 179